JOURNALS OF JOHN D. LEE

JOURNALS OF
JOHN D. LEE

1846-47 and 1859

❧

Edited by
CHARLES KELLY

❧

Introduction by
CHARLES S. PETERSON

❧

UNIVERSITY OF UTAH PRESS
Salt Lake City   1984

CONTENTS

❦

Introduction by
CHARLES S. PETERSON

᪔

Charles Kelly had lived in Utah for a decade and a half when in 1934 he became interested in the journals of John D. Lee of Mountain Meadows Massacre notoriety. Kelly stayed on in the state until the time of his death in 1971. During most of his Utah years, the history of the West was an abiding passion with him, directing his life in all its professional, economic and personal facets. He was explosive in his energy, boundless in his interests, keen in his vision, and courageous in his statement. Yet, as anyone who knew him would attest, he was also an abrasive, crusty growler, an iconoclast of the first magnitude whose anger was rarely hidden and whose biases were ecumenical. As newspaperman and historian Harold Schindler, who was his friend, puts it, "He ate Mormons for breakfast, chewed Catholics, Capitalists, Jews, Negroes, and public utilities for lunch, brunch and supper."[1] Another friend, former director of the Utah State Historical Society, A. R. Mortensen, has written, that Kelly was "a man with a barbwire personality, an individualist" who lived "in a society that was orthodox and conformist."[2]

---

1. Harold Schindler to Charles Peterson, July 25, 1984. In addition I am indebted to Mr. Schindler for calling several of the quotations from the writings of Kelly and his friends to my attention.

2. A. R. Mortensen, "Charles Kelly: In Memoriam," *Utah Historical Quarterly* 39 (Spring 1971): 196–200; hereafter the *Utah Historical Quarterly* will be cited as UHQ.

If Kelly's anger was intense, so was his interest in Western and Utah history. He was formally untutored, utterly without most of academia's approving stamps. He was hard pressed throughout his life to make a living but did more for history in his leisure hours than most professionals do in a lifetime. During his long writing career he approached history from at least three vantage points. He was a polemicist, avid and shrill; he was a romantic regionalist, snared in the webs of the West's heroic tradition; and he was part of what has recently come to be known as "the New Mormon History," although he and many of the school's current practitioners would shudder at the thought of being colleagues. He wrote, collaborated in or edited eight books and more than 120 articles. He was unflagging in his research, astute and enthusiastic in his explorations, gifted and colorful as a writer, ardent as a promoter of Utah, and in significant ways a pacemaker who marked historiographic trails others would follow.

Charles Kelly was born in 1889 at a Michigan logging camp. His father was an itinerant Baptist preacher, unstable, quick to fury, and heavy handed. Other than teaching young Kelly to set type in the small print shop where he produced religious tracts, thus giving the boy an occupation he pursued throughout his life, the father succeeded only in opening festering sores of resentment. Opportunities for childhood education were often interrupted as the elder Kelly was taken by the winds of chance from one place to another. After a brief college experience, Charles jobbed his way westward, did a World War I hitch in the army, and married Harriette Greener before settling in Utah where he became a partner in the Western Printing Company. He earned a scant living as a printer until about 1940 when he sold out and moved to Wayne County in the canyonlands of eastern Utah. There he planned to do a little fruit farming and indulge his passion for history. As it turned out, he became custodian of the Capitol Reef National Monument, where the Park Service encouraged the local color thrust of his historical interests.[3]

To understand the scars Kelly's father put on him and to see beyond them to his approach to history, one could well pay attention to a notation in his diary on August 20, 1936, at the time of his father's death. "The old man is dead. I've waited for a good many years to write that *good news* and at last it has come. . . ."[4] That the sentiment of this entry was no fluke is borne out by a coldly revealing letter written to him a few weeks after his father's passing by his confidante and coauthor, Hoffman Birney.

> I presume that congratulations are in order as to the blessed event of August 1 in Worchester, Mass. I'm not razzing. Only too clearly do I recall one night on a sandbar somewhere along the Colorado and you telling us the full tale of your late and unlamented sire. To me it explained *you* better than years of study might have done—your savage atheism (no God is infinitely superior to the one you were clubbed into serving during your boyhood), your hatred for shams and fakes and charlatans, and your confession of the realization that you were robbed of a rather priceless thing. Being more or less materialistic it wouldn't do for me to admit the existence of a hell—but if there is one the crime for which the late and unlamented rev. will sizzle the longest will be his treatment of his sons—his robbing them of a very precious thing, the memory of a father they could love and respect.[5]

---

3. The personal data on Kelly's life before he moved to Utah is taken largely from A. R. Mortensen, "Charles Kelly," and Harold Schindler, "Writer-Pathfinder Charles Kelly Possessed by a Driving Spirit," *Salt Lake Tribune,* Dec. 28, 1969; see also Authors' Note in connection with Charles Kelly and Hoffman Birney, "Killer for the Saints," *The Reader's Digest* (Sept. 1934): 101–4.

4. Charles Kelly, Diary, Aug. 20, 1936. The Papers of Charles Kelly (1889–1971). Manuscript collection (MS 100), University of Utah Library, hereafter cited as UUL. Italics added.

5. Hoffman Birney to Charles Kelly, October 12, 1936. Charles Kelly Collection (B-114) at the Utah State Historical Society, hereafter USHS.

One sees much of Charlie Kelly in these lines. They are especially important in understanding the vitrol with which he sometimes approached his historical writing. But in justice, it should be stressed here, that while Kelly's work exhibits anger and even meanness, a full reading displays growth, self-control, and a realization that sound history, not attack, was after all the most useful implement in telling his message. His development in this context is especially apparent, as we shall presently see in the pointed, but restrained tone in which the Journals of John D. Lee were edited.

As far as the record shows, Kelly's interest in history first surfaced in the late 1920s, after he had been in Utah about a decade. It was a time when laymen and professional historians alike were tracing routes of Spanish padres, mountain men, prospectors and emigrants through the West in what may be called the romantic regional movement. Unsuspecting, Kelly was caught in the mood of the time. Apparent from the first was his keen sense for the dramatic, for the uncommon, for the spectacular event or course of events that enlivened and gave body, meaning and interest to the broader, less gripping course of affairs. A chance ride into Utah's salt deserts precipitated this development. A brother had acquired a new car. Kelly rode with him west from Salt Lake City along what was then called the Old Lincoln Highway to the little town of Grantsville where he met old-timers Frank Durfee and Dan Orr who recalled local traditions of a weathered wagon track across the barren flats west of the lake and of discarded equipment from a time long past which still littered the trail.[6] His attention riveted to the trail of the Donner Party or the so-called Hastings' Cutoff

---

6. Charles Kelly, "Treasure Hunt on the Salt Desert," *Desert Magazine* 10 (Dec. 1946): 11–14, and Everett L. Cooley, "Charles Kelly Interview," Apr. 30, 1969 (Mss. 100), Western Americana Collection, UUL.

to California, Kelly read everything he could get his hands on about early exploration, hung around Dick Shepard's bookstore in Salt Lake City and corresponded avidly with librarians and trails experts throughout the West.[7] Perhaps more important, he set out to trace the trail foot by foot and to assess, register, photograph and collect the artifacts that lay along its course. This was a direct and intensely moving experience, an exercise in discovery that profoundly influenced Kelly, turning his attention even more emphatically to what may be termed field history.[8]

While he was by no means the first to respond to the enticements of trail lore, it quickly became apparent that he was wonderfully adept at it. His work soon attracted other trail scholars including Irene Paden and George Stewart, who were at the height of brilliant careers in regional writings in those years. Both discussed their own research and fieldwork with Kelly and became increasingly dependent upon him for the geographic understanding that enlightens their works. Other correspondents of the early 1930s suggest the growing breadth of Kelly's interests and the seriousness with which a wide variety of writers regarded his scholarship. Mountain men specialists who sought him out included Charles L. Camp, editor of numerous fur trade diaries including James Clyman's and George C. Yount's; H. C. Dale, author of *The Ashley-Smith Explorations . . .* (1941); and John G. Niehardt, Nebraska's poet laureate,

---

7. Ibid.

8. Ibid. Evidence of Kelly's enthusiasm for trail work as well as his correspondence is found throughout the Papers of Charles Kelly at UUL and in Charles Kelly Collection (B-114) at USHS. Both collections are extensive and complement each other. The USHS papers are somewhat richer in terms of Kelly's personal correspondence about trail work. In addition there is a substantial collection of "Charles Kelly Writings" at the Capitol Reef National Monument Library in Torrey, Utah.

whose epic poetry would soon memorialize the exploits of Jedediah Smith, William H. Ashley, and other Rocky Mountain fur traders and explorers. Canyonland and southwestern authorities included Earle Forrest of Arizona range war and Painted Desert fame, Frederick S. Dellenbaugh, member of the John Wesley Powell Colorado River expedition of 1871 and author of numerous canyonland books, and A. E. Douglas, the University of Arizona scientist who was just then developing dendrochronology as a means of dating historical and archaeological events. Even Harold Lamb, classicist and author of popular biographies of Alexander the Great and Hannibal, exchanged letters with Kelly about the cultivation of tobacco in Turkey.[9]

Locally, a Falstaffian collection of river runners, prospectors, ranchers, desert recluses, and history buffs began to be Charles Kelly's intimate associates. With him they traveled, yarned, studied, wrote and published, creating an impressive body of historical literature that appeared in weekly newspapers, official Utah tourist brochures, historical journals and increasingly in *Desert Magazine*, which ultimately published at least fifty-two of Kelly's offerings.

Perhaps the closest of these associates was fellow-journalist Frank Beckwith, who had come from Evanston, Wyoming, to found a land-boomer's newspaper at Delta, a late-blooming farm town that had risen miragelike out of the alkali dust along the Salt Lake and Los Angeles Railway line in west central Utah's Millard County about 1910. Between them, the journalist cronies made archaeological digs, which to them seemed to disprove Book of Mormon teachings about the origin of native Americans, located the famed Chief Walker's grave, speculated about geological

---

9. This correspondence is found at USHS. While most of it dates to 1930 and 1931, the Harold Lamb letters were written in 1923 and the John G. Neihardt letters in 1935.

finds, and ferreted out the sites of long-abandoned stage stations.[10]

Other Kelly intimates included local history enthusiasts like A. O. Kennedy of Ogden, who rescued Utah's first white resident, Miles Goodyear, from obscurity, and sometime Utah journalist Maurice Howe, who together with Kelly improved upon Kennedy's research to publish *Miles Goodyear* (1937). Kelly and Howe credited Goodyear with trapping and trading in the Central Rockies during the 1830s and with establishing a trading post at the confluence of the Weber and Ogden Rivers in 1846. This was later taken over by Mormon founders of Ogden, thus giving that city claim to being the state's oldest permanent community. Important in another way was Josiah Gibbs, an ex-Mormon and onetime newspaperman at central Utah's Marysvale, who saw it as his calling to promote publication of broad and often negative views of the Mormon experience. Gibbs became an important source of information and encouragement in Kelly's Mormon studies.[11] Quite different was J. Cecil Alter, a meteorologist who emerged during the 1930s as the most important figure at the Utah State Historical Society and as one of the state's most significant historians when he published *Utah the Storied Domain* (1932), a three-volume work. With Alter's encouragement, Kelly became one of the *Utah Historical Quarterly*'s regular contributors,

---

10. The Kelly-Beckwith correspondence is extensive. On at least one occasion they collaborated on an article. See Kelly and Beckwith, "We Found the Grave of Chief Walker," *Desert Magazine* 9 (Oct. 1946): 17–19.

11. Gibbs was born in Nauvoo, came to Utah in 1857, served as a Mormon missionary in England in 1867, but was disaffected by the 1890s and was excommunicated in 1907. A partial bibliography in the "Expanded Register to the Kelly Collection" at USHS reveals Gibbs' interest in the Mountain Meadows Massacre and polygamy, as well as his determination to expose what he took to be wrongdoing in the Mormon church.

issuing articles on Jedediah Smith, Chief Hoskannini, Denis Julien, and Antoine Robidoux, among others.[12]

Outlawry, a subject much talked about by Utah's folk historians, but little recognized in the state's historical literature, also occupied Kelly's attention, especially as he came to know Utah's backside, the Colorado Plateau, in the years after 1930. Charmed and intrigued, as well as sensing a good story, Kelly pursued the career of Butch Cassidy and the Wild Bunch, locating their haunts and turning up the rich folklore that clustered about them on the desolate Plateau from Wyoming's Hole-in-the-Wall country to Robber's Roost in southeastern Utah. With no sophisticated theoretical superstructure, such as E. J. Hobsbawn's theory of social banditry, to give Butch and the Wild Bunch a dignifed context, Kelly nevertheless knew a good story, and better yet he knew the country and the spirit of its people.[13] Lore, country and spirit, he wove into a significant book, *The Outlaw Trail* (1938), giving direction and form to what has proven to be one of the most durable of the Old West's outlaw traditions.

A sense for the underdog that expresses itself in one way in Kelly's affinity for Butch Cassidy took a somewhat different form in his long studies to pin down and identify Caleb "Old" Greenwood, an octogenarian explorer who was something of an anomaly among the youthful fraternity of mountain men and western guides of his day. Kelly first became aware of Old Greenwood during his Salt Desert

---

12. See "Jedediah S. Smith on the Salt Desert Trail," UHQ 3 (Jan. 1930): 23–27; "Chief Hoskaninni," UHQ 21 (July 1953): 219–26; "The Mysterious 'D. Julien,'" UHQ 6 (July 1933): 82–88 and "Antoine Robidoux," UHQ 6 (Oct. 1933): 115–16.

13. E. J. Hobsbawn, *Primitive Rebels: Studies in Archaic Forms of Social Movement in the 19th and 20th Centuries* (New York, 1965), pp. 13–29; also see Richard White, "Outlaw Gangs of the Middle Border: American Social Bandits," *Western Historical Quarterly* 12 (Oct. 1981): 387–408.

studies, finding vague evidence that led him to believe Greenwood had been a notable figure in opening the California Trail. Once on Greenwood's track, Kelly pursued him relentlessly, gradually assembling bits and pieces to find a classic frontier story—the courageous fidelity of an Indian wife, Greenwood's victory over blindness and age, sons and daughters who followed the old man's peregrinations, and Greenwood's persistence at the cutting edge of the frontier long after the comforts of a home somewhere in the Missouri settlements or Oregon's climes had claimed lesser men. As the Greenwood story was a prime example of the West's heroic tradition, Kelly's detective work was a prime example of historianship in the heyday of the regional romantics. Sensing that publication would serve as a research vehicle, Kelly placed his book *Old Greenwood* before the public in 1936. In due time new information was unearthed, largely from interest sparked by the book. Encouraged, Kelly secured the old maverick's place in the annals of the West when he rewrote the Greenwood book in 1965, this time collaborating with Dale Morgan, another Utahn, who combined "poetic imagery . . . with . . . exactness of expression" in historical writings that had justly earned him a place at the head of western historians."[14]

Not only did Kelly attract fellow Utahns like Morgan, but his expanding interests thrust him into a relationship of correspondence and cooperation with widening circles of the West's best historians in the decades after 1935. Two of Kelly's correspondents, who for different reasons and from different vantage points made monumental contributions to the history of the West, were Carl I. Wheat and Herbert E. Bolton. From his professorial chair at the University of California Bolton had written brilliantly about the institutions

---

14. Ray A. Billington, "Introduction," to Dale L. Morgan, *The Great Salt Lake*, new edition (Albuquerque: The University of New Mexico Press, 1973), p. viii.

and personalities of the Spanish Borderlands, and in the 1940s turned his attention to the Domínguez and Escalante expedition, the first-known European exploration of Utah. Puzzled at the intricacies of the geography described by the Padres and unable to do fieldwork himself, Bolton took advantage of Kelly's intimate knowledge of the canyonlands, inquiring of him for help and direction.[15]

Similarly, a need for detailed trails information made Kelly a necessary ally to Carl I. Wheat, a San Francisco lawyer whose superb five-volume work on mapping the West (1957–63) may well be said to be the connecting tissue between the romantic regionalism of the pre-World War II period and the increasingly scientific-cultural approaches of more recent western historians such as Turrentine Jackson, Wallace Stegner, and William Goetzman. In the late 1930s Wheat's attention was focused on Death Valley and the tragic experience from which its name was derived. As the Gold Rush rolled west in 1849, a large party of wagons hired the celebrated veteran of the Mormon Battalion and Utah guide, Captain Jefferson Hunt, to lead them on west over the southern route. Dissatisfied with Hunt's caution, most of the anxious gold hunters broke with him near Pinto Creek in southwestern Utah, heading directly west into southern Nevada's unexplored deserts. Shattered by the terrible country they encountered, the breakoffs divided again and again, some reeling back from various points to pick up Hunt's longer but safer trace. Others straggled on in fractured groups to test their destiny in Death Valley. It was the lines laid out in this desert jigsaw that Wheat tried to reconstruct. Even at this early time he probably had no peers in understanding the West's geography generally. At hand in California's Bay Area, he had the best libraries, the best written accounts and the best maps, but Kelly's

---

15. H. E. Bolton to Charles Kelly, June 8, 1938, USHS.

command of the ground led to a quick flurry of letters in which timing and content attest to the intensity of the two men's interest and the value of their exchange.[16]

Kelly's broadening circle of friends opened doors for publication in popular periodicals, as well as the pulp westerns. Especially after the later 1930s, he wrote for a wide array of magazines including *Saturday Evening Post*; *Arizona Highways*; *Pony Express Currier*; *Frontier & Midlands*; *True West and Pioneer*, as well as for *Desert Magazine*. In Kelly's papers, one finds no evidence of transactions in which money changes hands, but can only assume that he devoted a good deal of his time to promoting historic Utah, and that he did it for pay.[17]

While he looks very much like part of Utah's promotional establishment in the context of his periodical publications, Kelly was the rankest kind of an iconoclast and individualist in his monographic publications. Like many of the era's historians, he came to history with little or no formal training. It is true his growing circle of friends provided excellent on-the-job training, but either by choice or by force of circumstances in the hard times of the 1930s, Kelly did not develop any lasting relationship with a publishing house. In part, this seems likely to have been due to the roughness of his early monographs, which sometimes bristled with his biases and were often overly dependent on quotations, lacking in footnotes and citations, and in some cases had only the crudest organization and skimpiest transitions to bind them together. The fact that his periodical offerings and some of his later monographs show great polish suggests that the rawness of his first books may after all have been

---

16. Carl I. Wheat to Charles Kelly, Nov. 5, 10 and 17, 1938, USHS.

17. UUL and USHS: for a list of Kelly's 121 articles see Howard Foulger, "Bibliography of the Writings of Charles Kelly," USHS.

due to the lack of appropriate editorial help. This leaves the strong likelihood that Kelly's early experience as a tramp printer and his independent ways may well have led him to believe that the best mode of publication was after all the most direct. In any event, he published all of his books in their first editions on his own press, the Western Printing Company.[18]

In the beginning, at least, there can be no doubt that he was a better publisher than historian. Cramped for time and money, he did his own designing, set his type and ran his presses. His editions were small, several of them issuing as few as 250 numbers. Paper quality and binding were good. Layout and design, photo reproduction and index, and most of all the printing show the hand of a craftsman, one who knew his trade and took pride in it. Few who have worked the vineyards of western history have been less subject to the control and influence of others. Even the demands of the marketplace appear to have paled by comparison to Kelly's fierce independence. His was, in effect, a one-man operation. For those who gainsaid or found fault, academic or Mormon in persuasion, he made few concessions, meeting criticism with even more determined applications of individualism.

In view of this it is not surprising that Charles Kelly turned to Mormon history, nor that he did it with a vigor and abrasiveness that may well have made him "public-enemy-number-two" in Utah, second only in these years to Bernard DeVoto, whose ruthlessly negative appraisal of Utah, Mormons and his hometown, Ogden, which appeared in the *American Mercury*, occasioned an especially angry outcry

---

18. Books he published through his Western Printing Company include *Salt Desert Trails* (1930); *Old Greenwood* (1936); *Miles Goodyear* (1937); *The Outlaw Trail* (1938); and *Journals of John D. Lee* (1938).

in the mid-1920s.[19] Tutored initially in his Mormon studies by Josiah Gibbs, Kelly quickly established interests that clearly bear the stamp of his own predilection for color, action, controversy, and the uncommon common man or archetypical figure whose history could become a vehicle for a broader meaning.[20] In this context, more perhaps than any other, Kelly was a polemicist, a man with a cause. He was wired differently than his Mormon neighbors. He saw things differently than they, and in many respects was offended at their representation of their past. Typically he undertook to put the story right, and in so doing he picked at sore spots on the corpus of the Mormon experience—thus his attention to Orrin Porter Rockwell and John D. Lee.

There is no evidence to indicate when he became interested in Orrin Porter Rockwell, whose reputation as a Mormon hit man continues to attract biographers. But it is certain he was well into his Rockwell studies by 1931 when Hoffman Birney, another of the important associates in Kelly's career and an individual who featured directly in his editing of the John D. Lee journals, came to Utah to do research on his history of the Mormons, *Zealots in Zion* (1931).[21] With roots in the Midwest, Birney was younger than Kelly, but was an established writer with an eye for the sensational

---

19. This paraphrases Wallace Stegner's treatment of DeVoto's *American Mercury* articles. These three articles, Stegner writes, "marked DeVoto as Utah Enemy Number One, the contemporary avatar of all the Missouri Pukes and Illinois mobbers who had attained immortality in the Mormon memory for their persecution of the Saints." See *The Uneasy Chair: A Biography of Bernard DeVoto* (Garden City: Doubleday & Company, Ltd., 1974), p. 65.

20. Kelly and Hoffman Birney dedicated *Holy Murder: The Story of Porter Rockwell* (New York: Minton, Balch & Company, 1934) to Gibbs, who had died in 1932. They eulogized him as "hater of fraud, despiser of hypocrisy, champion of truth."

21. By 1931 Birney was an established writer, having written among other things, about George Armstrong Custer.

and a capacity for quick, smooth-flowing, if sometimes superficial, prose. He had a special flare for sarcasm, hyperbole, and polemic expression.

By 1933 Kelly had pulled a manuscript together on Porter Rockwell. Typically, he set it in type at the Western Printing Company and apparently ran at least one prototype or galley copy which is at the Princeton University Library now. This he showed to Birney, who expressed an interest in it. Together, the two men delivered themselves of a real philippic, *Holy Murder* (1934). A comparison of the original Kelly prototype and the published work suggests that the sarcasm and invective, and much of the flow of the book's hard-hitting style are Birney's, but that the conclusion that the Mormon church's complicity in Rockwell's killings and other criminal acts, including Mountain Meadows Massacre, ran clear to the top church leaders is clearly Kelly's.[22] Indeed, Birney seems to deftly put distance between himself and the source of responsibility for the book's allegation of Mormon criminality as he concludes his description of the Mountain Meadows Massacre with this paragraph. "The junior author of the present narrative, while far removed from admiration for Brigham, has asserted on several occasions that the rascally Old Boss was too shrewd, too farsighted, to have ordered deliberately so wholesale a slaughter as that at the Mountain Meadows."[23]

Doubleday, which had published some of Birney's earlier books, turned the Rockwell manuscript down, writing

---

22. Harold Schindler, author of *Orrin Porter Rockwell: Man of God, Son of Thunder* (Salt Lake City: University of Utah Press, 1966), a superb biography of Rockwell, has a photocopy of the Princeton galley of Kelly's Western Printing Company biography of Rockwell. I have compared it with *Holy Murder* and have discussed the similarities and discrepancies of the two works with Schindler. Both of us agree that research and content are substantially the work of Kelly.

23. Kelly and Birney, *Holy Murder*, pp. 166–67.

"there is a book here but it is not for us. Porter Rockwell is not a name to conjure with the book buying public. He is not well-known."[24] Minton, Balch & Company, which finally published *Holy Murder*, looked for it to sell well, and to that end hoped the Mormon church "may be provoked into a withering denunciation."[25] Although the First Presidency of the church did issue a brief statement styling it a "demonical untruth," no real controversy ensued.[26] Reviews elsewhere were generally negative, and *Holy Murder* failed to become a good seller. Even some of Kelly's personal correspondents damned it with faint praise or chucklingly referred to its potential as an irritant to Mormon power brokers. As one writer put it:

> I got a tremendous kick out of it, but as much as anything else, I admire the whatever-it-takes to wave the red flag of fact in front of the big bad bull of the C. of J.C.-L.D.S. As I told Birney, a friend remarked when handing the book back to me, "I never knew there were so many ways to call a guy an SOB without actually using the words." . . . I wonder if you didn't have to take care not to get between the lights and window for a while after the book came out.[27]

If *Holy Murder* sold poorly, Kelly did get one thing out of his collaboration with Birney. It was the latter who called his attention to the John D. Lee journal of 1846–47. Birney was informed that the journal existed by Rolla B. Watt, a prominent San Francisco lawyer who, on reading *Holy Murder*, wrote to him. Birney manifested some interest in the journal himself, but it was Kelly who pursued the matter, contacting Watt late in the summer of 1934. Watt responded, telling Kelly that an uncle of his, W. W. Bishop, a lawyer practicing in Pioche, Nevada, at the time, had been among

---

24. Russell Doubleday to Alan C. Collins, 1933, USHS.
25. Lynn Carrick to Hoffman Birney, Apr. 10, 1934, USHS.
26. *Deseret News*, Sept. 12, 1934.
27. E. G. Connely to Charles Kelly, Feb. 15, 1936, USHS.

Lee's defense attorneys. As Kelly knew, Bishop had published the *Confessions of John D. Lee* in 1877, the same year Lee was executed. Although Bishop's introduction appears to have been done in haste and is certainly a prime example of anti-Mormon polemics, the *Confessions* themselves bear the authentic mark of Lee's authorship and were doubtlessly the most enlightening and useful thing available on the Mountain Meadows Massacre in 1930, and have been heavily depended upon by modern scholars, including Juanita Brooks in her *Mountain Meadows Massacre* (1950) and *John D. Lee, Zealot-Pioneer Builder-Scapegoat* (1972). However, as the statement of a condemned man, the *Confessions* were suspect and were little known, especially in Utah. The Mormon church's position had been that the trial and execution of John D. Lee had officially closed the issue, and that the less said the better. When the Massacre was referred to at all, it was passed off as the work of Indians led by John D. Lee. To the extent that Lee was remembered in Utah, he was recalled as the man who was executed for the Mountain Meadows Massacre and was stereotyped as a criminal of the worst sort who had justly met his desserts. Even serious scholars did little to give Lee a hearing.[28]

Now in 1934 Kelly was informed of a journal in which John D. Lee spoke for himself. Rolla Watt explained that the journal dealt with the Mormon experience in western Iowa and eastern Nebraska in 1846–47, that it had every mark of authenticity, and that family tradition held that other Lee materials once in W. W. Bishop's possession had been destroyed in the San Francisco earthquake and fire of 1906.

---

28. For typical treatments of the Mountain Meadows Massacre and John D. Lee, see Andrew Love Neff, *History of Utah 1847–1869*, edited by Leland H. Creer, (Salt Lake City: The Deseret News Press, 1940), pp. 410–32, especially pp. 413 and 414; and Levi Edgar Young, "Mountain Meadows Massacre," *Dictionary of American History*, edited by James Truslow Adams, Vol. 4 (New York: Scribner's & Son, 1940), p. 36.

There the matter rested until early in 1936 when Watt wrote Kelly again informing him that "the records of the trial at Cedar City" had been sold to the Huntington Library at San Moreno, California, by a son of Judge Jacob Boreman who had presided at the trials of John D. Lee. Watt went on to indicate his own intention to place the Lee journal in his possession in the same library.[29]

From this point Kelly and Watt quickly moved to a decision to publish a small private edition of the journal with the two sharing costs. A trusted friend of Watt's, Salt Lake attorney Beverley Clendennin, carried the journal to Utah in November 1936. Kelly transcribed it immediately, completing the job before the first of 1937. About this time, the second journal (for 1859) and certain Lee family letters that also appear in the *Journals of John D. Lee* were made available by Edna Lee Brimhall of Thatcher, Arizona, and were appended to the larger Watt manuscript.[30]

To let Lee speak for himself, Kelly transcribed the journals literally, "carefully" preserving them "exactly as written," although punctuation marks, which were largely lacking in the originals, were "supplied by the editor for ease of reading, wherever their use was obvious" and "words omitted" were also inserted in brackets.[31] Kelly maintains his low profile in all his introductory material, presenting Lee in a straightforward fashion. Totally lacking are the strident tones W. W. Bishop had employed to condemn the Mormons in his publisher's preface of the *Confessions of John D. Lee* and the pyrotechniques of *Holy Murder.* Footnotes are limited in number and content and are, in the main, factual and explanatory. Although they sometimes overreach

---

29. Rolla B. Watt to Charles Kelly, Sept. 25, 1934, and Jan. 27, 1936, USHS.

30. Charles Kelly editor, *Journals of John D. Lee, 1846–47* and *1859* (Salt Lake City: Western Printing Company, 1938), p. 202.

31. Ibid., pp. 14–15.

verifiable fact, as for example when Kelly explains that friend of the Mormons Thomas L. Kane had "joined the Church and received his patriarchal blessing," they serve more to enlighten points of development or geography than to carry an argument.[32] Yet Kelly's point of view is clear. Brief margin notes make his case, calling attention to frictions and tensions, highlighting contradictions of polygamy and alcohol consumption, and playing up Lee's utter subservience to Brigham Young.[33]

Old trails man that he was, Kelly had interested himself in the geography of Nebraska and Iowa by the first of 1936. Again, Birney provided an essential contact, introducing him to E. G. Connely, a retired Corps of Army Engineers officer who knew the Omaha region like the back of his hand, and who himself was no mean trails sleuth.[34] While it does not appear that Kelly ever examined the area himself, the two men began to correspond immediately. Connely's early letters clearly reveal the dominance in his mind of abandoned army forts, trading posts, and various relics. For example, he wrote on March 11, 1936,

> There are not many surviving evidences of the Mormon and other early trails in this part of the country. Building materials were highly perishable—logs, sod, some mud or 'dobe—and what the elements did not destroy the early settlers appropriated as soon as 'fort', stage station, or whatever, was abandoned. The trails themselves have been obliterated by rain and cultivation, except a very few places, such as the South Platte Crossing, and a few where travel was especially heavy, and cultivation difficult on account of terrain. I know of one such spot on the Nebraska City-

---

32. Ibid., p. 89.

33. The tone of Kelly's attention to polygamy is apparent in such marginal notes as "Lee Goes Courting Again," (96); " 'Nancy Tarried Till Morning' " (106); and " 'Whores of the Twelve' " (108). A brief comparison of the published *Journals* with the handwritten original at the Huntington Library suggests that Kelly took no liberty in his transcription.

34. See E. G. Connely to Charles Kelly, Feb. 15, 1936, USHS.

Denver Route. Considerable remains of old Fort Laramie, but the only remains of old Fort Kearny is a mound of earth and cottonwood plantings. Fort Atkinson, about twelve miles up the Missouri from my home, was the first fortification west of the Missouri—occupied in 1819, abandoned in 1827. Because the site is near I have 'prospected' it a good many times, and have a few 'relics' of it, especially army uniform buttons, which, being bronze, have resisted decay. Also, a little iron workcut nails, a few gun parts, lead ball, flints . . . I should have some snap shots. . . . Will take a few at the old Mormon Cemetery and thereabouts and send you copies.[35]

But it did not take long for Connely to become a thoroughgoing student of the Mormon hegira, and he was soon combing libraries and archives throughout the area and delving into map collections of private and official agencies, especially the files of the Corps of Army Engineers, which were generously opened to him by his former associates. He also spent such time as dismal weather permitted during the winter and spring of 1937 doing fieldwork to establish locations, measure distances, assess topographic changes caused by shifts in the Missouri River and in talking with old-timers in an attempt to substantiate his growing understanding of Mormon geography through local traditions and folk history.

Meantime, Kelly was working with the history of the Mormons in western Iowa and eastern Nebraska himself as he tried to get the full picture of the 1846–47 Lee journal. Again and again he wrote, posing problems and listing sites in which nomenclature and geography were obscure. Connely whittled away at these lists. Especially useful to his efforts were local publications and a superb set of manuscript maps said to have been drawn by General G. M. Dodge of Union Pacific Railroad fame, which were in 1937 the "treasured possessions of the Council Bluffs Library."[36] Apparent

---

35. Ibid., Mar. 11, 1936, USHS.
36. Ibid., Jan. 20, 1937, USHS.

to both Kelly and Connely was the fact that the key to the geography of Lee's journal was Summer Quarters or "Brigham's Farm," a site some fifteen miles from the better-known Winter Quarters, where Lee and other "adopted sons" of Brigham Young had been assigned to plant upwards of six thousand acres of crops during the summer of 1847 with the intent of supplying the expected migration of the coming fall and year.[37]

Initially, Connely found no reference to Summer Quarters and seemed to doubt the possibility of a farming operation having been of the magnitude described by Lee. Reference to a fishing pond within three miles of the site and a nearby burial ground further complicated the matter. These and other engimas were ultimately resolved, permitting Connely to offer a well-substantiated opinion of the location of Summer Quarters and explain its relationship to other important points of reference in the Lee journal.[38] He granted that he was "not only an amateur historian but also an amateur draftsman" but insisted that "while my maps are by no means handsome" they were accurate. As he put it, *"I have not guessed at a damd thing* and have not only checked one source against another, but have discarded poor sources." To drive home this final point, he concluded that he had more than a "fair nose for authenticity."[39] Satisfied, Kelly presented Connely's opinion on the whereabout of Summer Quarters and other important sites as his own. Later historians have not improved on solutions developed by Connely and Kelly through their long-distance fieldwork of 1937.

37. From March 31, 1847, until the 1846–47 journal ends on July 23, Lee was at Summer Quarters most of the time. See Charles Kelly, *Journals of John D. Lee*, pp. 141–97.

38. Kelly, *Journals of John D. Lee*, n. 127, p. 141, also maps following pp. 144 and 160.

39. E. G. Connely to Charles Kelly, Jan. 20, March 11 and May 8, 1937, USHS.

Thus the *Journals of John D. Lee, 1846–47 and 1859* came off the presses of the Western Printing Company in 1938 in a limited edition of 250 copies. It was a significant event in the development of both Mormon and frontier historiography. It took a distinguished place in an era of great achievements in publishing the narratives of the westering process. More important, the *Journals of John D. Lee* stimulated interest in Lee, the Mountain Meadows Massacre, and the westward movement of the Mormons that is unfolding yet. It also gave human dimensions to John D. Lee and placed an issue in Mormon history that had long been tabled in active discussion again. Furthermore, it accomplished this with a sense of honesty and restraint that did much to ensure the responsible discussions that followed, especially in the work of Bernard DeVoto, *Year of Decision* (1942) and of Juanita Brooks *The Mountain Meadows Massacre* (1950), *A Mormon Chronicle: The Diaries of John D. Lee, 1848–1876* (with Robert Glass Cleland in 1955), and *John Doyle Lee: Zealot-Pioneer Builder-Scapegoat* (1961). In this context, then, Charles Kelly emerges as anything but the "public enemy" that opinion in some quarters once held him to be. Indeed, in his determination to reopen all phases of the past, Kelly was the forerunner of the best of a current crop of historians who traffic in what they style as the new Mormon history.

Those who read this new edition of the *Journals of John D. Lee* will share in Kelly's enthusiasm for the history of Utah and the West, as well as sense his feeling for fair play and his appreciation for setting, drama, and meaning in human events. Prepared and presented with an eye to letting John D. Lee speak for himself, the *Journals* accomplish even more. They combine a clear picture of the values and character of Charles Kelly, editor and historian, with a wealth of sound primary information about a crucial phase of the frontier experience, as narrated by John D. Lee, one of the best contemporary observers of the pioneer Mormon scene. The new edition makes widely available a work found previously only in research libraries. With the "barbwire" of Kelly's personality lending vividness to the real stuff of Lee's journals, readers of today will find its pages important and meaningful history, as readers did in the 1930s.

JOURNALS OF JOHN D. LEE

JOURNALS OF
JOHN D. LEE

1846-47 and 1859

ツ

Edited by
CHARLES KELLY

ツ

Privately Printed for

ROLLA BISHOP WATT

By

WESTERN PRINTING COMPANY
SALT LAKE CITY

1938

JOHN DOYLE LEE
September 6, 1812
March 23, 1877
From a photograph taken December 26, 1857 in Salt Lake City.
Courtesy Edna Lee Brimhall, Thatcher, Arizona

Biographical Sketch of

JOHN D. LEE

❦

John Doyle Lee was born at Kaskaskia, Randolph County, Illinois, on September 6, 1812. His father, Ralph Lee, was a relative of the distinguished Lee family of Virginia. His mother was a daughter of John Doyle, who came to Kaskaskia in 1796 and was for many years Indian agent in southeastern Illinois. Both parents were of the Catholic faith.

While John D. Lee was still a small child his mother died. His father, having wasted his fortune on liquor, sent young John to live with an aunt, who treated the boy with savage cruelty. At the age of sixteen he left his aunt's home and obtained employment at $7.00 a month with a mail contractor. At the age of eighteen he joined Captain Jacob Feaman's company for the Black Hawk campaign, saw action at the battle of Bad Axe, and was mustered out in September, 1831. For a time he worked as fireman on a Mississippi river steamboat. He next obtained employment as clerk with William Boggs, a merchant of Galena, Illinois. Returning for a visit with his cousins, he met and married Agatha Ann Woolsey, on July 24, 1833. He then settled on Luck Creek, Fayette County, Illinois, where he farmed and engaged in what was then called "trading."

The new prophet, Joseph Smith, and his followers, recently expelled from Kirtland, Ohio, made a new settlement at Far West, Missouri, in 1837, from which place missionaries were sent into the surrounding country on proselyting tours. Mormon missionaries visited Lee's section and were invited to preach at his house. Levi Stewart, Lee's most intimate friend, was converted to the new faith and persuaded Lee to accompany him to Far West. John D. Lee and his wife, Agatha Ann, were baptized into the Mormon church on June 17, 1838, and settled near Ambrosia, twenty miles from the new settlement. From that time until the day of his execution, he was a faithful and devout Mormon.

Lee was a charter member of the Mormon secret organization known as "Danites," or "Avenging Angels," organized in 1838 for

7

the purpose of carrying out the orders of Joseph Smith, Mormon prophet, and participated in the incidents which led to the expulsion of Smith's followers from Missouri, detailed at length in his "*Confessions*" and other records.

With his friend Levi Stewart, Lee went on a "mission" for the Mormon church in 1839, traveling through Ohio, Kentucky and Tennessee, where he made several converts. In October he returned to his old home in Illinois and was engaged in trading until April, 1840, when he and Stewart took their families to Nauvoo, Illinois, newly established church headquarters.

In 1841 Lee again went on a mission through Illinois, Kentucky and Tennesse. At Overton, Tennesse, he baptized Mrs. Nancy Gibbons Armstrong, who later abandoned her wealthy husband to become Lee's Wife No. 12. On another mission in 1842 to Clinton County, Illinois, he baptized Emmeline and Louisa Free, the latter becoming his wife No. 3. In 1843, at Readyville, Tennessee, he baptized a ten-year-old girl who four years later became wife No. 4. In 1844 he was sent out to campaign for Joseph Smith's election as president of the United States, but his mission was cut short by the prophet's assassination at Carthage, Illinois. During his residence at Nauvoo, after the prophet's death, Lee acted as bodyguard for Brigham Young, who had assumed leadership of the Mormon church.

The doctrine of polygamy, introduced by Joseph Smith at Nauvoo, was enthusiastically accepted by Lee. Between 1844 and the spring of 1847 he married twelve polygamous wives. On one occasion, as recorded in Journal No. 6, he took three in one ceremony. In later years he took six more.

Lee assisted in building the Temple at Nauvoo, and in 1845 was appointed chief clerk to record the "endowment" ceremonies given therein. About the same time he was made an "adopted" son of Brigham Young, the second to receive that honor.

In the early spring of 1846 the Mormons were driven from Nauvoo. Wandering westward in search of a refuge the main group spent the winter of 1846-47 at Winter Quarters, where Lee made most of the entries recorded in Journal No. 6.

In the summer of 1846 five hundred men were recruited for the Mormon Battalion, to assist in the conquest of California. Lee had been selected captain of one company, but his name was withdrawn by Brigham Young, who required his services for confidential missions. After the Battalion left Fort Leavenworth, Lee and Howard Egan were sent to overtake the soldiers in order to bring back their first pay, received at Santa Fe. Lee fulfilled that mission with satisfaction, returning to Winter Quarters on the evening of November 21, 1846, the day previous to beginning Journal No. 6.

Lee's activities from that time until July 23, 1847, are recorded in detail in the Journal. Most of his time was spent in the service of Brigham Young, and he conferred with his "adopted father" nearly every day until the Pioneer company left for the mountains. Few men, even among the "Twelve Apostles," were closer to the Mormon leader. As shown by frequent entries in Journal No. 6, Lee considered Brigham Young infallible; his merest suggestion as a command. Never did Lee express the slightest criticism or mistrust of his leader. His close relationship to Brigham Young during this period—which continued until a few months before his death—and his absolute obedience to the orders of his church superiors shed new light on Brigham's responsibility for the act which brought about Lee's execution.

When Brigham started west with his first band of Pioneers in the spring of 1847, Lee was ordered to take charge of farming operations on the "Brigham Young Farm" at Summer Quarters, 16 miles north of Winter Quarters, where grain was to be raised for the benefit of the Mormon prophet's many families.

Together with most of those remaining at Winter Quarters, Lee emigrated to Utah in the spring of 1848, where Brigham gave him a square mile of land at the mouth of Cottonwood Canyon in Salt Lake Valley. As Mormon settlement was extended southward Lee was put in charge of various groups of settlers. He was one of the founders of Provo, near Utah Lake. On December 16, 1850, he left Provo with a party of 120 men, 30 women and 18 children to found the settlement of Parowan in Iron county, where he occupied the position of major of militia, chief farmer and historian.

In 1852 he founded a settlement at Harmony, just over the rim of the Great Basin. Due to Indian trouble the settlers moved to Cedar City the following year, where Lee was commander of the Mormon military forces. Returning to Harmony he built a fort and was elected "president" of the settlement, a position he held from 1861 to 1864. Brigham Young appointed him Indian farmer and sub-agent. He was later appointed probate judge for Iron county and his records while in that office are still preserved. He was a member of the Territorial legislature and a delegate to the Constitutional Convention of the free and independent "State of Deseret."

9

Between September 13 and 18, 1857, John D. Lee participated in the Mountain Meadows Massacre, under orders of his church and military superiors, Isaac C. Haight, John M. Higbee, William H. Dame and Philip Klingen Smith, when an emigrant party of 130 men, women and children were murdered in the most coldblooded manner. It had originally been planned to incite the Indians to wipe out the emigrant train, and Lee was ordered by church authorities to assemble the natives from surrounding territory and direct their attack. When the Indians met stubborn resistance and fled, the Mormon militia completed the bloody business, after disarming the emigrants under promises of protection, leaving as survivors only sixteen small children. In his *"Confessions"* Lee admits his participation in the affair, but denies having personally committed any murders.

For nearly twenty years after the massacre Lee continued to enjoy the confidence and favors of Brigham Young, to whom all the horrible details were well known. As a reward for faithful service, Brigham gave him three new wives. In 1858 he was sent to the mouth of Santa Clara river, near St. George, to plant cotton, a new agricultural experiment in the Territory. He built homes for some of his families at Washington, Utah, and at Panguitch, near Bryce Canyon, a fine cattle country.

Major J. W. Powell, who had been exploring the canyon of the Colorado since 1869, left it at the mouth of the Paria river in the fall of 1871 to go to Kanab, Utah. When his party returned in the spring of 1872 they found Lee, who had built a cabin and was preparing to operate a ferry at that point, to assist Mormon colonists in founding new settlements in northern Arizona. Fifty men, at Brigham's orders, built dugways and roads on both sides of the river and assisted in anchoring the ferry cable. Lee made his headquarters at the ferry from that time until his arrest.

On November 17, 1874, while visiting his families in Panguitch, Lee was arrested for his participation in the massacre. At his first trial, in July 1875, eight Mormons voted for acquittal, four Gentiles for conviction. His second trial came up in September, 1876. In the meantime Brigham Young had been arrested as accessory-before-the-fact. Knowing it would be impossible to convict Lee with a Mormon jury, the prosecution made an agreement whereby charges against Brigham would be dropped if he instructed the jury to bring in a verdict of guilty. Lee was promptly convicted, and on March 23, 1877, was executed at Mountain Meadows, scene of his crime.

Rachel, Wife No. 6, and Emma Batchelder, No. 17, lived with Lee at the ferry. Caroline, No. 4, was also there for a year. Between the time of the massacre and the first trial, all his wives left him except the three named above. After his execution Emma continued to operate the ferry.

Surviving children of various wives are still living in Utah, Arizona and New Mexico. At his death fifty-four of his sixty-four children survived. His grandchildren and great-grandchildren are scattered from coast to coast, some of whom occupy prominent positions.

Because of his confession implicating Brigham Young and other church officials, and because he was the only participant tried and executed, the name of John D. Lee has been the recipient of more abuse than that of any other man in western history. Even today, eighty-one years after the massacre, he is remembered as one who was an instrument in the blackest crime ever committed on American soil. For that reason, if for no other, these journals, penned by his own hand, will be of unusual interest to every student of history.

LIST OF WIVES

This list has been compiled from Lee's *"Confessions"* and from the Journal. However, statements in the two sources do not agree in some respects and Lee exhibits considerable confusion as to names and consecutive order. The two different lists in *"Confessions"* do not agree, but the Journals are more reliable evidence and the following list is believed to be correct with one possible exception.

1—Agatha Ann Woolsey, daughter of Joseph Woolsey. Born Jan. 18, 1814. Married July 24, 1833, before Lee became a Mormon. She was then 19, and Lee was 21 years old.

2—Nancy Bean, daughter of James Bean. Married Lee in the winter of 1844, after living in his family several months. Was sent back to her parents, with an infant daughter, Cordelia, in 1847, and with them came to Utah in 1848, where she married Zachariah B. Decker, a member of the Mormon Battalion, and settled at Parowan.

3—Louisa Free, daughter of A. P. Free. The Free family were converted by Lee in Tennessee. He brought them to Nauvoo where he expected to marry both Louisa and her sister Emmeline. Brigham Young, however, demanded the latter. Louisa married Lee in April, 1845, but feeling she could have done better for herself, left him, probably in 1847, to become the first wife of Daniel H. Wells, commander of the "Nauvoo Legion." She later offered to return to Lee, but Brigham Young would not give his permission.

4—Sarah Caroline Williams. Lee baptized her at Readysville, Tenn., at the age of 10. He married her at the age of 14, on the same day he married Louisa Free. On Dec. 2, 1846, he sent her to Missouri to live with a Mormon family, for reasons not stated. She rejoined him later and became the mother of twelve children. She lived at Lee's Ferry for a year, then moved to Panguich.

5—Abagail Sheffer Woolsey, mother of Agatha Ann, Rachel, Andora and Emmeline Woolsey. She was an old woman and was "sealed" to Lee for "eternity only."

6—Rachel A. Woolsey, daughter of Abagail. Lee raised her in his own family from the age of 5, then married her in the spring of 1845, at the age of 14. She was his favorite in later years and lived with him at the Lee's Ferry hideout.

7—Andora Woolsey, daughter of Abagail. Listed as No. 7 on page 289 of the "Confessions" but found nowhere else. Her name does not appear in the Journal. Page 167 of "Confessions" mentions Rachel Andora. Rachel A. and Andora may be the same person, yet they are separately listed on page 289. Nos. 5, 6 and 7 were married on the same day.

8—Polly Ann Workman. Married late in 1845 or early 1846. Lee abandoned her at Mt. Pisgah when he went to Santa Fe. She was later brought to Winter Quarters by W. M. Kimball, but Lee cast her off on Feb. 10, 1847.

9—Martha Berry, daughter of John Berry. Married Lee in the Nauvoo Temple about the same time as No. 8.

10—Delethea Morris. Probaby married in Nauvoo late in 1845. While Lee was in Santa Fe she married a trader at the Pottawatomie Indian agency.

11—Emmeline Vaughn Woolsey, another daughter of Abagail. Married Dec. 21, 1846. She attempted to run away while at Summer Quarters, but was brought back. She later left with Charles Kennedy, Lee's chief enemy, in August, 1847.

12—Nancy Gibbons Armstrong (Nancy the 2nd), sister to Sarah Gibbons, wife of A. O. Smoot. She abandoned her former husband, a wealthy merchant of Louisville, Ky., expecting to marry Smoot. When the latter delayed, she proposed to Lee and was accepted. He married her for what money she had left, although she was 48, his senior by 13 years.

13—Lovina Young and

14—Mary Vance Young (also called Polly), daughters of David Young, from Tennessee. Nos. 12, 13 and 14 were all married on the same day, Feb. 27, 1847.

15—Mary Lear Groves, 1851.

16—Mary Ann Williams, 1856.

17—Emma Batchelder. Started to Utah in 1856 with the Willis Handcart company. Was abandoned by them at Ft. Laramie and brought on by the Paul Gourley family in the Martin company. Survived the terrible ordeal of Martin's Hollow, reached Salt Lake City, and was given to Lee by Brigham Young "as a reward for faithfulness" in 1858. Lived with Lee at Lee's Ferry and operated it after his death. Later married a Mr. French, moved to Holbrook, Arizona, and became a famous frontier midwife and nurse.

18—Teressa Morse, 1859.

19—Ann Gordge, 1866 or 1867.

History of Journal No. 6

❦

John D. Lee kept a series of journals from 1844, when he became a Mormon, until 1860, three years after the Mountain Meadows massacre. The journal first reproduced here is labeled No. 6, indicating that it was preceded by five others. No. 5 would have contained the details of his journey to Santa Fe and return, in the summer and fall of 1846. The second document reproduced is a fragment of a journal written in 1859. The one which preceded it contained entries for the years 1857 and 1858, including his own account of the massacre. Previous to his first trial in 1875 Lee gave some of his journals to Brigham Young—at the latter's urgent request. Because of the damaging evidence it contained the 1857-58 record undoubtedly was destroyed.

During his imprisonment Lee wrote the story of his life, confessing his participation in the Massacre. After having been sentenced to die, he intrusted the document to William W. Bishop, his attorney, together with all papers, letters and journals then remaining in his possession. All the journals were returned to the Lee family except No. 6 which Mr. Bishop retained. Because of his possession of Lee's confession, Bishop's life was in danger, but secretly leaving the Territory he safely delivered the manuscript to a publisher in St. Louis, thus fulfilling a promise made to its author.

William W. Bishop, who conducted Lee's defense and edited his published confessions, was considered the leading attorney of Nevada, with offices at Pioche. He had been admitted to the bar in Clay County, Illinois, on March 19, 1858. On September 6, 1862, he was appointed Drafting Commissioner by President Lincoln. Leaving his native state soon afterward for Nevada, whose mines were then flourishing, he was admitted to practice in the First Judicial District, United States District Court, on May 29, 1863. On April 2, 1883 he was admitted to practice in the United States Court for the Ninth Judicial Circuit, District of California.

In the late 60's a sister of Mr. Bishop's wife living in Ohio was left a widow, with two young sons, Rolla V. and James Alva Watt. Mr. Bishop brought them to Pioche, where they lived several

13

years. In 1872 they moved to San Francisco, where Mr. Bishop had established an office in addition to the one in Pioche. James Alva Watt studied law in the San Francisco office and was admitted to practice in 1883, becoming a partner in the firm of Bishop and Watt with offices at the corner of Pine and Sansome Streets.

When William W. Bishop died, the practice was continued by James Alva Watt, who fell heir to Journal No. 6, preserved by Mr. Bishop. During the fire of 1906 all records in Mr. Watt's office were destroyed, but the journal happened to be at his home and fortunately was preserved. Upon Mr. Watt's death it came into possession of his son, Mr. Rolla Bishop Watt, a distinguished member of the legal profession in San Francisco.

The authenticity of the document is thus established beyond question. The handwriting corresponds with the script of other documents on file in Utah written by John D. Lee. The contents speak for themselves, needing no other authentication; the subject matter could have been written by no other person, and corresponds in date and detail with other records of the same period.

Ever since the publication of Lee's manuscript, *"Mormonism Unveiled, or the Life and Confessions of John D. Lee,"* the Mormon church has persistently attempted to discredit that document. Church authorities have, and still continue to claim that the entire document was fabricated by Mr. Bishop, for purposes of personal profit, and that Lee left no journal or manuscript. The discovery of these two original journals, in Lee's own hand, not only clears Mr. Bishop's memory of any attempt to deceive the public with a spurious document, but furnishes definite proof that the *"Confession"* was Lee's own statement, published as written except for punctuation and corrections in spelling supplied by the editor. Its statements are verified, during corresponding periods, by these journals.

Mr. Rolla Bishop Watt has placed the original Journal No. 6 in Huntington Library, Pasadena, California, where it may be inspected by any authorized person.

Because of their historical importance, and to circumvent any charge of altering the text, it has been thought advisable to transcribe the journals exactly as written. Lee's spelling and grammar, frequently inconsistent and erratic, have been carefully preserved. The originals contain no punctuation marks, which have been supplied by the editor for ease in reading, wherever their use was obvious. Words

14

omitted in the original text have been supplied and inserted in brackets.

In order to make the record more clear and informative to those not familiar with Mormon history, many footnotes have been supplied by the editor from information contained in various other records of the period. Information on landmarks near Winter Quarters mentioned in the Journal, has been supplied by Mr. E. G. Connely of Omaha, whose painstaking research and accurately drawn map have been of great assistance. Much credit is also due Mr. J. Roderic Korns, of Salt Lake City, for proofreading and checking of historical data contained in the accompanying footnotes.

These journals not only claim the distinction of being the only surviving diaries in the handwriting of John D. Lee, a participant in the Mountain Meadows massacre, but are also the only Mormon records of their kind to be published without Mormon censorship.

THE EDITOR.

15

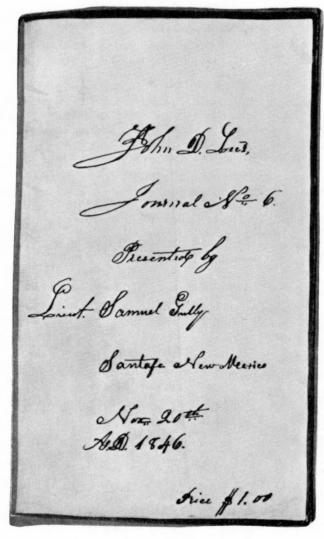

TITLE PAGE OF "JOURNAL NO. 6"
The blank book was purchased in Santa Fe by Lieut. Samuel Gully
and presented to John D. Lee, but no entries were made until
after his return to Winter Quarters.   (Actual size.)

JOURNAL No. 6—1846-47

☙

Winter Quarters, Omaha Nation, Nov. 21st, '46

Morning clear, cold, wind high N. west. This morning
when I arrose from sleep, dressed myself and walked out,
I was astonished when I looked arround and saw what
serious enterprise and industry had brought to pass within
6 weeks past. A city of at least 400 houses had been erected
in that short space of time, through the ingenuity and industry of the Saints. No other people but the Saints of
God has ever been known to acomplish as much in so short
a time.[1] After an absence of 2 months and 25 days I again
reached the camp and presant home of the Saints in health
and safety, according to the prediction of the servant and
prophet of God (my father in Iseral Pres. B. Young) who
when setting out on my journey blessed me saying thou
shalt go and prosper and return in safety. Our deliverance,
protection and return certainly was as great a meracle as
has been wrought in Iseral in this the last dispensation, for
co's [*companies*] of above 40 men have not only been robbed but many of them murdered on our rout, while we
were permited to pass unharmed. About 7 morn. [*a.m.*]
Pres. Young sent requesting me to come to his dwelling
before crossing the river for my mules and conveyance
which I had left the previous night. Acordingly at 8 I responded to his wishes and spent 2 or more hours in relating
the circumstances connected with my travels. On entering
the room, he met and blessed me with the warmth and affection of a father. At 12 noon the Saints assembled at the
stand [*in meeting*]. Prayer by Elder B. L. Clapp. Pres.
Alpheas Cutler said that he was requested by Pres. Young

17

to say that inasmuch as the day was cold and disagreeable that we would omit singing and preaching, but do the business necessary, then return home. Elder O. Pratt read off a mail of 283 letters and 17 packages, direct from the army [2] [*brought by Lee*]. While crying off the letters Pres. Young observed that he did not want any person to take letters that did not belong to them and keep them 2 or 3 weeks in their pockets or about their houses before sending them to the owners. A package of about 15 letters came in by the Eastern Mail and was cried off on the stand. The Marshal advertised [*advised*] the meeting that an ordinance had lately passed by the municipal council requiring all persons to penn their horses, mules, cattle, sheep and all forefeeted animals each night, or they will find them in the stray penn and will have to pay 25 cts each head, the avails of which will go to support the police. Pres. Young

---

[1] After many clashes with their "Gentile" neighbors, and to avoid threatened destruction of their city, the Mormons agreed to evacuate Nauvoo and began their historic trek in February, 1846. After crossing the Mississippi their first temporary camp was made on Sugar Creek, 9 miles from Nauvoo; the second was at Garden Grove in Decatur County, 145 miles; third at Mt. Pisgah in Pottawatomie County, 175 miles; fourth at Council Bluffs on the east bank of the Missouri, near present Council Bluffs, Iowa. Crossing the river at Sarpy's Ferry they established a semi-permanent camp called Winter Quarters, consisting of 538 log cabins and 83 sod houses or dugouts, containing a population of 3500 persons. Winter Quarters, seat of church authority in 1846-47, was located on land set aside for the Omaha Indians but was occupied through a temporary arrangement with that tribe, contrary to government regulations. In 1848 the Mormons who had not emigrated were compelled to move east of the river, but in 1854 the land was opened to settlement and old Winter Quarters, renamed Florence, continued to be a gathering place for Mormon emigrants for several years. It is now a northern suburb of Omaha, lying along both sides of Thirtieth Street (Arterial Highway No. 73).

[2] The Mormon Battalion, organized by the government to assist emigration and considered by Mormons as an act of Providence on their behalf, left Fort Leavenworth for California on Aug. 12-13, 1846. John D. Lee and Howard Egan, commissioned by Brigham Young to follow the Battalion, collect the soldiers' pay and bring it back to Winter Quarters, overtook the Battalion on the Arkansas river about Sept. 13. Due to lack of small change, pay day was postponed until Santa Fe was reached. On the Arkansas Lee and Egan met William Crosby and John Brown (eastbound) from a group of Mississippi Mormons which had started west in 1846, expecting to join the main body of pioneers on Platte river. Brigham's decision to postpone the journey another year upset their plans and they were advised to winter with a group of trappers at "The Pueblo." After collecting the soldiers' pay Lee and Egan left Santa Fe on Oct. 19 and started east, accompanied by Lieut. Samuel Gully who had resigned, and Roswell Stevens, a private. These four reached Winter Quarters on the evening of Nov. 21. Lee's dates in this journal are often in error; correct date of his first entry should be Nov. 22, 1846.

18

said that a police has been appointed in consiquence of the unexperience of the divisions, for the protection of property. Bro. Lott has taken quite a No. of sheep to take care of for the brethren. While they could be hearded on the prairie the sheep done well enough, but now they certainly would do better in smawler No's. I would recomend those that have sheep to take them back and pay him for his trouble. I am told that some of the women whoes husbands are in the army, are suffering for the want of food, raymond [*raiment*] and fuel. What the bishops are doeing I know not. I want Bishop Whitney to call a meeting of the bishops in each ward, that they may learn their duty. I expect him here today to make an appointment, but inasmuch as he is not I shall not make one. It is not to be expected that the bishops will supply the cases of all that are made out of his own means, but it is their duty to see that they are attended to out of the means that are in their ward, and were I a bishop I would go to those waggons that are loaded down with flour, pork, and that have been bought with the money of those very individuals that are now destitute [3] and would have provision if I had to take an ax and burst their waggons and barrels oppen if they would not hand it out. The time has now come when we must help each other, and those that do not will regret it in sorrow and deep lamentation. There has been a mericle wrought in Iseral. We have [*sent*] 2 men to the army for money. Their mission was kept a profound secret in the breast of about 2 or 3 persons. They have now returned in safety, while co's of 40 have perished, and you are welcome to the secret. Had their mission been public property

---

[3] A clothing allowance of $42.50 had been paid each soldier of the Battalion when he enlisted at Fort Leavenworth. A large proportion of that advance had been collected by Parley P. Pratt and turned over to Brigham Young, presumably for the benefit of the men's families. Part of that money had apparently been given to certain individuals to buy provisions, which they had kept for their personal use instead of distributing it to the needy families. No distribution of the funds brought by Lee and Egan had yet been made.

19

the Mo'r [*Missourians*] would have followed them, robed and likely have killed them. Their journey was an arduous and dangerous one and I am determined that they shall be paid for their services out of this money [4] and it is just justice that each person should bear a portion. One thing more, then I have done. We want the brethren to turn out on the morrow and help complete the race before the earth freezes that the mill may soon be put in opperation. Closed about 3 p.m. by Pres. B. Young. After the close, the presidents of the Seventies by request remained at the stand and took into consideration the wants of the poor; enjoined upon the Pres. of each Quorum to search into the situation of those in their several Quorums. The committee that had been sent to enquire into the circumstances of each one in their several wards &c reported that several persons were destitute. Some help was volunteered to finish Pres. Jos. Young's house. Closed at 4. At 15 minets to 5 Pres. Young, Phinahas, his bro. and myself went to and administered to Mother Angel who was low and feeble, then walked to Bro. H. C. Kimble [5] and spent a few minets. Bro. L. Stewart [6] came in while in conversation and reported that the Omaha Indians had killed 4 of the cattle out of his drove within a few days past and the probability is that they will continue to kill cattle. At 7 I met in council [7] at Pres. Young's. Presant: B. Young, H. C. Kimble, G. A. Smith, W. Woodruff, A. Lyman, O. Pratt, Egan and myself. Dr. Richards would have been

---

[4] In *"Mormonism Unveiled, or the Life and Confessions of John D. Lee,"* (p. 195), it is stated that the soldiers paid Lee and Egan $100 each for their services before leaving Santa Fe.

[5] Heber C. Kimball, one of the "Council of Twelve" (afterward called Apostles), until his death Brigham's chief assistant.

[6] Levi Stewart was Lee's closest friend. They had been old neighbors and joined the church at the same time. Stewart was bishop at Kanab, Utah, at the time of Lee's execution in 1877.

[7] The "Council of the Twelve" then consisted of Brigham Young, Heber C. Kimball, George Albert Smith, Wilford Woodruff, Amasa Lyman, Orson Pratt, Parley P. Pratt, Orson Hyde, Willard Richards, E. T. Benson, John Taylor and Lyman Wight.

there but did not know of it, yet within 6 rods, being sick. Pres. Young requested me to give a history of my journey to Santafe, which I did. They appeared much interested at the history of the country, manners and customs of the Mexicans, our own prosperity, deliverance and protection. But when I relate the sufferings of the Bat.[8] [*Mormon Battalion*] and the cause of their oppression, the manner in which Capt. Hunt [9] and others of the officers submitted the command of the Bat. to Lieut. A. J. Smith, a poor wolfish tyranicle Gentile, who was a second Nero; how they rejected the council of the 12 and thretned to put me under guard for telling their tyrant and the Dr. (Death) [10] of their meanness and threatening to cut their infernal throats if they did not cease to oppress my brethren, Pres. Young could no longer keep his seat. Asked me why I did not take his head off then, and wished that his arm was long enough to reach the Bat. The yoke of oppression and bondage would soon be broken. About 10 the council dissolved, when I paid Pres. Young $1277 in check Bat. money; $50 from Capt. and $16 I paid him, it being my 10th [11] while absent. I told him of the conduct of my partner which was nothing more than what he expected.[12] Expressed entire satisfaction with the course that I had taken while absent. Returned home at 11 at night.

---

[8] See *"A Concise History of the Mormon Battalion"* by Daniel Tyler, and *"March of the Mormon Battalion"* by Frank Alfred Golder.

[9] Jefferson Hunt, a captain in the Battalion, returned to Utah from Los Angeles in 1848 over the "Southern Route," or Old Spanish Trail, and because of his knowledge of that trail was selected to guide the Death Valley Party of 1849. See Manley's *"Death Valley in '49."*

[10] Dr. George P. Sanderson, Gentile army doctor, known to the Battalion as "Dr. Death" because he prescribed calomel for every ill.

[11] "My tenth" refers to the tithe or 10% income tax levied by the Mormon church on all members. Lee apparently received $160 for his trip to Santa Fe.

[12] Refers to Howard Egan. In *"Confessions"* Lee says Egan was drunk all the time they were in Santa Fe, and when they left stole Dr. Sanderson's mules. Egan was later Utah's champion horseman, superintendent of the Deep Creek section of the Pony Express, and Brigham's nurse and bodyguard at the time of the latter's death in 1878. See *"Pioneering the West,"* Egan's own journal.

21

Morning cool, wind high N. W., clear. At 9 morn. I was
at Pres. Young's. Two men just from the Rocky Mountains, old trappers 16 years in the employment. They or
one of them, Mr. . . . . . . appeared quite intelegent.[13] At
12 noon Pres. Young and Kimble was an hour or longer
at my tent. Read a letter from Lieut. Lytle, another from
E. Averett certifying that the course taken by me was just
and upright and that likely an influence might be used
against me by Hunt and others and should such an attempt
be made it is without foundation in truth. The letter here
referred to was written by Capt. Hunt, signed by Hunter,
Davis and Lieut. Willis.[14] Multitude of ladies came daily
to enquire after their husbands in the army. About 6 Dr.
Richards was at my tent, asked me to loan him $3.00 for
a few days. I presented him $2.50 from Lieut. Lytle and
$2.50 myself, for which he blessed me saying that I should
receive an hundred fold, and bread to eat, when I otherwise would not have had. At 5 Truman Gillett and myself was at Pres. Young's. Read a letter from Wm. J.
Phelps, an apostate from my family,[15] Strangism and infi-
delity. Pled for acceptance back again into the church and
to his former standing. (See letter on file under date Oct.
3rd, '46). Returned and wrote an answer instructing him
to come to camp as soon as circumstances would alow.
Wrote history till 1 morning.[16]

---

[13] Brigham was gathering all possible information about the west. From these
mountaineers (Groseclaude and Cardinal) and other trappers from Bellevue, he
obtained facts which formed the substance of his "revelation" concerning the
western move.

[14] Instead of delivering the money to soldiers' families, Lee turned it over to
Brigham. This and many other entries refer to that transaction, which caused Lee
endless trouble and apparently some twinges of conscience.

[15] For the "Law of Adoption" to which Lee so frequently refers, see Brigham's explanation on pages 80-88. J. J. Strang claimed to be the rightful Mormon leader after Joseph Smith's assassination, but was excommunicated by Brigham.
He later founded an independent colony on Beaver Island, and was himself assas-
sinated. See *"Kingdom of St. James"* by Milo Quaife.

[16] Lee was historian of the "Seventies" at this time.

Winter Quarters, Omaha Nation, Teus., Nov. 23rd, '46.

Morning cold, wind high. At 9 I was at Pres. B. Young who offered to send me help to build my houses, and counseled me to send the remainder of my stock to the Rush Bottom,[17] to send the family to take care of them. Acording about 2 p.m. I started 6 mules and some 15 head of cattle by Bro. L. Stewart and Wm. Lee. Wind high N. W.

Winter Quarters, Omaha Nation, Wed., Nov. 24th, 1846.

Morning clear and cold in N. W. At 2 p.m. at Pres. Young's those two men from the mountains were calculating to set owt on the morrow in co. with Bro. Samuel Gully and E. Kay, to the Puncaw villiage.[18] Was at Howard Egan's and effected a settlement. In evening divided my goods among my family, there being about $200 worth's that I brought from St. Jos. After candle light wrote in Journal till midnight. Still cold.

"Puncaw" Expedition

[17] The Rush Bottoms along the Missouri above Winter Quarters were covered with a growth of rushes or jointed grass which remained green through the winter and furnished good feed for stock. The plant was easily destroyed by plowing and is now practically extinct. The Mormon herd was probably pastured on the bottoms east of Tekamah, Nebraska.

[18] Before his assassination Joseph Smith had planned an exodus to the Rocky Mountains and had appointed James Emmett leader of a secret scouting party. After the prophet's death Emmett remembered his commission and organized an expedition with John L. Butler, James Holt, Zachariah Wilson and a few others. Although their destination was supposed to be a secret, they were soon joined by "a whole settlement located on Bear Creek." In September, 1844, the party started up the Missouri in a flat boat. At the mouth of Iowa river they sold the boat and continued up the Iowa with wagons and oxen. Ten miles above Iowa City they built cabins and made winter camp. In February messengers from Brigham Young ordered them to return. Instead, they continued their journey up the river in March, 1845, leaving it on May 15. Soon they were far north of Council Bluffs, their supposed destination. Emmett commandeered all food supplies and property in his party and put them on scanty rations. Due to this act and his petty tyranny, the party, which then numbered 130 persons, split and many returned to Iowa City. Emmett and his starving contingent continued on to Fort Vermillion, operated by Bruyere, at the junction of the Vermillion and Missouri rivers, near present Vermillion, South Dakota. They reached the post on June 17 and were fed by the French traders. The party planted crops, intending to move on west the following season. However, at Brigham's orders they returned to Council Bluffs. Emmett and part of his group, on July 9, 1846, joined Bishop George Miller's party which was instructed to build a way-station along the emigrant route. At the recently raided

Winter Quarters, O. N., Thurs., Nov. 25th, 1846.

Trappers and Messengers Leave for "Puncaw"

Morning clear, cold wind S. At 8 Jacob Woolsey and family set out for the Rushes. This morning I paid 6 cts per lbs. for beef, flour and meal scarce in market. About 12 noon I was at Pres. Young's, all was well. At 2 and 30 minets S. Gully and the two mountaineers started for the Ponckaw village. I remained working on my house till 11 at night. At 3 p.m. Bro. Bean brought Nancy [*Wife No. 2*] home and engaged to bring me 40 bushels meal from the Pottowatomy mill for which I paid him $20.00. Evening rather clowdy.

Winter Quarters, O. N., Friday, Nov. 26th, 1846.

Morning clear, W[*ind*] S. I spent the day in labour on a cabbin. At 7 eve. I went to Dr. Richards, delivered my records and rendered an account of my stewardship to him. At 12 retired, went to Bro. F. Free's and spent the night.[19]

Winter Quarters, O. N., Sat., Nov. 27th, 1846.

Morning clear, wind south, pleasant. I sent some teams to the forest and one for hay. Myself in person laboured on my building through the day. I bought about 3 & 50 lbs. beef at 3 cts.

Pawnee village Miller sent his wagons back to Bellevue with the Methodist missionaries while he harvested their abandoned crops. The returning wagons were accompanied by many families sent by Young and Kimball, increasing the company to 600 persons. At this time Miller received written instructions to proceed to California, but had only reached Grand Island when he was ordered to halt there for the winter. Visited by the Ponca chief, he was advised against the location and invited to winter near the Ponca village, at the mouth of the Running Water (Niobrara), about 60 miles west of Vermillion and 180 miles from Winter Quarters. Miller walked to Winter Quarters at Christmas, the Poncas having "borrowed" his horses, returned, and was again called back, with Emmett, on Jan. 28. Emmett and Miller, claiming orders from Joseph Smith, denied Brigham's authority, which resulted in a quarrel. Thoroughly disgusted, the expedition returned in April, 1847 and scattered to various points in Iowa. Miller apostatized and joined Lyman Wight's scism in Texas, then went to Beaver Island, Mich., to join J. J. Strang's colony. After Strang was killed he moved to Maringo, Ill., where he died in 1856. (See "Biography of James Holt," MS.; "Expedition of the Emmett Company," by Wm. D. Kartchner, MS.; George Miller biography in So. Calif. Hist. Soc. Annual, 1917; Anson Call biography in Tullidge's History of Northern Utah and Idaho.

[19] With Louisa Free, Wife No. 3.

Winter Quarters, O. N., Sund., Nov. 29th, 1846.

Morning clear, pleasant wind S. At 11 I was at Dr. Richards's tent. Found him comfortabley in bed though somewhat ill. At 20 minets to 12 noon the Saints assembled at the stand. Prayer by Elder J. D. Lee. Elder H. C. Kimble addressed the meeting. Said that this people no doubt considered themselves oppressed, because of poverty and privation, but not so much as we in times passed have been; and some are allmost driven to desperation and become careless and indifferent and forget to pray. This should not be but we should be helps to each other and pray for one another and thereby become saviours on Mount Zion. Are our enemies to come up on Mt. Zion? I say no. My brethren, the council are laboring and striving all the day long, then why find fault? They will not be with you many years hence unless you are united and take hold and help them bear of this kingdom and take care of the poor. If you do not you will probably fall out by the way and will have to atone for all your misdoings if it is 200 thousand [*years*] hence. Elder E. T. Benson, who arrived in camp on Friday eve at 9, Nov. 26, '46, said that he was glad to [*live*] and dwell in the midst of Iseral, which is fast becoming a terror in the midst of the nations and that delight my[?] we are now considered a distinct nation. Witness the title of our brethren in the army (Mormon Bat.) Bro. Kimble says that mericles are wrought in Iseral. I know it. Miericles were wrought in the deliverance of our brethren in the Battle at Nauvoo, when men stood where bullets flew arround them like hail and but few were hurt.[20] A bullet struck Br. Hyrum Kimble on the top of his head and knocked him down. He jumped up and went at [*it*] again and likely knocked some sense in. The Lord struck Paul down before he could see as he ought. Many of the enemy saw the deliverance and

Remarks by Kimball and Benson

---

[20] The "Battle of Nauvoo" took place Aug. 24, 1846.

went down into waters of baptism. If we are only united nothing will harm us, but a corrupt man cannot be saved in the Kingdom of God. I never enjoyed myself better in my life before, than I have while on this mission East, and have learned to be at home wherever night overtakes me, content myself with whatever I am favored with. I am determined to build up the heads of this church. As Joseph said, Build me up and I will build you up. As a man said, Bro. Benson, how do you know when you council right? I answered, How do your children know what to do? Answer: By your telling them. Just so it is with me. When my president counselled me I then counsel others. I am not as the Methodist sister was, that she wanted to get a little bit of glory in some corner about as big as a little twinkling star, but I want to get all the glorey that I can. If [I] should get the glorey of the sun I should not rob anyone because there is all sufficient for all who walke upright before the Lord. Truly my heart rejoiced when I came to the bank of the river to see the lights that luminated the Saints, here [hear] the doges bark and wolves howl. Now when I look arround and see what has been done within 3 months past plainly declares that the Lord is with Iseral. No people could build up a city of this magnitude in the same time but the Nephites [Mormons], and that, too, without means, as the sectarian God created the world out of nothing. There are many good Saints in the east that will come out in the spring if it is council, and my heart is with them. Bro. Lytle laid our case before the Pres. of U. S. and has written the Pres. views on the subject to the council. I had an interview in person with our old friend Tindall, the postmaster general. He assured me that he would do [all] that was in his power for us without charge, but should he fall in our way, rember him, for he did not no what might hapen. Pres. Young said that the preaching was excellent and as the day was unpleasant

26

and the people wanted to go home he would therefore directly bring buisiness before them that he wanted. It is known that we have a mill to build, responsiblety of the same rests upon me. We have done all we could and I have hired all that would come but for the want of houses, wood, hay &c, we were unable to accomplish it; but now I want the brethren to turn out and do it without pay.[21] Let their be no excuse rendered or taken. Let the 12 bishops, Seventies, H. P. and E.[22] turn out. Let the bishops divide the wards into 3 divisions and let 1 part labour tomorrow, the 2nd next day, 3rd the day following. The eighth quorum of Seventies published an appointment on this evening 5th. Closed at 2 by prayer per Elder J. M. Grant.[23] Several cases of the sick were presented before the Lord. After meeting Pres. Young and myself walked to Father John Smith,[24] A. Lyman, G. A. Smith, W. Richards, and notified them to meet in council at 3 at Pres. Young's. Went home where I met Bro. W. M. Kimble, who requested me, or rather demanded $5 of me, for bringing Polly Ann Workman [*Wife No. 8*] from Pizgah.[25] I told [*him*] to look to her for his pay as she went off contrary to my council and I did [*not*] employ him to bring her, but would give him $5.00 to take her back. I received a letter while on the stand stating that he could bring the meal that I sent for. Start 12 days. Pres. Young counselled me to open a trade between us and the Mo's [*Missourians*] and if you have not sufficient capital I will furnish you and will have you furnish my mill and purchase

Offers $5 to be Rid of Polly Ann

---

[21] They were requested to work without pay on the mill, Brigham's private property, but were charged regular toll after it was in operation.

[22] Bishops, Seventies, High Priests and Elders—divisions of the church organization.

[23] Jedediah M. Grant, father of Heber J. Grant, president of the Mormon church since 1918.

[24] John Smith, uncle of Joseph Smith and father of Apostle George Albert Smith. "Patriarchs," such as John Smith, supported themselves by issuing "blessings" at $5 each.

[25] Mt. Pisgah, in Pottawatomie County, Iowa, 175 miles west of Nauvoo.

such articles as I need. At 4 p.m. met in council at Pres. Young's. Presant: B. Young, H. C. Kimble, G. A. Smith, O. Pratt, W. P. Woodruff, A. Lyman, W. P. Richards, E. T. Benson, and J. D. Lee. Bro. E. T. Benson gave an interesting account of his mission. Said that Strang and G. J. Adams [26] was at Pittsburg endeavering to stir a smoke. The apostates and whoremongers are ralleying arround Strang's standard. Elder O. Pratt read a leter from Elder J. C. Little stating that the president had read a letter from the Bat. requesting him to appoint Capt. Hunt or J. B. Backenstos [27] to take command of the Bat. Pres. Polk replied that he had no power to appoint any man to take command of the Bat. The Bat. alone had the right to appoint by vote whom they chose; that his feelings was warm toward our people and Judge Kain [28] of Philadelphia said that he would do all in his power for us in the cabinet or elsewhere. About 3 hours were spent conversing on var-

Strang and Adams, Apostates

Judge Kane Expresses Friendship

---

[26] George Jones Adams had previously been high in church councils. In 1843 he had been sent to Russia as a Mormon missionary. Like many other ambitious fanatics, he aspired to leadership after Joseph Smith's death, and was excommunicated by Brigham Young in 1845. Joining J. J. Strang, another disappointed aspirant, he toured the East lecturing against Brigham and proselyting for Strang. When Strang was shot, the colony on Beaver Island disintegrated. Nothing is known of Adams' activities until 1865, when he appeared at Jonesport, Maine, representing himself as founder of the "Church of the Messiah." With a large company of followers he set sail from Jonesport on Aug. 25, 1866, to found a colony in Palestine. The new settlers were landed at Jaffa, where a number of buildings were erected. But crops suitable to Maine failed in the desert climate and many of the settlers died of starvation. With all available funds Adams deserted his followers, who were finally rescued by Moses S. Beach of the New York Sun, and the survivors, some of whom are still living, returned to their own land. Mark Twain, then a young reporter, returned on the same vessel, but failed to appreciate the news value of the tragedy. Adams later started a "five-cent bank" in California and was apprehended while trying to abscond with its funds.

[27] J. B. Backenstos, sheriff of Hancock County, Ill., during the "Mormon War," was married to a relative of Joseph Smith and although not a Mormon, was a Mormon sympathizer for political purposes. He went to California in 1846.

[28] Judge John K. Kane of Philadelphia had been personal advisor to several United States presidents and acted in that capacity for President Polk. His son, Thomas L. Kane, had accompanied J. C. Little from Washington, D. C. to Fort Leavenworth to study the Mormon problem. Taken with a fever, he was nursed back to health in a Mormon camp on Papillion Creek, joined the church and received his "patriarchial blessing." Posing as a friendly Gentile, he was active in behalf of the Mormons during the "Johnston War" of 1857 in Utah. Kanesville, Iowa, and Kane County, Utah, were named in his honor.

ious subjects; the council enjoyed themselves well. At 7 the council dissolved and walked to the High Council. Pres. Young reported or rather called for the report of H. Stout before the High Council. 28 men that he had selected as a police which were accepted. Upon motion the committee was discharged. Bishops were ordained in each ward. Pres. Young instructed the bishops to see that houses were built for the widows immediately, that the sisters stop paying out what money they have for buildings. Let their means be laid out for provisions which can not be had without money, but houses can be built by the wards. Voted by the council that the police receive 1.50 cts. for each night servis, and that Hozea Stout (capt.) receive 75 cts per day. The above revenue to be raised by levying a tax on the citizens. That the marshal, H. Eldredge, be the police cessor and collector to receive in payment (E. I.[29] the tax) wood, cash, clothing, provisions &c. That Capt. H. Stout be the wood inspector. That 1.25 cts be allowed for wood. Pres. Young said that he wanted the gates shut down for a few days, still a few droves of hogs could be brought in for the benefit of the camp which can be had for 2 cts per lb., whereas now it is selling from 4 to 6 and 2 to 3 down in Mo., because of the imprudence of the brethren that go trading and raising the price by telling them that the camp will consume all the pork that can be had in the settlements 200 ms. round. Let word be communicated to the ferrymen not to cross any more teams that are going to Mo. to trade until we instruct.[30] Several bishops were ordained to supply the vacancies in the different wards. Council dissolved to Wed. eve 6. Now 9 at night, pleasant, bright moon.

---

[29] "E. I." is intended for "i.e."

[30] An example of Brigham's complete control over church members.

Winter Quarters, Mond., Dec. 1st.

Morning mild and pleasant. I was employed through the day mudding or daubing my little cabbin. At 6 eve several families of my children met at Wm. Pace's where I gave them a discourse on the law of adoption. Lucy [31] and I prayed together till about 12. The spirit of the Lord softened and cemented our feelings together, till we were almost like angels.

"Almost Like Angels"

Winter Quarters, Teus., Dec. 2nd, '46.

Cold and clowdy. Wind N. W. Engaged in building. About 3 p.m. Sister Marcia Allen and Caroline W. Lee [32] started for the English Grove [33] in the settlements of Missouri. It was not, however, without feelings of sorrow that she left and went away, notwithstanding Sister Allen promised to be a mother to her and see that she had a good home.

Caroline Is Sent to Missouri

Winter Quarters, Wed., Dec. 3rd, '46.

Cool, bleak wind from the north all day. Bro. Wm. Pace and myself were engaged in cutting and hauling house logs.

Winter Quarters, Thurs., Dec. 4th, '46.

Morning rather clowdy, bleak, piercing wind N. W. Employed today in the forest cutting house logs. 3 teams drawing.

Winter Quarters, Frid., Dec. 5th, '46.

Clowdy, cold, W. east. I commenced laying the foundation of my house No. 2.

---

[31] Lucinda Pace, wife of Lieut. James Pace of the Battalion. The Pace family had been "adopted" by Lee, who assumed the responsibility of looking after Lucinda.

[32] See sketch of Caroline W. Lee (Sarah C. Williams), No. 4 in list of Lee's wives. She was about 15 years old at this time. No reason appears for sending her away. Family tradition is to the effect that his older wives gave Lee a horse-whipping for marrying so young a girl. She joined him in Utah in 1848, traveling with a Mrs. Gillum, and became the mother of twelve children, some of whom still live in Utah (1938).

[33] English Grove was 65 miles above St. Joseph.

Winter Quarters, O. N., Dec. 6th, '46.

Cool, clowdy. At 7 wind shifted north, day uncomfortable. At 11 Sister Steavens came to me in tears requesting council to know what to do saying that she intended coming into my family and claimed me for her counsellor. The case was not only critical but difficult. I told her that I would lay the matter before my father in Iseral and get his mind, then advise her accordingly. At 12 noon I was [at] Pres. Young's, spent about 30 min., walked with him to his store house that was then building, visited the family; in the meantime interduced Sister Steavens case concerning Truman Gillet Lee. Obtained his feelings, returned back at 1 p.m. Sent 3 teams for wood. At 6 I received a letter from Bro. Levi Stewart stating that my stock was doeing well in the Rushes, that he would do all to take care of my stock and to benefit me. He therefore wishes me to do in like manner for him.

Trouble in "Adopted" Family

Winter Quarters, Omaha Nation, Sund., Dec. 7th, 1846.

Morning cold. Hail, snow and sleet. W[ind] N. E. In the forenoon I was engaged in drawing my account against the Bat. About 8 Pres. Young was at my tent. About 1 p.m. I was at the Historian's tent; found him bedfast. At 2 Pres. Young was at the store. At 3 he returned home where he sat and counciled some 2 or 3 hours. Instructed me to write to Wm. Crousby and John Brown [34] with re-

---

[34] Fourteen families, together with several single men, left Monroe County, Miss., April 8, 1846, with instructions to "proceed through Missouri and fall in with the companies from Nauvoo in the Indian country." Reaching Independence, Mo., they were joined by Robert Crow and William D. Kartchner, both Mormons, with their families, and fourteen non-Mormons bound for Oregon. This party of 25 wagons, with William Crosby as captain, followed the Oregon Trail across Kansas, reaching Ash Hollow on the North Fork of Platte river, where they learned from a former trapper, James Clyman, eastbound from California, that there were no Mormons west of that point. The disappointed Mississippi company, then numbering about 100, exclusive of the Oregon emigrants who had gone ahead, continued to Fort Bernard, 8 miles east of Fort Laramie, where they learned from the trader Richard (or Richieu), Bill New and other trappers, of a good wintering place on the headwaters of Arkansas river. Guided by Richard they reached The Pueblo (Pueblo, Colo.), Aug. 7, 1846, where they found several mountaineers living with

lation to our policy in the spring, that the church in that vicinity may know what course to pursue, &c. At 4 I went to Truman G. Lee, counselled them relative to families affairs. Supped with them. Truman and I went to Bro. Free's and wrote the letters that Pres. Young instructed to be written. About 9 Sister Free, Louisa [*Wife No. 3*], prepared supper. At 11 I retired to rest. Staid Bro. Free's.

Winter Quarters, O. N., Mon., Dec. 8th, '46.

Cold and clowdy. Wind N. Spent the [*day*] on my building.

Winter Quarters, O. N., Teus., Dec. 9th, '46.

Somewhat more pleasant. Sun shone through light clowds. At 8 I paid 56 cts for meal. At 9 Pres. B. Young was sitting in his room counselling those that were or had called for that purpose. At 10 I returned, having received a present from my father [*Brigham Young*], a good piece of pork. Spent the remainder of the day on my house. About 5 eve. John Gheen came with only a part of my . . . . . .

John Gheen Confesses

Confessed that he had gambled off money and made way with part of the cargo. The loss that I sustain was about $50. At 8 I was at Pres. Young's. Presented Sister Young a demijohn fitted with ebony. [42]

Winter Quarters, O. N., Wed., 10th

Cold. Wind N. Clear. At 8 morn. Pres. Young sent us a

---

their Spanish and Indian wives. After assisting in the erection of cabins, William Crosby, John Brown and others left Sept. 1 to return to Mississippi for their families via Bent's Fort and the Santa Fe Trail. Encountering the Mormon Battalion at the crossing of Arkansas river, and advising of the settlement at Pueblo, they continued eastward, meeting Lee, Egan and Lieut. James Pace the following day, Sept. 13. On his return to Winter Quarters Lee advised Brigham Young of the Mississippi company's intentions. Brown and several new recruits, with their negro slaves, were members of Brigham's pioneer party of 1847. Robert Crow and family met and joined Brigham's party at Fort Laramie; the fourteen families of Mississippi Saints traveled with the sick detachment of the Mormon Battalion, arriving in Salt Lake Valley July 29. About 300 Mormons wintered at Pueblo. Mrs. Manomus Gibson Andrus, living (1938) in St. George, Utah, who as a child accompanied her parents from Mississippi, remembers with gratitude the kindness of the trappers' Spanish wives who saved her family from starvation at Pueblo. Bill New, the trapper, married Mary Gibson, an older sister, by whom he had two children. (See John Brown's Journal, MS.; "James Clyman," edited by Camp; "Oregon Trail," Francis Parkman; Journal History of L. D. S. Church; William Clayton's Journal; statement of Mrs. Manomus Gibson Andrus, MS.

pail of first rate molasses. Half of my time has been used since my return in hearing and counseling.

Winter Quarters, O. N., Thurs., 11th.

Morning cold, clowdy.

Winter Quarters, O. N., Frid. Dec. 12th.

Clowdy, cold W. North.

Winter Quarters, O. Nation, Sat., Dec. 13th.

Clear, cold. Wind N.

Winter Quarters, O. N., Sund., Dec. 14th.

Clear weather, mild, W. south. At 12 noon the Saints assembled in public meeting, at the stand. Prayer by H. G. Shearwood. Elder C. P. Lott addressed the meeting. Spoke with reference to the duty of the Saints in their several capacities, places and stations. Bore record that we now have a prophet in Iseral who declared while in the Temple of the Lord last winter that we (the Saints) would escape in the wilderness and that wickedness and abomination and corruption and blasphemy would be the doings of those who were left behind. The Temple [35] which we have built unto the Most High God for the endowment of the Saints and the furtherance of his cawse, shall be turned into a money changer and the habitation of thieves. At the close of C. P. Lott's remarks Pres. Young gave an invitation for others to speak who wished. Pres. B. Y. said that in as much as there is no one occupying the stand I will do my errand and retire, on account of the inclemency of the atmosphere. It will be advisable to meet here often, therefore the bishops will have to prepare a large room in each ward and meet once a week and the instructions necessary be delivered in this way. Yesterday we had a council with those (O.N.) Indians through Major [*Mitchell*] and

A Prophet in Isreal

---

[35] The Temple at Nauvoo was abandoned and later burned down.

the interpreter, and they have agreed to move some 6 or 8 miles below here, provided we will build them houses, but they are afraid to go without, as their lodges are not bullet proof as has been proven here when the Iowas attacked them and wounded 3 of them. Last evening an express arrived, saying that a party of Sious fell on a party of about 50 Omahas and out of that No. about 8 only escaped, which makes those Indians that are here begs leave to remain till morning, when we want the brethren to turn out and help build those houses. I cannot do it all, yet I will send some help. Come, brothers, bear each other's burdens that you may reap the reward of the faithful. I want the bishops and High Council to adjourn to Dr. Richard's, the room is large and commodious and I will meet them there to give the necessary instructions at candle light. There is a request that I should like to make provided I could get it answered, but that I cannot; and that is that those who have money sent them from the army that are dissatisfied could have it back again; but this cannot be because the means have been sent to St. Louis and laid out for goods.[36] It is true the goods are much higher than what we anticipated but it is an unavoidable occurrence. The low stage of the river raised the price of freight to $3.00 when it should be 1.25 only. I see [no] cause of complaint whatever and had not Bro. Parley and those brethren that were with him, happened at the Fort, at the payment, and urged the necessity of sending a part of their

---

[36] Advances paid to the 500 soldiers in the Battalion at Fort Leavenworth amounted to $22,500. The amount brought back by Parley P. Pratt and turned over to Brigham was "between five and six thousand dollars." Instead of distributing that sum to the soldiers' families, Brigham invested part of it in goods, as admitted by this entry, and the goods were sold at a stiff profit through the store operated by Brigham Young, Albert Rockwood and William Clayton. Part of the money brought from Santa Fe by Lee was also invested in goods (see Note 52). Final pay of the sick detachment was collected in 1847 by Capt. James Brown, at Monterey, Calif., and used by Brigham's orders to buy out the claim and improvements of Miles Goodyear, at Ogden. Families of men in the Battalion received little of the money paid by the government, although some individuals sued for its recovery. From Brigham's viewpoint, organization of the Battalion was a decided financial success.

means back, you would not had any money to have troubled you about. Who caused your husbands and bro. to enlist? Was it not me?[37] Have I received any remuneration for taking care of their family? No, not a cent,[38] and there is Bro. Wm. Clayton shall be paid for his services. There is but few that know how he fares. He has neither coffee, nor sweetening nor meat for 6 weeks, all the fall. Yet without a murmur.[39]

Winter Quarters, O. N., Sund., Dec. 14th, '46.

Report of "Quorums"

At 35 min. to 8, the Council of the First Presidency of Seventies. Prayer by Pres. J. Young. Pres. Jos. Young [40] said that on last Sabbath it was resolved that the Seventies should visit the poor in their wards or Quo's [*Quorums*], and that their contributions should be left with him. Some flour and beef has been brought which he sent to those that were destitute, since which time the wards have been set in order and bishops have been appointed to attend to the wants of the poor which will probably release us from this burden, as it belongs to the Bishoprick. Also counseled the presidents to rill all vacancies that had occurred in their several Quo's and right up their Quo's.

15th [*Quorum*]. President John Lytle reports that he found none destitute in his Quorum.

13th. Pres. Solon Foster reported all efficient in his Quorum.

29th. Pres. O. M. Allen reports that his Quorum donated 30 lbs. flour and 35 lbs. of beef; that Sister Brow-

---

[37] After arrival in Utah, to foster the persecution complex, Brigham and other church authorities claimed that the Battalion had been organized by the government to cripple Mormon emigration. That falsehood is still propagated by the church, but all contemporary documents, including the above, prove that the contrary was true. Mormons enlisted only after Brigham had issued specific orders.

[38] He had taken charge of the entire amount of advance payment.

[39] For William Clayton see his published "Journal," which contains numerous "murmurs." (See also Note 44).

[40] Joseph Young, brother of Brigham. All the "Twelve" and various other church officials were entitled to the prefix "Pres."

ett was destitute of provisions and was [*without*] a house and that she has no means to assist herself. Pres. Rockwood said that Sister Browett need not suffer for anything as she has abundance of good property sufficient to make her comfortable. Voted that Pres. O. M. Allen take such articles as she has to spare and build her a house by her consent and that Mrs. Browett have the privilege to redeem them.

5th. Pres. W. Brown reported that all were able to take [*care*] of themselves in his Quorum. The Widow Ott which is now on the opposite side of the river . . . .

10th Q. Pres. Royal Barny reported that he was aware of the measures taken by the Council at the last meeting.

Pres. Daniel Allen, 24th Quo., reported that all could sustain themselves.

Pres. S. H. Earl, 20th Quo., reported all was able to help themselves.

Manufacture of Baskets

Pres. A. P. Rockwood by request of Pres. Jos. Young reported that on the last meeting the policy and economy of securing labor or employment for poor making willow baskets was thought to be the most proffitable, whereupon Pres. J. M. Grant was appointed to select some person to open a school and instruct such as should want employment. Pres. J. M. Grant reported that he went in person to Bro. S. H. Earl's, found him employed in making baskets with his partner. Had completed 40 odd dollars worth making at least $3 per day for the benefit of the Seventies. Proffered to open a school and instruct such as want employment for $1.25 per day and board himself. Whereupon he was employed and his bro. also. A sample of the baskets was brought before the Council and pronounced good. After hearing the report the brethren presant approved of the measures taken. Pres. A. P. Rockwood said that he considered admissible to build a house 20 feet square for that purpose. It was approved. Pres. Jos. Young suggested the propriety of establishing the instruction upon a liberal principle that all Saints may benefit, that there be no selfishness or tenacity in prefference to the Seventies. The Council have employed Bro. Sylvester H. Earl and we will see that he is paid, out of their means. The man that is to get and prepare the willows is entitled to 1/3rd of the baskets made, which he can take at any time, which releases us for his services. But Bro. E. must be paid in provisions. Let every man endeavor to do what is right and have no division. Pres. Earl said that difficulties may arrise. Call on all the Seventy to build this house, then every man will have a claim and consiquently will want their children schooled, and to take too large a school it will not be proffitable. Upon motion [of] Pres. Rockwood that all scholars taken to learn the art of basket making shall be subject to the Council; that they be required to remain in the service of the association so long as the Council shall deem expedient and that they shall receive baskets in payment for their service. Carried unanimously. Voted that Pres. A. P. Rockwood receive 24 dollars in baskets at 20 cts discount for having the basket house, 20 x 14 feet, 3 feet underground, covered with willow and sod, a chimney to each end, window and 24 lights sash, all fitted for servis but the glass, $24 if done within six days and if not within 10, $20. Dissolved at 30 m. to 10. Meeting adjourned to Teusday eve., same place. Walked to Pres. B. Young's, found him writing a letter. Had the pleasure of drinking a glass of wine made by himself [42] and eating some rye and cheese presented by the hand of Mother Young. Spent 2 hours conversing with him and hearing him explain the law of adoption. In the meantime he suggested to me the propriety of taking some 20 or 30 of the brethren down into the settlements and take contracts of threshing and cleaning wheat and thereby procure an out-

Brigham's Home-Made Wine

37

fit for the journey in the spring;[41] in the meantime have teams employed in hauling grain, tallow, butter, lard, soap, whiskey [42] and other articles that are in good demand here and can be purchased at a low rate, leaving them in the hands of Brother Rockwood to dispose of and make returns, and so keep up the trade and trafick through the winter, and that he would advance a part of the capital and share in the profits, and told me that I should have his blessings and approbation and prosper in the undertaking. My reply was to him, father, thy will be done. He blessed me and I returned home about midnight. About 3 p.m. Bro. James Bean [*father-in-law No. 2*] brought me 37½ bushels of meal from the Potawatimie mill which cost me about 56 cts cash per B. on the opposite side of the river. The remainder of the evening Thomas Johnson, Wm. Swap and Harvey Pace was employed in getting it home from the river..

Winter Quarters, O. N., Dec. 15th, '46.

Morning cold, wind N. W. Some snow on the ground. About 8 o'clock had some talk with Bro. Maginnis. Received insulting language from him concerning a waggon that he put in for the benefit of the Saints. I told him that I had acted in accordance with the council of Pres. Young, and if he was not satisfied he must quarrel with him and not me. He replied that he had nothing to do with Pres. Young and that he should look to me for the waggon and if I did not produce it with all things with it, this people

---

[41] Referring to the Pioneer emigration of 1847.

[42] Whiskey and all alcoholic drinks were prohibited by Joseph Smith's "Word of Wisdom." The prohibition has always been a dead letter. Lee's journal shows that whiskey was a regular stock in trade at Brigham's store, and its use is frequently mentioned. Later, in Utah, Brigham Young and Heber C. Kimball opened the first saloon. Brigham Young owned both a distillery and brewery, and was granted a liquor monoply for the Territory of Utah by an act of his own "legislature." See "*Lights and Shadows of Mormonism.*" (Gibbs); "*A Quaker Forty-niner,*" (Pancoast); "*Lucky Baldwin,*" (Glasscock); "*An Excursion to California.*" (William Kelly).

should know that I had lied. I told him that he was an ungrateful child and as the Lord lived I would not bear any more of his insulting and unbecoming language and that he should atone for what he had already said. In about ½ hour Pres. Young sent a messenger requesting to see me immediately. I responded to the call, found Bro. Maginnis and Bro. Brooks at Pres. Young's, doubbly entering a complaint against me. Pres. Young asked me what was the difficulty with Maginnis and me and I laid the whole matter before him, whereupon he asked Bro. Brooks if Maginnis had got the waggon of him. Bro. B. replied he had. Pres. Young said that he would make it all right with him, leaving Maginnis out of the scrape, and did so. Maginnis, finding that he did not succeed as he expected, offered some apologies, at the same time attaching the blame to me. Pres. Young replied that I was not to blame; that he kept the waggon on his own responsibility. Bro. Brooks went away satisfied while Maginnis was left to torture under the pangs of a guilty conscience. At 9 o'clock information came to me that articles could be purchased reasonable at the Point [43] by making a bill of 1 or $200. Sugar by the barrel can be had for 13 cts, coffee 12½, salt $1.25 bushel, molasses from 63 to 75 cts per gallon, &c, &c. Pres. Young advised me to send immediately and purchase from 300 to 1000 dollars worth. Acordingly through the day I fitted up some teams, purchased a load of beef hides at 4 cts and made ready to start on the morrow. Light showers of snow through the day. Evening cold, wind east.

Sarpy's Trading Post

[43] "The Point," or "Point & Poles" as written by Lee, refers to Point aux Poules, possibly so named because of the wild turkeys found in that section. It was located on the east bank of the Missouri, opposite Bellevue. P. A. Sarpy maintained a trading post and ferry at Point aux Poules, which had developed into a small Indian village and was then a sub-agency for the Pottawatomie Indians. It was also sometimes called "Pull Point" and "Trader's Point." The ground on which the post stood has been washed away and partly replaced by the river since 1846. The Mormons used Sarpy's ferry until they established one of their own 15 miles upstream, opposite Winter Quarters.

Winter Quarters, O. N., Teusday, Dec. 16th, '46.

Morning cold and snowy. At 8 o'clock Bro. Charles Bird started for the Point for the groceries, goods, &c that we had engaged. I sent by him $250 dollars cash exclusive of the load of hides. The remainder of the day I was employed in building a chimney to my house. Evening cold and some snow. About 9 Bro. Thomas Johnson and George Gillett started for Stewart's herd with 2 and ½ yoke cattle. On account of a press of business I sent Truman Gillet as a reporter of a meeting which convened at Bro. Pulcipher's agreeable to previous appointment. Presant: Pres. Joseph Young, Jedediah Grant, and Welcome Chapman. After waiting until 8 or 9 o'clock for the rest of the brethren of the council and conversing on various subjects, dispersed and retired home without any further business. Now about 11 o' and I have just finished laying my hearth. Truman Gillett, clerk for the evening.

Winter Quarters, Om. Nation, Dec. 17th.

Clear, mild and pleasant. Engaged in plastering or rather mudding my house.

Winter Quarters, O. N., Thurs., Dec. 18, '46.

Lee as a Merchant

Clowdy, cool, wind N. At 9 morn. at Pres. B. Young's, proposed going and returning immediately with a load of groceries, in the meantime look arround and learn the moves of the times and trade. He decided that I was right. Teusday morning T. Johnson and G. Gillett started to the heard with 2 yoke oxen to bring my mules down. They have not yet returned, the cause of their delay I no not. Borrowed $250.00 to secure a contract of groceries at the Point. Sent Bro. C. Bird to lay in the goods. About 2 p.m. Bro. C. Bird arrived with the goods which I deposited at Bro. A. P. Rockwood's for sale on Main Street. Spent the eve. in taking an invantory of them and at 6 met in council at Dr. Richards. Pres. B. Young and the council of the 12 presant. At 9 I took supper at Bro. A. P. Free's and spent the night [*with Wife No. 3*]. Took them some sugar and coffee.[44]

Winter Quarters, O. N., Fri., Dec. 19th, '46.

Clear, keen, piercing from the N. At 8 morn. I [*was*] at Bro. Rockwood. Left with him another smawl cargo of goods. This morning commenced selling. Retailed molasses at 80 cts per gal., first article. Sugar and coffee at 16⅓, salt 1.75, brown domestics at 11, drilling at 18, bleached muslin from 16 to 25 cts. At 6 Pres. B. Young was at [*my*] humble cottage, then attended meeting at Bro. Leonard's. Gave the bishop of the ward a sentimental lecture on the subject of each man and duty, women not excepted. Meeting closed at 9. Pres. B. Young and W. Woodruff stopped a few moments at my dwelling, said that he wished that I could go immediately with them to the changes[*?*] and get the spichain[*?*] as it is much wanted. My boys have not yet returned. I am somewhat uneasy fearing that some accident has happened. Pres. B. Young said that I had better go and see about them, that he would furnish me a mule and anything else that they had at command. Blessed [*me*] and returned home. The remainder of the Omahas returned.

Winter Quarters, O. N., Sat., Dec. 20th, '46.

Clear, cool, rather more moderate than the day previous. At 9 I was at Pres. B. Young's who belted arround me a brace of 6 shooters to protect my person against savage depredations. At 10 I obtained Dr. Richard's riding beast and started to the Rush bottom in pursuit of my lost boys

Blessed and Armed by Brigham

---

[44] Prohibition of tea and coffee among Mormons by Joseph Smith's "Word of Wisdom" was not observed by the prophet himself, nor by many of his followers until after the settlement of Utah, and then principally to prevent cash from leaving the Territory. They are still theoretically prohibited. See sermon of Apostle George Albert Smith, March 8, 1855.

or supposed to be. Passing the mill then building, Pres. came and said, I bless you in the name of the Lord and say that you shall go and prosper and return back again in perfect safety. At 1 p.m. I passed the Fort at what is called Old Council Bluffs [45] and at 2 and 30 min. I arrived in the neighborhood range, and point of my destination. Learned from Bro. L. Stewart (who was collecting his) that my boys missed their way while going and was compelled to take refuge for the night in thick cluster of willows for the night and forced to ascend the branches from the ravages of the wolves who set out a hideous yell while all arround them. The night was tremendous cold, yet these sufferers survived it without much serious injury. About 7 the next morning they came into camp where they were rested and refreshed. Nothing more serious occurred. On reaching the camp of the heardsmen I found all well and doing first rate. The cattle and mules were in the rushes almost waist deep and thriving, remarkably fat. Bro. Stewart who had just returned from the battle grounds between the Omaha and Seu Indians said that the Omahas had a regular slaughter yard where they butchered our beaves without reserve until they were defeated by the Seus and 5 of their Nos. slaughtered, which together with revelation that their prophet had saying that 20 Seus were then in the valley and on the morrow a larger band would

---

[45] Chittenden says: "The particular situation always known in those early years as Council Bluffs was 25 miles above the modern city of that name and on the opposite side of the river about where the little town of Calhoun is now located." Mr. E. G. Connely says: "Old Council Bluffs is a correct appellation for the Fort Atkinson site. Fort Atkinson was about ten miles up the river from Winter Quarters. It adjoins the present village of Ft. Calhoun. It came into being as a result of the failure of the Yellowstone expedition of 1818-19, was garrisoned for eight years, abandoned and succeeded by Ft. Leavenworth in 1827. It was first called Camp Missouri, then renamed in honor of its commander. It had a lime kiln and brickyard, and the surrounding land was cultivated extensively enough to export grain to Missouri. The sites of Lisa's and Cabanne's old trading posts both lay between Winter Quarters and Ft. Atkinson." Passing the place in 1833 Nathaniel Wyeth remarked: "It is grown up with high weeds, a memento of much money spent to little purpose. The magazine and three or four chimneys only remain." Council Bluffs was so named by Lewis and Clark, who held a council there with the Indians in 1804.

be on them and calling his band together made known what he had seen and advised them to escape for life which was done and then were our brethren and heards released from a band of thieves and robbers who had long infested our country.[46]

Winter Quarters, O. N., Sund., Dec. 21st, 1846. Clear, mild and pleasant. At 10 we started home with our mules. Sister Emoline came down to camp with us. About sunset I was in council at A. P. Rockwood's with Pres. B. Young. Paid Wm. Clayton $76.00. Was with Pres. Young in his different apartments. He told me that he wished me to start to St. Jos., Weston and probably Ft. Leavenworth in the morning, take with me 2 4-mule teams and between 3 and 4 thousand dollars in check on the bank of Mo. to exchange for the cash. Advised me to engage all the corn delivered in camp at 40 cts, wheat 60, also from 500 to 1000 head of fat hogs at 1.50 per cwt. at home or 2.00 delivered. About 6 eve. Pres. B. Young by permission, not according to law, as the sealing ordinances were stopped when the Endowment stopped in the Temple for that ordinance belongs to the alter and Temple alone, solemnized the right of matrimony between Emoline and myself.[47] Charged the family to lock these things up in our breast and there let them remain. After attending to the ordinance I presented him with a box of saridins. He blessed us and retired. Bro. Smith Workman has just arrived from Pizgah. Said that the apostates were stealing from the Bros. and carry[ing] to Mo. Also recd. a letter

Trading Expedition to St. Joe

Secret Marriage to "Emoline"

---

[46] Lee now refers to the Omahas as "thieves and robbers," and the land on which the Mormons had settled by Omaha permission as "our country."

[47] The "ordinance of endowment" or "sealing" to polygamous wives had ceased by Brigham's orders when the Nauvoo Temple was abandoned. Brigham here broke his own law for Lee's benefit. It was to be kept a secret for two reasons: to protect Brigham Young, and because polygamy was being publicly and officially denied. In England, that same year, Parley P. Pratt said: "Such a doctrine is not held, known or practiced as a principle of the Latter-Day Saints. It is but another name for whoredom; and is as foreign from the real principles of the church as the devil is from God." (Mill. Star, Vol. 6, p. 22). Pratt had seven wives at that time.

from Bro. J. Workman. It is now 1 at night and must close.

Winter Quarters, O. N., Dec. 22nd, '46.

Teus. morning. Clear and cold. Left the camp of Iseral about 10 o' a.m. on business to S. Joseph. Crossed the river on the ice and proceeded on my journey. Arrived at

Business with P. A. Sarpy

Point & Pole about 4 o' p.m. Tried to acomplish some business with Mr. Sarpy [48] but could not effect much that night, consiquently tarried till morning and laid in a load of goods to the amount of $158 and some cts in salt, a little sugar, coffee &c which Br. Wm. Pace received to convey to camp. After closing my business with Sarpy I started about 10 o' a.m. on my journey for St. Joseph (this being Wensday 23rd, '46). Morning clear and little cold. Wind south. Traveled this day about 30 miles and camped in company with a No. of brethren that was on their way to Mo. to work for provisions. Tarried this night in the open prairie and started at sunrise Thursday morning 24th and proceeded on my journey. Day somewhat clowdy. It thawed some which made it hard traveling for our mules. Traveled about 25 m. and stoped at Lindon for the night with Br. Mathews. This was Christmas Eve. Considerable shooting about town. [49] A drunken rabble assembled about 10 o'clock p.m. before the house where I lodged. Sung and danced, hallowed and yelled like the wild Indians which served in a measure to show the folly and depravity of this Gentile world. This evening made a bill

---

[48] Peter A. Sarpy, clerk for the American Fur Company since about 1834, was in charge of the post at Trader's Point or Point aux Poules, opposite Bellevue, but was practically independent of the company in 1846-47. He was brother to Thomas L. and John B., and son of Gregoire Berald Sarpy, first to navigate the Missouri with keel boats. He had formerly been a clerk at Cabanne's post a few miles north of Winter Quarters. In 1855 he had a store at St. Mary's, Iowa, and one at Decatur, Neb., in 1856. He had an Omaha Indian wife, Ne-ko-ma. Sarpy was eccentric and excitable, loved fast horses and liquor, but died wealthy. Sarpy County, Nebraska, was named in his honor.

[49] It has long been the custom in the South to shoot guns and fireworks on Christmas day.

of $18 and better with the merchant in Lindon (Booth).
Left a check with him (on the Mo. bank) of some $800
to be lifted on my return from St. Joseph. About 12 o'
commended ourselves to our Heavenly Father and retired
to rest.

Lindon, Friday, December 25, '46.

After brakefast about 8 o' a.m. started again for St. Joseph. Morning warm and plesent. Wind So. Continued
warm through the day. Met Br. Grover P. Sessions. Paid
Br. Grover $10 in gold and received a fifty dollar note of
him to take to St. Jos'h to exchange for goods. Roads verry
bad and hard traveling for mules. Drove to Sister Marcia
Allen's [50] and put out our mules about 3 o' p.m., having
some business with Sister Allen and it being Christmas. I
found Sister Rosecrans with Sister Allen. We had some
conversation with her about hard sayings against the
Twelve or the authorities. She denied saying anything
against the Twelve but had said something about Br.
Whitney but was sorry for it and said she was willing to
do just what Brigham said she must. I exhorted her to be
careful what she said about the authorities of this church.
After prayer we retired to rest.

*Sister Allen is
Reproved*

Saturday, December 26th, '46.

Morning clowdy and cool, wind from S. W. Started again
about 7, traveled about 25 miles, camped in the timber
near Galispies. I went to the house to engage some pro-
vender for my teams and the gentleman invited me to take
supper with him to which I acceded. After supper returned
to my waggons (accompanied by Mr. Galispie) (found
the company which consisted of some 6 or 7, one of my
teamsters and C. Decker having taken in 4 or 5 brethren

---

[50] Sarah Caroline Williams, Lee's 15-year-old Wife No. 4, was supposed to
be with Marcia Allen, but is not mentioned in this entry.

that was going to Mo. to work) enjoying themselves first rate. After the boys had taken supper we conversed on various subjects and related some anecdotes and passed the evening off quite merry (it being Christmas eve) and retired to rest about 10 o'.

Sunday morning, Decr. 27th, '46.

Started about sunrise, day warm and pleasant. Road some better. Crossed the Nodaway R. at Lackey's Ferry. Paid 20 cts for 2 waggons, passed on, arrived about sunset at Savannah, the county seat of Andrew Co., Mo. I called on Gen'l H. Rodgers, one of the principal merchants of this place, havieing a letter of introduction on business from Prest. B. Young. Mr. Rodgers received me verry cordially and invited me to spend the night with him, to which I acceded with pleasure. Mr. R. informed me with refference to the number of fat hogs that our people wish to purchase on foot could not be had at presant at 1.50 pr cwt. as was anticipated. That some of our members had unwisely raised the price of pork by paying exhorbitant prices but that he could have delivered us all the pork that our people wanted at the camp at 2.25 pr cwt. provided we could have contracted with him in season; but now he would not like to engage it at 3 dollars delivered, yet he thought probable that small lots could yet be bought of an inferior quality at 1.50 pr cwt. but would be quite inconvenient to obtain any large lots at that price and would not justify the purchases and that he had contracted quite a quantity of white beans and wheat at 37½ cts per B. and beans from 50 to 62½ cts per bushel and that we should have them at the same price; but to deliver wheat at our camp for 62½ cts and corn at forty cts he could not do it unless we would wait until navigation opened in the spring, then he would do it for considerable less. After supper I introduced to them the Gospel of the Kingdom,

Business with
Gen. Rodgers

Prices of
Commodities

reasoned upon the Scriptures and predictions of the prophets, bore record of the truth of Heaven. After hearing the testimony in so solemn a manner the family, which consisted of Mr. R., lady and one child, appeared much interested and listened with intense interest till near 1 o'. Mr. Rodgers is a professor of the new school Presbyterian faith, yet a man of reason. Before retiring to rest he invited me to pray in his family. Eve. pleasant. Dis. of the day 30 ms.

Monday, Dec. 28th, '46.

Clear and pleasant. Mr. R. invited me to pray, after which I partook with them of the rich bounties of the earth. At 8 o' I took leave of Mrs. R. who insisted on my calling whenever I passed that way. Mr. R. also said to make his house my home whenever I came that way. Mr. R. accompanied me and introduced me to the different merchants of the place and assisted in changing 2 checks of $1600 dollars. Proffered to lend me any aid that I might need. About 10 I reached Mr.[51] David P. Abbott's, 1½ mile on the road to St. Jos'h where my teamster had put up. Truman Gillett, my clerk, informed me that C. Decker had gone to St. Joseph which caused me to take a mule from my team to convey me to St. Jos'h. Left Truman with 1 team at Mr. Abbott's until I return as I intend to lay in a part of my goods here. About 3 p.m. arrived in St. Jos. Soon after I had a New Mexican blanket taken off my mule. Commenced trading at Mr. Smith's and Donald's. Stayed at night with Br. Jacob Peart's. Found articles low. Wednesday I met with a chance of having some 3000 lbs. hauled to camp for 30 dollars by Br. Huston who had been disappointed in getting a load. I loaded him with salt, dried fruit, and whiskey,[42] molasses, honey, tallow, fish, &c &c.

A Load of Whiskey for the Saints

---

[51] The prefix "Mr." denotes a non-Mormon.

Continued my business in St. Jos'h. At night commenced raining, sleeting, hail and snow till Thursday noon, when the wind shifted N., turned cold. Wed. noon C. Decker left with his load. Thurs. Br. Houston started with 2 loads and at noon I settled my bill with Smith and Donald which amounted to near $600 dollars. When leaving them they presented me a fine finished pocket knife, pair of scissors and a bottle of French brandy, also paid me $200 dollars on check that I left with Mr. Booth, clerk of their store at Lindon. This he did that I might not be disappointed in getting the change for the check. At 3 p.m. I came up with C. Decker who was waiting for the roads to freeze, being unable to travel in its present state. At 7 eve. I arrived at Mr. D. P. Abbott's where I found my clerk, T. Gillett, enjoying himself with singing and preaching. This family were remarkably friendly and strong believers in the faith of the gospel.

Friday, Jany. 1st, 1847.

Too Cold to Travel

Arrose in the morning, found the wind blowing strong from the N.W. and snowing hard and quite cold and blustering. Concluded that we could not travel this day without much suffering, so by the warm and pressing invitation of our kind host we concluded to remain and contented ourselves to tarry through the day. I went up to Savannah. Staid all night again with Gen'l Rodgers. Traded to the amount of $135 dollars.

Sat., Jany. 2nd, '47.

Quite warm and pleasant. Took our leave of our friend in Savannah about 12 o' (having tarried some 7 or 8 days, for which friend Abbott kept my clerk and mules free of expense). Traveled some 7 or 8 miles and camped in the timber.

Sunday, Jany. 3rd, '47.

After brakefast Truman and I took our mules and went back about a mile and bought 4 B. of white beans for which I paid 50 cts pr B. and the man gave us what oats we could carry to our wagons. I having hired a man that camped with us at this place to haul some 10 or 12 cwt. to camp intending to load him with beans and corn, but came on to the Nodaway and loaded him with pork, as I purchased 6 hogs of Mr. Smither weighing about 1200 lbs. for which I paid 1.62½ cts per cwt.

Price of Pork

Monday, Jan. 4th, '47.

I tarried to help dress and weigh the pork. Truman and Charles Decker took the teams and started ahead having [*left*] my lead mule for me to overtake them, consequently I overtook them about 12 miles ahead. Day cold and blustering, the wind blowing strong from the N. W. We traveled this day about 18 m. and stoped for the night at Mr. A. McCoy's. Eat our supper and went to bed in our waggons. Very cold night. Slept quite cold.

Teusday, Jany. 5th, '47.

Started again about sunrise. The roads verry rough, being quite cold and the ground froze hard. Drove to Mr. Mathews and camped for the night having traveled about 18 miles. I went to the blacksmith shop to get some repairs for my waggon (which had broken) and staid by request with Mr. Blackburn. About 7 at night it commenced snowing. Wind hard from the N. and turned very cold.

Continued so all next day, Wed. 6th, which compelled us to lay bye. In the meantime I repaired my waggon and fixed ready for a start as soon as the weather should moderate sufficient. About 9 morn. one of the mules drove by C. Decker broke loose and ran away. He employed C. Peck to pursue it. Returned after traveling 6 miles but without success and almost perished with the cold, in fact it was unsafe to venture out a mile from fire. Through the day we enjoyed ourselves as well as we could considering the cold. About 4 eve. the stray mule was taken up and returned according to the morning contract.

English Grove, Wed., Jay. 6th, '47.

Morning cold. Thermometer 13 deg. below zero. W. N. Entirely unsafe to travel especially in the open prairie. Concluded to remain till the morrow. Sold some things to defray expenses. About noon the storm began to abate. Eve. clear.

English Grove, Thursday, Jany. 7th, '47.

Clear this morning, W. N. Some warmer. At 8 o' a.m. we took leave of friend Mathews and family and traveled to Lindon. Rec'd the money on the check that I left with Mr. Booth. Traded considerable more with him and proceeded homeward. Traveled about 4 miles when unfortunately the right fore wheel of my waggon run off and the fall broke the axel tree. C. Decker who was a short distance ahead with a more serious accident. His wagon run off the bridge about 14 feet high, capsized, bursted the waggon box as well as the goods boxes. About 8 at night after much difficulty I arrived at the fatal spot where lay our goods scattered around in the snow exposed not only to the weather but to the stock. We made up a fire, took our mules down in the hollow from the storm, for it was remarkably cold. About midnight we succeeded gitting the load back into the waggon after a manner.

"Fatal" Accident

Fatal Encampment, Fri., Jan. 8th, 1847.

Morning clear and cold. About 8 Bro. Vanloover, E. M. Webb and myself commenced repairing the wrecks, got the

50

goods wagon and team again on the level. Evening clear and cold.

Fatal Encampment, Sat., Jany. 9th, '47.

Morning clear and remarkably sharp. About 9 after paying an extravagant bill we started. Bought by the way some 8 or 10 bushel corn to feed of Bro. Vanloover. Crossed the Nishnabothna at Worlden's Ferry and encamped for the night at a lone grove on the prairie by a lake. Distance of 18 ms. from the starting point. Here we fell in with Bro. Winchester who just had made up fires. Eve. cold. W. S.W.

Lone House Encampment, Sund., Jay. 10, '47.

Clear, Cold, wind west. Started at 7. Roads good. Crossed Keg Creek at the lower bridge and about 9 reached Mosquitoe Creek almost frozen where we encamped, leaving Bros. Winchester, Dixon and Samuel Rusell in the rear. The latter we passed near the bridge. Dis. 31 ms. W. W.

Musquitoe Creek, Mon., Jany. 11, '47.

Clear. Started by times. Stopped at Point & Poles and paid Mr. Sarpy $158.45 for groceries bought. Passed Bro. Jas. Bean and lady on the road. They going to Mr. Sarpy's. Reached Winter Quarters about 2 evening. Met Father B. Young who received me with the same cordial welcome as usual. Blessed me in the name of the Lord and said that he would have been uneasy had he not known me to be a man of wisdom and would not have ventured out in such extreme cold weather. I told him that I had laid out about $1200 in goods and groceries, about $1050 I took out of the check. He told me all was right and he would back me up in what I had done. At 5 I delivered $1576.69 cts which left me minas $970.63 cts. The money I laid out I did thinking to benefit the cause which will

51

doubtless have the effect as I bought the articles remarkably low. Evening clear and cool.

Winter Quarters, Teus., Jany. 12th, 1847.

Morning clear. At 8 I was engaged in the firm of Rockwood, Lee & Co. invoicing our goods. Pres. B. Young was in the store frequently through the day. Evening cool.

Winter Quarters, Weds., Jany. 13th.

Clear, strong wind W. Till the 16th I was engaged in getting up firewood, during which time about $700 worth of goods were sold mostly in payment of debts contracted by Pres. B. Young in building a grist mill.

[No entries for Jan. 14-15-16]

Winter Quarters, Sund., Jany. 17th, 1847.

Clowdy, keen wind north. Thermometer stood 17½ deg. below zero. I spent the day in the store selling with Bro. Wm. Clayton. Paid him $125.75 which still left me minas $744.87 cts. Some sharp words passed between us but soon over and forgotten. How to meet my demands at presant I know not. Goods had been sold to cover twice that amount but the returns were not in a shape available. We parted with good feeling to meet on the morrow.[52]

Sharp Words with Clayton

Winter Quarters, Mon., Jany. 18th, '47.

Cool, clear, wind N.W. At 9 met at the residence of Br. Wm. Clayton to arrainge the pay roll. Retired about 11. Weather rather moderate.

---

[52] Lee took to Missouri Battalion pay checks amounting to $2447.32. On his return he turned over to William Clayton, Brigham's bookkeeper, $1576.69 in cash, and in this entry $125.75 additional, leaving a balance of $744.88. $970.69 (including $744.88 of Battalion money), was invested in goods which were offered for sale in the store of Young, Lee, Rockwood & Clayton, but were mostly used to pay debts contracted by Brigham Young in building the mill, his own private property. These irregular transactions, authorized by Brigham, caused Lee considerable embarrassment, as indicated by subsequent entries (see Jan. 27). Lee was inherently honest and felt a personal responsibility for the Battalion funds.

P.S.—15th and 16th in council with the Twelve at
E. T. Benson's, when the word and will of the Lord concerning the journeyings of Iseral was first laid before the
Council as a revelation [53] to the church and acknowledged
by the Council of Fifty. The revelation was then presented to the First Presidency of the Seventies and so on
down and acknowledged.

Winter Quarters, Teus., Jany. 19th, '47.

A few days after J. D. Lee met in council with the Twelve,
Wm. Clayton and Bishop Whitney at Pres. B. Young's
house, in which the situation of the affairs relative to the
Battalion boys and their families was talked over. Pres. B.
Young said that he had furnished 2 mules and the harness
for the Santafe expedition. They were pretty much used
up, still he would not make any charge for them. [54] J. D.
Lee said that Pres. B. Young proposed to pay him and
Howard Egan $100 each for their services [55] rendered the
Bat. but he made no charge at all. That he had [not] received one cent for any servis rendered the church and that
he would not have anything now. He had received blessings for his servises and that was worth more than gold
and silver to him. Pres. B. Young said that some persons
had feelings because Br. Lee layed [out] so much money
for goods and provisions but that he would back up Bro.
Lee and make his contracts good for he done nothing but
what he instructed him to do and that it was all right and
that Bro. Lee had done as well as any man could do under
the same circumstances.

Trouble Over
Battalion Money

---

[53] This was Brigham's only recorded "revelation," but it did not specify the
actual location, which was left to his own judgment.

[54] He had already received most of the money sent back by the Battalion.

[55] According to his *"Confessions,"* Lee and Egan were paid $100 each by
the Batallion in Santa Fe.

[*At this point twelve pages of the Journal, intended for the entries of Jan. 20-21-22, were left blank. On one of these pages the following entry was inserted after Lee's arrival in Utah.*]

Vally of the Great Salt Lake, State of Desarett,
Sund., May 19th, 1850.

Young Marriage Record

John William Young was born March 23rd, 1828, Union Co., Ills. State.

Eathalinda Margarett Young, bourn March 12th, 1834, Gipson Co., near the town of Trenton, Tennessee State.

John William Young and Eathalinda Margarett Young was joined in the covenant of matrimony at 7 p.m. in the presence of Wm. Westley Willis and Joseph Adair.

John D. Lee officiated at the residence of Wm. Young, the father of the bride.

[*The Journal continues.*]

Winter Quarters, once Omaha but now
Potawatamy Nation,[56] Sat., Jany. 23, 1847.

At 6 eve. a convention of the Seventies assembled in the council hall. Previous to calling the house to order the clerk was sent for who in reality had previously sent in his resignation, consequently considered himself released from that office

2nd. The Prest. (Jos. Young) not having arrived, was sent for. At 28 m. to 8 the Pres. and clerk were ready for business.

3rd. House called to order and prayer by Counsellor Herriman.

---

[56] The Mormons had occupied land set aside for the Omahas. The Pottawatomies and later the Otoes claimed the same ground, but the basis of their claim is not clear. In 1848 the Mormons remaining at Winter Quarters were forced to move east of the river. The Omahas were moved 65 miles north in 1854.

4th. The names of each man (Seventies) were read, and there labor in laying the floor of the Council House reported (which amounted to about 90 days).

5th. Pres. Young said that some seats were yet wanted and other necessaries to make the room comfortable, leaving an opportunity for volunteers, whereupon some 12 men offered their services to labor the following Monday.

6th. Decided that those of the Seventies who assisted in the completion of this hall should occupy the room on Teus. 26th and Wednesday 27th eve. commencing at 2 p.m., dividing the Co. into 2 equal parts, correspondent with the days before specified, beginning with the first names on the list and so continue. Each one to bring with them their sweetmeats, nuts and cakes, that their hearts may be made glad while they dance before the Lord.[57] Let all things be done in prudence, modesty, humility and sobriety.

7th. The general clerk and recorder (J. D. Lee) addressed the meeting and said, Brethren of the Seventies, I have long been your historian and while in that office I endeavored to magnify the place. It was an honorable and a responsible station, one in which I took much pleasure, pride, and delight and would be glad to have retained the same standing, was I not satisfied that I could be far more beneficial to this church to serve them in another sphere of action and to act in both rendered inexpedient as the duties of a historian pressingly called forth the tallent and strict attention of the scribe to gather all passing events and circumstances necessary to be connected with a history of this kind, and ever feeling ready to step forward in the harness and work where I could do the most good, I resigned my

---

[57] This was the first introduction of dancing among Mormons. Brigham introduced it in order to furnish social recreation and keep the people's minds off their troubles. Dancing is still promoted by the church, nearly every "Ward House" having its accompanying dance hall.

station considering it more honorable so to do than to have retained it when I knew that I could not magnify it and respond to the duties assigned me in other spheres. This I believe is also the feelings of the authorities that are placed over me. I can assure you, brethren, though I am deprived of meeting so frequent with you, yet my spirit, my prayer, my faith and love is always with you.[58]

8th. Upon motion of Pres. J. Young, seconded by Pres. B. Young, unanimous vote of thanks were given to the clerk and recorder for his faithfulness in keeping the records of the Seventies and upon the acceptation of his resignation from that office.

Resignation as Historian

9th. Adgerned 25 m. to 9 to Sat., Jan. 30, 6 eve. In the meantime Pres. B. Young sent for the 12 and band who were on hand to execute his will and pleasure. The band were seated in the south part of the house. Pres. B. Young, after some brief though striking instructions, took the council of the 12 and Seventies, placed them on the floor in a dancing attitude (said; addressing himself to the multitude) I have as much interest in this house as any man so far as building is concerned, therefore I will take the liberty of showing you how to dance before the Lord. Having thus spoken riquested the multitude to uncover their heads, then bowed before the Lord, dedicated the hall to Him and asked Him to accept of their offerings this evening, after which the band [59] struck up a lively tune and in a moment the whole house appeared to me to be filled with the melodious sounds of the inspired harps of Heaven. Pres. B. Young led and went forth in the dance of praise before the Lord. About 10 Pres. B. Y. retired and about 11 the music ceased. Signed, J. D. Lee, Clerk for the evening.

First Introduction of Dancing

[58] Lee was asked to resign his office as historian in favor of Dr. Willard Richards.

[59] Pitt's Brass Band, converted in a body, had been brought to Nauvoo from England.

Winter Quarters, Sund., Jany. 24th, '47.

Morning clear, wind east. In the forenoon I was engaged in writing. At 11 morn. Elder H. C. Kimble delivered a first rate discourse on the subject of obedience to the Word of the Lord concearning Iseral and their journeyings west. At 20 m. to 2 p.m. Elder B. Young (after an exhortation by Br. Major who opened meeting) addressed the members of his ward; said that it was good to be called a Saint and have our names cast as evil that we may be No'd. with the transgressors as was Jesus in whoes mouth guile was not found, yet he was No'd. with the transgressors for transgressing the laws of the land and of foolish men. For the same purpose Paul was beheaded, Stephen stoned and Jos. Smith shot in jail. This is a trick of the Devil to cause the Saints to mingle with ungodly characters. The Bible says when the Saints or sons of God came up to worship, Satan came also and will continue to do so until justice is brought to the line and judgment to the plumet which will bring to pass the saying of the apostle when speaking [of] the time when every plant that offendeth or worketh iniquity should be plucked out, then we shall build up the Kingdom of God in purity. Then we shall no longer have thieves in our midst and devils and wicked men to seduce every woman that they can. Such characters the Devil has always rushed in our midst to try to overthrow the truth. Jesus had such to follow him, eat, drink with, still were devils from the beginning. Geo. J. Adams, John C. Bennett [60] and others never had any faith nor interest only to prostitute every female that they could; men that were ordained unto this condemnation.

Woman Trouble Among the Saints

Winter Quarters, Sund., Jan. 24th, 1847.

Daniel Spencer, born July 20th, 1796, in the town of West Stockbridge, Berkshire Co., Mass.

---

[60] For John C. Bennett, see his *"Mormonism Exposed."*

Emily Spencer, born Aug. 13th, 1819, town of Mansfield, Tolland Co., Conn.

Hyrum Spencer, born Dec. 30th, 1799, town of W. Stock-bridge, Berkeshire Co., Mass.

At 15 m. to 5 eve. at the residence of Bro. D. Spencer's, Sister Emily Spencer (wife of Hyrum Spencer, deceased), was sealed to Daniel Spencer for time, he acting for and in behalf of his Bro. Hiram Spencer (deceased).[61]

Brigham Young officiated.

John D. Lee and Claudius V. Spencer, witnesses.

Claudius V. Spencer, born April 2nd, 1824, town of West Stockbridge, Berkshire Co., Mass.

Maria Antinetta Spencer, born Jany. 22nd, 1826, T. W. Stockbridge, Berkshire Co., Mass.

On Sund. eve. at 5 m. to 5, Jany. 24th, 1847, Maria Antinetta Spencer was sealed to Claudious V. Spencer for time and all eternity by Pres. Brigham Young. John D. Lee and Daniel Spencer, witnesses. After the rites of matrimony were solemnized between the parties above specified the wedding cakes were handed round. Pres. B. Young and myself received each a piece of gold from Bro. C. V. Spencer as token of friendship. About 6 Pres. B. Young returned to the High Council. I walked to Bro. Free who had walked to Bro. Jas. Duncan and H. Dayton. Returned to Bro. Free and at 10 returned home.

Winter Quarters, Mond., Jany. 25th, 1847.

Morning cool and clowdy and occasional snow. At 8 I received a letter from Nancy counselling me to take care of my family, having reference to herself, who was only on a visit to her father's. I was not pleased with the spirit

---

[61] According to Mormon doctrine a woman can be "sealed" to but one man for "time and eternity." If her husband dies she may be sealed to another for "time" only. Children of subsequent marriages are credited to the first husband.

of the letter, knowing that she had no right or cause to do so. I presented the letter to Father (B. Young) who was of the same mind and counselled me to treat her letter with silent contempt and by so doing she and her father and mother will find that something is meant. Practice of this, said he, and she will soon learn to attend to her own business and do as I should say.[62] I spent the remainder in fitting up my waggons and teams to send to Mo. for grain. At 6 eve. Pres. B. Young met the members of his Co. (presant of the 12, B. Y., H. C. Kimble, O. Pratt, E. T. Benson, W. Woodruff and W. Richards). After reading over the names of those that had given in a schedule of his property Elder E. T. Benson took the stand, asked the members whether they wished to appoint their officers or whether the President should do it or not. Voted that the Pres. make the appointments. Whereupon Isaac Morly, Pres. Reynold Cahoon and John Young, Daniel Spencer, Jedediah M. Grant, Edward Hunter and Williard Snow, Caps. of Hundreds.[63] Jacob Gates, Ira Eldredge, Jos. W. Cumming, B. L. Clapp, Jos. B. Noble, Erastus Snow, Benj. Brown and Chas. Bird, Capts. 50's. The forementioned appointments having been made Pres. B. Young asked the multitude if they would acknowledge the several appointments; voted in the affirmative. Pres. B. Young then instructed the several Capts. to make out their companies and prepare to journey west when the spring should open and grass get sufficient for cattle to travel. Adjourned sine di.

Organization for Emigration

Winter Quarters, Teus., Jan. 27th, 1847.

Clear and cold. At 7 I was engaged in fitting up my teams

---

[62] The suggestion of Wife No. 2 that Lee provide for her and her child, was considered by himself and Brigham an unprovoked insult. Polygamous wives were in most cases required to live with their parents or support themselves.

[63] Preparing for the emigration of 1847 the people were organized into bands of hundreds, fifties and tens, with a captain for each group, as outlined in Brigham's "revelation."

to send them to Mo. for grain. At 9 morn. Elder H. C. Kimble met and appointed a president and two counsellors over his Co., Alpheus Cutler, Pres., and Winslow Farr and . . . . . counsellors. At 2 p.m. the 1st Co. of the Seventies commenced gathering for the dance. About 5 I had the

More Trouble Over Battalion Money

pleasure of unbosoming my feelings to Father B. Young, which afforded me no smawl degree of comfort and relief as I was very much depressed in spirit on account of the money that I laid out belonging to the Bat. although the goods which was purchased with the money have been sold at a heavy per cent and the avails of which has went to liquidate the debt of building the mill.[52] Notwithstanding there has and still are feelings on the part of some who has but interest for this church. Father B. Y. said that he was fully satisfied with what I had done, it was for the best and that he could safely say that I had done more for him than any other man in this Kingdom; not that he wished to find fault with any one of his family, they all done well. I told him that I had 6 good mules and some new waggons that I could cash if it was best. He replied that he did not wish me to sell either, that he would back off all that I had done; to be comforted and let not my spirit be troubled, for he knew that I, like him, sought the interest of this people. I replied that his words reminded [me] of a dream

Troubled Dreams

that I had about the money; that I said, Bro. Wm. Clayton, the most precious coin which was the gold, had cankered to such an extent that by a slight pressure of the finger and thumb it readily crumbled to dust. I chew and spit it out on the ground. This, I thought, left me in an awful situation plunging and involving me deeper in debt than ever. While in consternation a friend approached me, but from him refused to be comforted, not supposing it in his power. But following me up he handed me gold of the pure metal, which replaced my loss in part. At this I began to take new courage. This dream still puts in hopes.

60

Bro. Miles Anderson (one of my first converts in Rutherford Co., Tenn.) seeing the depressed state of my feelings,
offered all the means and property that he could command
to relieve me from embarrassment. Pres. B. Y. said that
money at the present would be very acceptable and when
he starts [*the mill*] he would soon replace it again as it
would certainly neat him $20 per day. We parted with the
promise of meeting at the council room 1 hour hence to
join in the dance of praise before the Lord. Agatha and
Louisa [*No. 1 and No. 3*] accompanied me. The band
was refreshed during the 4 days recreation at the expense
of J. D. Lee and A. P. Rockwood. Room crowded. Pres.
B. Y., Kimble and Benson returned after dismissing the
Saints with their blessing. Heavens clear.

Winter Quarters, Thurs., Jany. 28th, 1847.
Weather moderate though snowing like a torrent. At 2
p.m. I, in co. with Bro. M. Anderson, took a span of mules
and drove to the settlements on Booe [64] river to obtain
money for the church.

Booe Bridge, Friday, Jay. 29, '47.
Heavy frost. Morning clear and warm, day pleasant.
Spent the day at Br. M. Anderson's. Brought up my journal. Evening clear. At 6 I addressed an attentive congregation on the subject of the organization and the necessary
requisites to prepare us to build up Zion. Entire satisfaction, I believe, was rendered.

"Entire
Satisfaction"

Booe Bridge, Sat., Jany. 30th, '47.
Clear and pleasant. W. S.W. At 8 morn. I, with Bro. M.
Anderson was at the house of Sister Ruth Stewart. Had
some conversation with her about her estate in Alabama
of some $4000. She wished me to take the matter in hands.

---

[64] Lee's attempt to reproduce the French pronunciation of Boyer river, on the
Pottawatomie reservation, where the Mormons had been permitted to make a
temporary camp.

61

I took her pappers and promised to lay them before the Council at a convenient time. Borrowed from her and son $60.00 gold and silver which I promised to replace in time to fit her out for a journey. Returned to camp in co. with her son James and young Bro. Bass. Found Bro. John Berry [65] from Pizgah. From him I learned that my boys were preparing to come to camp, that all was well. My own health is somewhat impaired, having had a violent attack of a cold. Evening clear.

Winter Quarters, Sund., Jany. 31, 1847.

Morning clear, warm and pleasant. At 8 morn. I was at Father B. Young's. Found him verry unwell, having had a violent attack the evening before from the effects of a severe cold. About 1 p.m. I started Geo. Laub, T. Johnson and Wm. Woolsey to Mo. with a waggon and team of 4 mules. Sent with them $20.00 in gold and silver, a new waggon and quilted seated saddle worth $25.00. Blessed them and told them to go and prosper and return in safety. About 2 I received $15.00 from Bro. Miles Anderson. About 4 I was at Pres. B. Young's. Found him still verry unwell. Notwithstanding his illness he solemnized the rites of matrimony between Wm. F. Carter [66] and Sister Hannah Cordelia Meecham. See the following record:

Carter Marriage Record

Wm. F. Carter, born May 1st, 1811 in the T. of Newry, Oxford Co., State of Maine.

Hannah Cordelia Meecham, born Oct. 15th, 1829.

Sund., Jany. 31st, '47, at 5 evening in the house of Pres. B. Young, Hannah Cordelia Meecham was sealed to Wm. F. Carter for time and all eternity in the presence of Jos. Young and John D. Lee. Brigham Young officiated. Evening mild, wind low.

---

[65] Father of Martha Berry, Wife No. 7.

[66] William Carter plowed the first furrow in Salt Lake Valley on July 22, 1847. His plow has been preserved as a pioneer relic. All marriages listed by Lee were probably polygamous.

Winter Quarters, once Omaha but now Oto Nation,[67] Monday, February 1st, 1847.

Morning clear, warm and pleasant. At 7 I was at Father B. Young, found him still unwell. He said that he wished me to have Geo. Grant take the carriage (B. Y.'s) and go to the Point and redeem a $30.00 note that went from him, stating that he wished to leave the people with first rate feelings. At 11 morn. George Grant, Sister Powers, Rebecka Holman Y. and myself set out for the Point. Strong wind south W. About 2 p.m. reached Belleview,[68] an Indian and French village where at the residence of a missionary we left Rebecka while we crossed over to the Point and arranged our matters. Returned back to Mr. Lester. Feed and refreshed ourselves free of cost. At 25 m. to 5 we started for camp. Clowded up, W. shifted N.W., blew like a tornado, accompanied with snow. Turned cold as Greenland. Traveled 4 ms., took up for the night at Bro. Jos. Allred. Sisters Powers and Rebecka lodged at Bro. Homan Hyde's. His daughter, Bro. G. Grant's consort, was lying a corpse when we arrived. Sat and detailed my narrative to Santafe. I spoke of the firmness of Bro. Wm. Hyde which was gratifying to them. At 11 I retired to repose on a cottonwood puncheon. Had for a covering (Bro. Grant and I) a buffalo robe.

Trip to Bellevue

---

[67] The Otoes now claim the former Omaha land.

[68] Chittenden says of Bellevue: "Crooks and McLellan seem to have been the first to locate there [1806]. The next occupant was the Missouri Fur Company under Joshua Pilcher. Fontenelle and Drips apparently bought Pilcher's post and established it under their own name which it retained for many years. At a date between 1830 and 1840, which is not exactly known, the American Fur Company moved to Bellevue from Cabanne's post some distance above, and established a new post there under the management of P. A. Sarpy. The Indian agency of John Dougherty was also located near there at about the same time. The agency was at Cote a Quesnelle just above the American Fur Company post." Proximity to the Omahas, Pottawatomies, Otoes and Pawnees, and Sarpy's sagacity in dealing with them, made Bellevue an important place. It is now some distance inland, due to changes in the river.

Mormon Point, Teus., Feb. 2nd, 1847.
Pottowatomy Nation.

Cold and clowdy, wind north, high and verry piercing. At 8 we ventured out, traveled 6 ms. when we lost one of the linch pins.[69] Stopped and substituted one of wood in the storm. Suffered considerably with the cold. Arrived in camp about 2 p.m. Found Father Young rather more feeble. Had about 1 hour's conversation with him. Walked to Bro. Free's. Found [*Louisa?*] rather unwell, and myself with much difficulty could be about. Aggathiam[70] was also taken quite sick but now better. Bro. J. Berry is here from Pizgah. I had some conversation with Bro. Chas. Bird relative to taking a contract of removing and selling a portion of the Pottowattomie's Indians to the amount of $6000.00. I told him it was the Pres. feelings to have him do so.

Winter Quarters, once Omaha but now
Oto Nation, Wed., Feb. 3rd, 1847.

Young Family Dance

Clear and rather cool, W. S. About 8 I paid some money to Bro. C. Bird to help him out on a church contract. At 2 p.m. the Young family assembled at the council room to dance and praise the Lord. The festival was rich and sumptuously furnished. Father B. Young is some better of his sickness. After spending an hour with him I walked to T. Gillett's. He was absent. Sister Gillett told me that they had nothing for 2 days except a little brand. I advised him (T. G.) to go to the settlements in Mo. and take up a school, that I would attend to his family in his absence. Returned home. Stopped a short time at Br. Free's. Sent Sister Gillett a bushel of meal, about 10 lbs. of salt

---

[69] In the old style "linch-pin" wagons, a pin was passed through the end of the axle to hold the wheel in place.

[70] The name of Lee's Wife No. 1, Agatha Ann, is written "Aggathiam," "Aggathian," or "Aggathiann."

SARAH CAROLINE WILLIAMS

Married Lee in April, 1845, at the age of fourteen, as Wife No.
4. Was the mother of twelve children. Lived at Panguitch,
Utah, after 1877. This is her only known portrait.

Courtesy Edna Lee Brimhall

pork. This evening I wrote a letter to my children [71] at Mt. Pizgah instructing them to remove Sister Lucinda Pace to Winter Quarters. Sent $2.50 in gold to her. John Berry will lodge with tonight. Now 11.

Winter Quarters, Oto Nation, Thurs., Feb. 4th, '47.

Morning clear, weather moderate. About noon while in conversation with Sister A. D. Young, I felt quite feeble and lay down. About 2 Bro. Rockwood and G. Grant came and said that it was the will and pleasure of our father for us 3 to collect his adopted children at some convenient time when the council room would not be engaged by previous appointments, have each one bear a part by bringing their proportion of cakes, pies, sweetmeats &c, all to be done under our superintendance. About 3 I began to drink herb teas which threw me into presperation. In this state I remained about 3 hours. About dark Louisa [No. 3] came in to see and comfort me. She lay and embraced me in her arms near 2 hours.

Winter Quarters, O. N., Frid., Feb. 5th, 1847.

Morning pleasant. Pres. B. Young's health is improving. At 10 Alanson Allen, my grandson, [71] arrived in camp from the settlements in Mo. Brought in a load of meal. Said that Caroline [No. 4] and his mother's family were all well. Today at 1 p.m. the aged men of Iseral, called the Silver Grays, met and celebrated the praise of Zion's kings at the hall. Pres. B. Young, Kimble and others of the 12 participated in the worship. About 9 I was washed in salaratus and water from head to foot, afterward in spirits, then anointed in like manner by Louisa [No. 3] and Rachel [No. 6] (as I told them) preparitory to my burial. They both were verry kind and attentive to me. In the eve. I felt some better. Weather warm.

Lee Is Anointed for Burial

---

[71] By "adoption."

Winter Quarters, O. N., Sat., Feb. 6th, '47.

Weather mild. At 7 Bro. Levi Stewart and Leucinda, my grand daughter [71] from the heard came in with Bro. Stewart. I had considerable conversation on matters of importance.[72] This morning I sent and requested a favor of Bro. A. P. Rockwood which was to let my affairs be known to Father B. Y. Sent to him twice afterwards, urging my petition. He replied that he had not said anything about it, but would at a convenient time. Finding that the confidence that I had reposed was not about to effect what I most desired, I sat up in bed by the assistance of Rachel [No. 6] and wrote the following lines:

Requests Brigham's Presence

Winter Quarters, Sat., Feb. 6th, 1847.

Pres. B. Young:

Dear Father: Should it be agreeable with your feelings and your health permits, nothing could afford me more comfort in the hour of affliction than your presence. I requested Bro. Rockwood to say a word for me but I presume that he has other things that he considers of greater moment that calls his attention. I have been confined to my bed 3 days, which is the longest since I have been a member of this church.

Your afflicted though faithful son in Iseral's cause,

J. D. LEE.

The above lines, with verry little variation I sent by the hand of A. Allen, my g. son. Sister A. D. Young and Bean were in to see me this evening. Through the day Bro. B. L. Clapp, Turbow, Haden, Carter, Father Glinnon and son, Sister Pace, C. Bird and some others called in. Alanson, by my counsel tarried another day. It is now 8 and I am getting up in bed bringing up my journal. Bro. A. P. Free called about dark, said Louisa [No. 3] was taken verry ill this evening and was confined to bed. Polly Ann

66

[*No. 8*] was also verry violently attacked of a fever and sickness at the stomach, but is now some better. About 8 eve. Bro. Levi Stewart came bearing the message from Father B. Y. Said that his health would not allow him to turn out that night but that he felt to bless me in the name of the Lord and say that I should recover and to pray for me in his behalf. I immediately after receiving the message revived and conversed till 10 with Bro. Stewart on his contemplated mission.[72]

Winter Quarters, O. N., Sund., Feb. 7, '47.

Mild and pleasant after a severe frost. In the forenoon the room was thronged with visitors to see me in my affliction. About 9 Bro. Jas. Bean came in—his lady the eve before— but no inquiry was made by myself of Nancy [*No. 2*] who had written me the insolent letter. A short time before this, I, in compliance to council, acted. Soon I expect to hear from her. About 2 p.m. Allen Weeks and Jas. Woolsey arrived in camp from Mt. Pizgah, brought a part of a load for Gen. Rich greatously. All was well. About 3 Father B. Y., W. Woodruff and W. Richards came in, Bro. L. Stewart also. Father B. Y. brought and laid on my breast a cane built from one of the branches of the Tree of Life that stood in the garden in the Temple.[73] This as a matter to be expected, collected my thoughts and centered them on sacred and solemn things. After assenting to my request relative to Bro. L. Stewart's mission—which will appear hereafter—he in connection with Bro. W. Woodruff &c anointed and blessed me with a promise of immediate health from my bed of affliction that my usefulness should continue a great many years on the earth; that my wakeful moments should be employed in contemplation of the glory and happiness of the Faithful and

Insolent Nancy Bean

Brigham's Magic Cane

---

[72] Levi Stewart, Lee's best friend, was to be entrusted with the "mission" of bringing Lee another wife from Tennessee, as will be shown by later entries.

[73] The only known reference to this magic cane.

while enwrapped in repose the Heavenly visions of Eternity should be opened to my view, to increase my glory and happiness. Bro. L. Stewart said that as far as the mission was concerned he was to act where he might be most profitable. Pres. Young said that he would doubly accomplish for himself and others by goeing there to stay and that he felt to give him his blessings and prayers and say that he should prosper in the enterprise; that he would send an epistle to the branches setting fourth our views relative to our moves in future. Retired about 30 minets to 5 eve, leaving their peace and blessings on my humble cottage. Soon after Br. Rockwood came in. I presented him with a fifty bill on the Mechanics bank (Boston) which I had redeemed for him, it being rather under par and hardly a circulating currency. He took it and credited me $50. Bro. Wm. Major came about 7, the same that was in about noon, and brought me a letter from P. A. Sarpy, merchant at the Point with a fifty dollar note enclosed in the same which I redeemed. He conversed with me till near 10 at night. My strength increased beyond expectation.

Miraculous Recovery

Winter Quarters, O. N., Mon., Feb. 8th, 1847.

Morning pleasant. At 7 got up, washed and dressed myself. Felt almost entirely free from pain. Eat a hearty breakfast. Felt to rejoice in the blessing of the speedy restoration to health. I employed myself in writing and conversing with those that came in among which were Bro. W. Richards, C. Bird, Sarah Gibbins and others. In the evening walked to Br. A. P. R. At candle light the historian (W. R.) came in, sat and chatted till bed time, when he blessed me and retired. Today Bro. Hathaway and Capt. Clifford got permission to use our store room 4 days.

Winter Quarters, O. N., Teus., Feb. 9th, '47.

Morning clowdy, bleak wind north. At 8 Lucinda returned to the Rush Bottoms with Bro. Wm. Empy, Sister Stewart and others. About the same time I started 6 head of catle to the heard by Bro. Snider. Assisted myself to start them. Spent this day mostly in writing. Made out a company schedule for the 4th Ten, 2nd 50, 1st 100rd, Pres. B. Young's Co., Miles Anderson, Capt., who were here. The girls [*Lee's wives*] were engaged in building Jas. Woolsey a bed blanket coat. The linings, trimmings, buttons, cutting and making were all done at my expenses. Jas. is somewhat unwell, being troubled with cold and the canker. Allen and Jas. chopped me some firewood. In the evening I wrote to G. W. Hickerson and family M. T. P. [*Mt. Pizgah*] after which I walked to Bro. A. P. Free's where I remained till morning.[76] At 9 weather growing colder.

Winter Quarters, O. N., Wed., Feb. 10, 1847.

Morning cold, clowdy, W. N. About 8 I sat down and had some conversation with Polly Ann [*No. 8*], who at the Cold Springs in the month of July last, contrary to my feelings, went to Pizgah. I at that time told her the consequences of such measures, still she persisted in going, and after a severe chastisement of sickness of 4 months she returned home where she has been till the present, at times verry turbulent and unruly and arbitrary, using unbecoming words in the family. I frequently advised her to refrain and be mild, until I found it useless to entreat further. I at length told her that she never had observed the conditions of her obligations in the Temple and had been heard to say that she intended to make a perfect hell for me and that my happiness should consist in misery, while she was permitted to remain connected with my family, and that her con-

Polly Ann Leaves By Request

---

[76] With Wife No. 3. Several of Lee's wives, like most polygamous wives of that period, lived with their parents and were supported by them. This journal nowhere indicates how many or which wives were living under Lee's own roof. (See also note 96).

duct certainly confirmed her words and inasmuch as that was her feelings I wanted her to take her effects and leave me and mine just as she found us, as she certainly could not take pleasure by persisting in the course that she had been practicing, and leave a coverlid to defray a bill of expenses that she brought on me since her first elopement. She at first refused to do either, but I told her that her Bro. would give her 1.00 per week to keep house for him and I would send her to him, so our conversation ended.[77] The day was quite cold, occasionally showering.

Winter Quarters, O. N., Thurs., Feb. 11th, 1847.

Clowdy, W. N.W., rather cool. At 9 I had conversation with Mary [*Polly*] Ann. She requested me to let my feelings remain in my own bosom and not expose her. Confessed that she had done wrong and although I had thrown her out from under my protection, yet she hoped that her further course of conduct would be sufficient to redress my injured feeling; that she was determined though banished from my presence and society to redeem herself should years of solitude be required to effect it, and so far as counsel was concerned she wanted none other than mine. I told her that it was grevious for me to take the measures that I have taken, though a sense of duty demanded of me, and that her future conduct alone would determine her happiness or misery; that words were but signs of ideas. She said that she would submit to her fate, though lamentable, and try to comfort herself in doeing my will. I left her heavy hearted. By Bro. Allen Weeks I sent Lucinda Pace some clothing, requesting them to come up immediately. At 12 noon Allen, Jas. and Polly Ann started for Pizgah. About 1 p.m. the Silver Grays met in the council room. I called in a few moments. The praise and worship of God was introduced by prayer, after which Pres. B. Young

---

[77] In his "*Confessions*" Lee bitterly regrets having expelled Nancy Bean and Polly Ann Workman from his family.

spoke on this wise: Brethren and Sisters, you have met here today to join in the dance, in a recreation that all people participate in except such as have been traditioned to believe it to be an evil. To some it is an evil. The prayers of some men are abominations before the Lord because they pray for evil things; but for a Saint to pray or dance is not sin. Why? Because they seek to do the will of the Lord and not their own will. Since this council room has been finished I have heard the music at all hours of the night and upon reflection I remembered that I had heard the axes throughout the city in building houses for the widows and fatherless at all hours of the night. How then could I find fault? So I then concluded inasmuch as they would labour all night, now they may dance all night, but the hours of recreation will soon be over with us here, when this room will be converted into preaching, organizing Co's. and preparing for what is before us. As I withdrew Pres. B. Young invited me in to spend the day, should my health allow, but not to expose myself too much. Returned home and employed about 3 hours in writing. About 5 walked to the hall, but finding my health to be rather delicate and feeble I soon returned. Pres. Young and Kimble walked into Dr. Richard's to arrange a council. Evening cool.

Winter Quarters, O. N., Friday, Feb. 12th, 1847.

Morning clear and pleasant. The fore part of the day I spent in writing letters to Rutherford Co., Tennessee. Wrote one to Isham Gilliam,[78] D. M. Jarratt and all the Saints and friends in that county. About 3 p.m. Dr. Richards, Jos. Young came in to see how I was getting along. Sat and chatted perhaps an hour about the outbrake on our heards of cattle and horses by the Sious. Said that a

---

[78] Isham Gilliam, husband of the woman Levi Stewart was being sent to steal.

71

report came to me to camp that the Sious had stolen 13 horses and killed 30 head of cattle; that Pres. Brigham Young ordered 40 men armed to go to the chief of the nation and demand the property and make them give them up. The cause of the Sious interupting our catle was from the fact that Bishop Miller sent out a Co. against them in favor of the Punckaws. This move only fulfilled what the Pres. said last March while encamped on the Charidon River: Bro. Miller will not stop until he runs against a snag and gets the camp into trouble and will yet call for help unless he stops running before the Council.[18] The report is now that the Indians have killed the most of the cattle of his Co. Evening mild.

Winter Quarters, O. N., Sat., Feb. 13th, 1847.

Morning clear, fine and pleasant. At 7 some 40 or 50 men collected in front of the council room to make arrangements about going to the heard and demanding the stolen horses from the thieves of the Sious. At [?] I was in at Pres. B. Young. He was in council with Bro. C. Bird. Advised him to take all the contracts of labour in removing the Pottowatomies Indians and building houses, mills, opening farms &c that he could. A few minutes after the Historian came in. At 9 I returned home. Let Bro. Potter have 3 bushels corn and some pork as he was hearding some of my cattle. My health slowly improving. Evening remarkably fine. Spent a part of the evening in conversation with Sister Nancy Armstrong who had sacrificed a large fortune of earthly substance, forsook her own dwelling habitation, merchandise and kindreds for the gospel sake, having spent a good portion of the substance that she succeeded in getting away, say somewhere between 4 and $600; was now about to be left. Requested me to take her on with this camp in the spring, which I in part consented to, by telling her that she was not without friends,

Nancy Armstrong

72

although the man that used her effects was about to leave her here—A. O. S. is the italics.[79]

Winter Quarters, Sund., Feb. 14th, 1847.

Morning rather clowdy, wind S. At 9 I was in at Father B. Y.'s who invited me into his sitting room. Said to me that while I was in the vigor of youth that my spirit, ambition, enterprise and perseverance, with a verry little faith, went a great ways in conquering sickness and decease, but that I would find, when my constitution began to break that nothing but the resurective power would keep me up. After some moments had been spent in conversation, by his request I read a letter that I just written to send to the branch in Ruthersford county, Tennessee, a copy of which will be found on file. After hearing the contents he said that it is good, it is first rate. I then laid before him the propriety of buying out about $1000 worth of goods in the hands of Bro. Hathaway & Co. The goods were not the articles that the camp actually wanted; he therefore thought that amount of money laid out for provisions would be far more to the interest of this camp. I then asked his feelings relative to the arrangements of the family meeting on Teus. and Wed. next, which would be the 16th and 17th of Feb. 1847. He said that he laid the arrangement of that matter on Bro. Rockwood, Grant's and my shoulders and should look to us. I told him that I had been confined to my bed with sickness which rendered me entirely inadequate to the task. He replied that he was aware that I had been sick. I insisted to know his mind and we would act accordingly. He replied that he intended

Conference with Brigham

[79] Nancy Gibbons Armstrong was a sister of Sarah Gibbons, wife of A. O. Smoot. She had abandoned her husband, a wealthy merchant of Louisville, Ky., to come to Nauvoo with her sister and Smoot. The latter had borrowed most of her money, but did not marry her in polygamy as she had expected. She later proposed to Lee, who accepted her because she still had a little money, although she was then 48, 13 years older than Lee. He already had one Nancy in the family (Wife No. 2) so he distinguishes between the two by labeling this woman "Nancy the 2nd." The expression "A. O. S. is the italics" refers to A. O. Smoot.

73

something better than dancing and frolicking. He expected to teach and instruct and show his children the relationship which they held to him and one another; that we had better have a table sat and furnished with boiled hams, corn beef, bread, sweet cakes, pies, fruits, tea and coffee [44] &c; that each one that came have their portion. I asked him and Mother Young to have supper with us which they readily consented. Returned about 1 p.m. after consulting Bro. Rockwood and Grant about what the Pres. said. Bro. Rockwood being unwell the burden of arranging the feast fell on Bro. Grant and myself. On reaching home, to my astonishment one side of the roof of my house had slid and blown off, filling everything with dirt. Some 8 or 10 persons dined with us. Finding the house uncomfortable I deferred Fath. B. Y. and Mother's visit to another time. Evening spent at Uncle David Young's, who was quite unwell.

Winter Quarters, O. Nation, Mon., Feb. 15, '47.

Organization of Pioneer Company

Morning clowdy, sharp wind N. At 9 morning Capts. of 100s, 50s and 10s assembled in the council room, handed in the reports of their respective companies. Whereupon Pres. B. Young said that he wanted the aggregate amount of the whole camp (E. I.) No. of persons, the number of families whoes husband are in the army also wants to be reported sepparate and apart, together with a schedule of all the waggons, horse, oxen, mules, cows, sheep, provisions, groceries, cash, seeds, tools and farming utensils &c. Then it will be the duty of the President (I. Morley) and his council together with the Capts. of 100s, 50s and 10s to decide who of that No. shall go and what portion shall be taken by each Co. (E. I.) of those families whoes husbands are in the army and the widows; but inasmuch as there is a deficiency on the account of some of the Capts. not having made their reports the matter must lay over till

74

Wed. morning next at 8 o'clock, which will give time to remove such officers that have not done their duty and put in others in their place, then let an exertion be made to have full reports by that time. Then let the Pres. and his counsellors, together with the 1st Co. including the officers meet and organize according to the will and word of the Lord which has been read repeatedly in your hearing and a copy of which will be at the meeting, then on Thurs. let the 2nd Co. meet and do in like manner and so on until the whole camp is organized. I further want some elders sent to the branches scattered arround to instruct them in those principles and organize them. Whereupon J. M. Grant, W. Woodruff, C. Bird, A. O. Smoot, Z. Coultrim and some few others were called upon to take a short mission but not being able to raise the No. wanted this was also laid over till Wed. morning's meeting. The marshal then called for the room, it being about 11 morning. At 12 noon the room was occupied by the dance, it being the hours of school from 12 to 6. Returned home and was engaged the remainder of the day in recovering my house. About noon Bishop Miller, E. T. Benson, P. O. Rockwell and others returned from the Puncaw river or rather arrived in camp.[80] B. Miller brought his family with him. Evening engaged in writing journal and wrote a letter to John Henigar, T. Gatewood and John Woolsey, Fayette Co., Ill.

Miller Returns from "Puncaw"

Winter Quarters, Teus., Feb. 16th, 1847.

Minutes of Pres. B. Young's family meeting. Morning clear, warm and pleasant. About 7 Bro. L. Stewart and lady came from the heard and took brakefast. I conversed upon the nature of his mission then in contemplation. I read him the letters of introduction and business of his

---

[80] See note 18. For biography of Orrin Porter Rockwell see *"Holy Murder,"* (Kelly-Birney). Rockwell was Brigham's personal messenger during this period.

mission. He felt much encouraged and firm in the enterprise. About 10 Chester Loveland one of my adopted
children who was with me at the altar whom I had not seen
since I left Nauvoo, came in. He told me that [he] had
been prospered and that he, his father and family, Brother-
in-law and Bros. wife were all ready to be disposed of according to my council as they claimed me to be their counsellor. At 30 minets to 1 p.m. the 1st Co. of Pres. B.
Young's family commenced assembling and at 22 minets

to 2 Pres. Young said it was time to commence the services of the day. Yet my wife [*No. 1?*] is not yet ready
from the fact that the house is thronged all the day long
so that I scarce can ever get her out. The object of this
collection is to show the relationship my family sustains
to me and each other which I will endeavor to do; when
we sing and pray. Presant of the 12: B. Young, H. C.
Kimble, O. Pratt, G. A. Smith, A. Lyman, W. Woodruff,
Wm. Richards and E. T. Benson. The house having been
called to order the hymn O Happy Souls That Pray &c
was sung by the audience. Bro. Stephen Goddard led the
hymn. The following prayer in substance was offered by
Pres. B. Young. Our Father which art in Heaven, hal-
lowed by Thy name, let Thy Kingdom come and Thy
will be done on earth as it is done in Heaven. Give us day
by day our daily bread and forgive us our sins as we forgive each other's wrongs; deliver us from temptation and
guard us against all evil by pouring out Thy Holy Spirit
upon us in all our tribulations, sickness and sorrows, for
Thou are our Father, Saviour and our God and in as much
as we approach the day we pray Thee in the name of Jesus
Christ our Saviour to let us [*not*] be disappointed in our
expectations while assembled in a family capacity before
Thy throne to worship Thee. May our souls be enlight-
ened and filled with understanding that we may be enabled
to comprehend and appreciate Thy handiwork in bringing

salvation to Thy children. Let Thy Holy Spirit inspire
the hearts of Thy servant this day that he may be enabled
to bring to the understanding of these my brothers and
sisters the beauty and glory of Thy kingdom when built
up in purity upon the earth. We thank Thee for Thy
spirit even the comforter of Thy people that flows down
through the channel of the Holy Priesthood to lead and
guide us into all truth and prepare us for all coming events
that awaits us. We pray the Father in Heaven to poor out
the Spirit on those of our brethren who have not the privilege of being here with us today. Comfort and gladden
their hearts that they may repose in Thy promise. We also
ask Thee to clothe Thy servant upon with power and authority who are called to preach the everlasting gospel (on
whose shoulders the keys of this Kingdom does rest) when
they may go forth in Thy wisdom, strength and power,
the isles of the sea and nations of the earth, that Jerusalem
may be rebuilt and Zion redeemed and become the joy and
praise of the whole earth. I now dedicate myself and these
my children unto Thee and pray Thee to prepare us for
immortality and eternal life in the midst of Thy Kingdoms
and Thy name shall have the praise, honor and glory of
our salvation through Jesus Christ our Lord, Amen. After
prayer the well known hymn, The Glorious Day Is Rolling On &c was sung. Pres. B. Young then addressed the
assembly, said: Now brethren, I will endeavor to talk a
little while and give way for my brethren, for if I talk
much I will be sick as my lungs are very much affected. I
want perfict order kept in the room while I am talking
that the minds of those that are incorrect may be corrected.
The 12 men whom I have invited, although they are not
of my family circle, yet I expect them to act free and speak
such things as the Lord may [tell] them too.

*Brigham
Instructs
His Family*

1st. Let me state a principle by which you may comprehend much by those who do not understand the same

and have learned to be passive, that is for the want of an understanding. Many have suffered jealousies to arrise which afflicted their minds, which borrowed trouble and unnecessary uneasiness for fear that the Lord loved some other person more than he did them. This I have seen almost since the rise of the church as far back at least as at Kirtland. When the first bishop was ordained this jealous feeling began to show itself and many was troubled saying I done a great deal for this church, still I fear I don't please the Lord. Others saying I do wonder if the Lord will ever think of me to ordain me a bishop. Father Morley and others that were at Kirtland can bear me record of this thing. When the 12 was called the same feelings were manifested and in fact I will not exempt all of them for some of them had feelings when the bishops were ordained. This spirit has been the overthrow of many in this church and in fact upon this principle thousands have fallen in all ages. God gives to every man all the power, influence and authority that he can wield in righteousness and all that his faithfulness and good works merits. Then why should jealousies arrise or what benefit can be in suffering such feelings to exist? None that I can percieve, but when such feelings does exist those that cherish them commences pulling down immediately every one that is prospering or gaining influence as Cain did. Instead of building up and nourishing every promising tree and thereby prove himself worthy and show to his brethren and to God that he loves the cause and by his passive, meek spirit that he is not only willing that others should prosper and gain influence but that he actually loves to see them prosper. For when he does all that he can through himself he helps advance it through others although they may receive the honor of it and he still be aware of it. Such a man will never be forgotten and to his honor, glory and exhaltation there shall be no end.

There is another principle that has caused considerable uneasiness and trouble (E. I.) the idea of some men having more wives than one. Such tremendous fear takes hold of some that they don't know how to live and still they can't die, and begin to whisper and talk arround saying, I am actually afraid to go on a mission for fear some man will be sealed to my wife,[81] or when they return home some will be babbling about you don't know but what you have got another man's wife. For my part some say I am afraid to speak to a young woman for fear that she belongs to somebody else or for fear somebody else wants her (others deny the faith as they think, but they never had any), and say that it is all from the devil and so on. Such foolishness ought not be cherished among a wise and prudent people. Admitting the Lord created the same number of women that he did of men in the beginning and commanded them to multiply and replenish the earth and to fill up the measure of their creation in righteousness, the question is, did they do it? Answer, no. They soon disobeyed every commandment and plunged thousands into wickedness and rendered themselves unworthy to raise up seed unto the Lord and in fact was every man to have but 1 woman would he answer the end for which they were created? (Answer) No. But 9 tenths of them would rebel against the very thing that he was created to do, hence you see the propriety of the Lord calling upon men who bears the priesthood to take to themselves wives from among the daughters of men and raise up a riteous seed unto him that he might fill up the measure of their creation and hasten the consummation of his purpose in righteousness in this dispensation, acording to his word previously spoken through his servants the prophets, but those that suffer

---

[81] Polygamy had not yet been announced to the Gentile world. That the fears of the missionaries were well founded is shown by Lee in *"Confessions"* where he states that the wife of one missionary had been stolen by Joseph Smith in Nauvoo (p. 132). Clayton, as church secretary, was reproved by Brigham for listing polygamous wives (Clayton's Journal, p. 28).

fears and jealousy to arrise in their bosoms either back right out or get to be mighty righteous and for fear that they are sleeping with some other man's wife they kick up a broil at home and perhaps abuse their companions through jealousy, then go to some woman that does not understand which is right or wrong and tell her that she cannot be saved without a man [82] and he has almighty power and can exalt and save her and likely tell her that there is no harm for them to sleep together before they are sealed, then go to some clod head of an elder and get him to say their ceremony, all done without the knowledge or counsel of the authority of this church. This is not right and will not be suffered. The God that I serve will reward every man openly without his being under the necessity of going secretly and privately palming himself on the credulity of innocent, ignorant females. Such jealousies do exist and were I to say to the elders you now have the liberty to build up your kingdoms, one half of them would lie, swear, steal and fight like the very devil to get men and women sealed to them.[83] They would even try to pass right by me and go to Jos. thinking to get between mine and the 12. Some have already tried to use an influence against me, but such jealousies and selfishness shall be stopped and if the brethren do not stop it I will blow it to the four winds by making them all come and be sealed to me and I through my father, and he and all this church to Jos. When I go astray, give wrong counsel and lead this people astray, then is time enough to put me down and their God will remove me as he has done all others who has turned from the truth. But to return.

I have gathered a number of families around me through the law of adoption and seal of the covenant ac-

---

[82] This is a fundamental doctrine of the Mormon church, the cornerstone of polygamy.
[83] See pages 81-88 for "adoption."

EMMA BATCHELDER

Came to Utah from England in 1856 as a Handcart Pioneer.
Was given to Lee in 1858 by Brigham Young (Wife No.
17). Operated Lee's Ferry several years after 1874.
Remarried, moved to Holbrook, Arizona, and
became a famous frontier nurse.

Courtesy Edna Lee Brimhall

cording to the order of the priesthood and others have done likewise, it being the means of salvation left to bring us back to God. But had the keys of the priesthood been retained and handed down from father to son throughout all generations up to the present time then there could have been no necessity of the law of adoption, for we would all been included in the covenant without it and would have been legal heirs instead of being heirs according to promise. The priesthood is eternal without the beginning of days or end of life (as the apostle has described it), but man through apostacy (which is entire disobedience) has lost or suffered the keys and privileges of the priesthood to be taken away from them and they left to wander in darkness and practice all manner of wickedness until thousands became the vessels of wrath and were doomed to destruction, for as long as they are without the priesthood they continue to wander from God and never retrace their steps until it is again done by the P. H., and the idea of the Saints being led by false prophets is just a notion according to the light in which they view them. All the false prophets we have are men that have turned aside from the truth. The man is the head and God of the woman, but let him act like a God in virtuous principles and Godlike conversation, walk and deportment, and such men will continue to gain influence in power and advance in glory through all eternity, but should they use their power in wickedness as a tyrant they soon will be called to render an account of their stewartship. If not found worthy they will be hurled down to perdition and their family and kingdom will be given to another that is more worthy. Some say that a woman can't be saved without a man. Neither can a man without a woman. Bro. Jos. said that he had taught the 12 all he knew concerning the order of the Kingdom but the difficulty was that they could not remember it as he could then, but when it was necessary they

81

would not be at a loss for understanding, and I bear record to the truth of his words before God this day, that I always had an understanding and everything was brought to my mind just as he taught them to us. All the ordinances of the Temple and building of the alter &c came to me just right when they were to be done; and could we now know Bro. Hyde, Pratt, Taylor's feelings you would say that they could read a man through as soon as they would cast their eyes on him. The Apostle Paul when speaking of the fathers and the ancients said that without us could not be made perfect. There was a lack in his day and still will be through all eternity until the chain of the priesthood is restored and every spirit take a tabernacle that was foreordained acording to the dispensation of the will of God. I am entitled to the King. of the Priesthood according to descent and so is brother H. Kimble and many others have taken kingly power and grades of the Priesthood. This we would have taught in the Temple if time would permit. Jos. Smith was entitled to the keys of the P. H. according to blood, still he was the 4 son and so was I the 4 son, but when we get another Temple built then we will teach you concerning these things. Sufficeth to say that I will extend the chain of the priesthood

A New Temple   back through apostolic dispensation to Father Adam just as soon as I can get a Temple built. Jesus could have restored the order of the priesthood in his day and have brought in the millinnial if the people would have hearkened to his instructions; but they rebelled and would not and it was for this cause that Jesus told them that all the blood that had been shed on the earth from righteous Abel down to Zachriah the prophet should be required at their hands. I have a request to make of my family and that is that they (especially old persons) omit calling me father. Call me Bro. Brigham. I shall feel better when you do for I do not consider that I am worthy of that appalation.

82

Father in the P. H. implies the Great Head. The term would be proper to Father Adam. Jesus had reference to the same thing when he told his deciples not to call any man on earth their father for their father was in heaven. The seal of the covenant that I have been speaking of today was what the apostle saw previous to the distruction of the wicked when the angel was commanded not to poar out the vials of wrath on the wicked untill the Saints were sealed in their forehead and when this was done they all became Father Adam's family.

Those that are adopted into my family and take me for their counsellor, if I continue faithfully I will preside over them throughout all eternity and will stand at their head and Jos. will stand at the head of this church and will be their president, prophet and God to the people in this dispensation. When we locate I will settle my family down in the order and teach them their duties. They will then have to provide temporal blessings for me instead of my boarding from 40 to 50 persons as I now do, and will administer spiritual blessings to them. I expect to live in the house of the Lord and receive and administer ordinances to my brethren and for the dead [84] all the year round.

Ordinances for the Dead

Elder H. C. Kimble said that he was highly entertained by the remarks of Bro. Brigham, snatched at his words as fish would at bate for they were true. I should be sorry that anything should ever exist between us to sever our union. If Bro. Brigham had not invited me here today that he would have asked him for the liberty of getting down in some little knuke or corner where he could have heard his counsel on the things that he talked today. Elder O. Pratt concured in what Elder Kimble said and so far as counsel was concerned that he was ready to do anything that might be required of him and that he knew of no man

---

[84] Ceremonies for the salvation of the dead still furnish a considerable portion of the Salt Lake Temple revenue.

that he preferred as a leader to President B. Young. Pres. B. Y. gave an intermission till after supper, 5 p.m.

The table was well furnished and sufficient large to acommode 40 persons. The men were seated on the right with their companions opposite them commencing with the 12 (Pres. B. Young at their head) then in order the adopted children beginning with the first that was adopted. The band and choir kept their seats and continued their sweet strains of music while the guests were partaking of the rich festival that were spread in great plenty before them.

Messengers from
the Battalion

Just after rising from the feast I heard my name called by a voice that I once knew. I sprang to the door and my astonishment I met Bro. Thomas Woolsey, my first adopted son, just from the Bat. Bro. John H. Tippets came with him. They left the Bat. 280 ms. south of Santafe on the river Riogrand on the 10th of Nov. 1846.[85] Piloted 56 sick men to Puerblo where Capt. Brown's detachment were stationed, from thence came in on pack mules. Were 50 days on the way, taken prisoners twice, once sentenced to be shot by the Pawnee Indians. Were 40 days without bread and 5 days without much of anything to eat. Brought a package of 137 letters. Good account from Ft. Purbelow but rather unfavorable from the Bat. Their faces were covered with hair and their persons resembled a mountaineer. This certainly was a mericle in Iseral or the lives of those men would never have been saved. The weather was cold enough to have frozen them to death aparantly. Pres. Young had them seated down at the table in their natural garb. Their arrival produced no smawl

---

[85] Many women had accompanied the Battalion soldiers. These were detached at the last crossing of Arkansas river and sent to join the camp of Mississippi Saints at Pueblo. John Tippets and Thomas Woolsey accompanied that group. At Santa Fe, on Oct. 17, 88 soldiers, the "sick detachment," and husbands of women, were sent to Pueblo under command of Capt. James Brown. Tippets and Woolsey rejoined the Battalion south of Santa Fe, and on Nov. 10 started back from the Rio Grande with 58 sick men. Battalion members believed they were being marched south into Mexico, but they turned west when within 90 miles of El Paso, Dec. 27, 1846. About 30 per cent of the Battalion force wintered at Pueblo.

stir in camp. Men and women came in every direction to inquire after their friends in the Bat. and to see the faces of those who had been so merichesly preserved from the dangers and perrils of their journey. After they (the messengers) had been refreshed by nourishing food, the 12, myself and the 2 messengers met in council in Pres. B. Young's sitting room. They delivered an interesting account of their [travels] a part of which I have already noted. Stated that the Bat. was but in verry little better situation than they were when Bro. Lee left them, that they had been on ½ rations for 3 weeks when they left them and no prospect of more than ½ rations should they attempt to cross the mountains this winter. However, report reached Santafe before we arrived that the Bat. had taken the Alpasio [El Paso][85] a stronghold between the Riogrand and the mountains without the firing of a gun. If this report is true (he continued) the Bat. will have abundance of supplies and likely take up winter quarters; that some of the officers were tyranical and oppresive. Brought with them a mail of 137 letters mostly from Purbelow which is the place where the sick of the Bat. have taken up Winter Quarters. I received a letter from Lieutenant Pace giving an account of the situation of the Bat. which was coroberative with the testimony of the messengers. Pres. Young said that could $500 have put him in the Bat. when Bro. Lee came up with it I cheerfully would have given it, but they were where I could not reach them at that time. But I trust that we will be able to reach them yet and save them irretrievable ruin.[92] Had they gone acording to our council not a man of them would ever have fallen, but they would all have returned to their families and friends in perfect safety. They might just as well all have wintered at Bent's Fort where their supplies were stationed and where they had marching orders for, had the officers been agreed when Bro. [Lee] reached the command; but no, they must

Mail from Pueblo

85

[*march*] right into unnecessary suffering and distress. It does appear to me that the officers lost sight of things that we taught them.[86] Decided that 15 cts postage be put on each letter for the benefit of the messengers. Dissolved about 7 o'clock.

"Law of Adoption" Continued

Returned to the council room, found the brethren enjoying themselves, bearing record to the things that had been taught them through the day. Among those that had spoken Elder Isaac Morley said that his soul was filled with rejoicing to see the beauty and harmony of the family connecting links of the priesthood that had been taught this day and when I look at the family connection I cannot but acknowledge him my leader in all things, and he looking to Jos. the martyred prophet who has gone to prepare the way for us and can do more for us than he could do provided he was here. This P. Hood spoken of is from all eternity and will lead to all eternity and will exalt to be gods through faithfulness. Pres. B. Young said that Bros. Thomas Woolsey and John L. Tippets had just arrived from the Bat. and from the brethren at Purblow. Have brought 137 letters for the brethren and sisters in camp. 15 cts postage will be required on each letter for the benefit of the messengers as they were robbed of their clothing by the Indians. Then continued his remarks on the law of adoption. Granted the brethren permission to ask questions when they did not fully comprehend his meaning. The Lord introduced the law of adoption for the benefit of the children of men as a schoolmaster to bring them back into the covenant of the P. H., not as some have supposed to add anything to his glory. This principle I ansre is not clearly understood by many of Elders in this church at the present time as it will hereafter be, and I confess that I have had only a smattering of these things, but when it is neces-

---

[86] Brigham Young insisted his orders were superior to those of the United States military officers. (See note 92.)

sary I will attain to more knowledge on the subject and consiquently will be enabled to teach and practice more and will in the meantime glorify God the bountiful giver. I have often heard elders say that they were [not] dependent on any man. I then considered and do now that they were saying more than what I in reality could say, for I consider that we are all dependent on one another for our exhaltation, that our interests is inseparately connected (for example) what can my family do without me? Supposing they were to all turn away from me, I hold the keys over them through which they are to receive their exaltation. Would they not be like sheep that are without a shepherd and would be devoured by the wolves? (Ans.) They certainly would. Then let us change the position and say that I would cut off all my family, then what glory would I have with nobody to rule over but my own dear little self? To tell you my feelings I would rather be annihilated than to be in that situation. This is another strong proof of the apostle's saying when he declared that they without them could not be made perfect neither can you without me nor I without you be made perfect, that is if we are faithful and without there is no perfection on any condition whatever. This rule applies to the whole human family. This is the torment and misery of the disobedient spirits that they cannot be made perfect unless some scheme should hereafter be introduced for their redemption. They are now without tabernacles to dwell in only such as they have unlawfully taken possession of and usurped power over, it being a part of their agency that was allowed them which they used to the consummation of their unhappy and wretched estate, it being the reward and fruits of their doings having been given over to all manner of wickedness permitted to afflict the handiwork of the Lord until they fill up their cup of inequity and the Lord says thou wicked and disobedient spirit, thou shalt not have power any

Brigham as "Ruler"

87

longer to afflict my people or destroy the works of my hands. You have forfeited your agency and wrought thy fullness. Depart hence to the pitt that I have prepared for you and this is their torment that their power and agency is taken away and they are left to regret that it was through their own disobedience that they cut the thread of their salvation, the reflections of which only serves to torture and increase their torment and that would be the situation of my family should they cut themselves off from me (I use my family for an example, not that I have the least fears of their ever doing so for I have none). I feel happy this night because we [are] of one mind, still should I believe that we were perfect and could not advance any further I should not be happy; but to the honor of power and glory of the faithful there is no end for your satisfaction. I will show you a rule by which you may comprehend the exaltation of the faithful. I will use myself as a figure and say that I am ruler over ten sons and soon each one of them will have 10 men sealed to them and then they would be rulers over them and that would make me ruler over ten presidents (or rather kings), whereas before I was ruler over 10 subjects only. Or in other words I ruled over one kingdom whereas I now rule over 10. Then let each one of those ten get ten more and then I would be ruler of 100 kingdoms and so on continue through all eternity and the more honor and glory that I could bestow upon my sons the more it would add to my exaltation but to clip the thread of your exaltation then where would be your glory.[87] It would be like the fallen angels or devils that kept not their first estates, were reserved in everlasting chains of darkness unto the judgment of the great day. Others fell from Heaven down to hell like lightning; but if you wish to advance, hold up the hands of your file leader and as the

"Law of Adoption" Elucidated

---

[87] This is Brigham's own interpretation of the "Law of Adoption" so frequently mentioned in this Journal. Like many other Mormon doctrines, it was but a passing fad, and is now ignored and forgotten.

Yankee says, boost him ahead and should you have 10 legions of trains follow on after you you should say to your file leader, push ahead for I am coming with my train, boosting up at the same [time] instead of trying to pass. To him the word would stimulate him and he would say, come on my boys, I will travel as fast as you can and on we would go in one solid train through all eternity.

Before I stop I will answer a question that has been repeatedly asked me (E. I.) should I have a father dead that has never heard this gospel, would it be required of me to redeem him and then have him adopted into some man's family and I be adopted to my father? (I ans. no.) If we have to attend to the ordinances of redemption for our dead relatives we then become their saviours and were we to wait to redeem our dead relatives before we could link the chains of the P. H. we would never accomplish it.

Elder E. T. Benson gave an interesting account of his mission to the brethren on the Puncaw river,[18] bore record to the truth of the day and evening's instruction. Elder Jos. Young readily concurred in the above remarks. Pres. B. Young spoke by way of explanation to what Bro. Jos. Young had said while speaking, turned his discourse and said: You Sisters, if you expect to call me Bro. Brigham I want you to be cleanly, keep your faces and hands and skin clean from head to foot, your clothes, dishes and houses clean and nice, also your children and learn them manners, and when you mix up bread don't have a dozen flies in your tray and when you hair your butter, do keep the hairs and flies on a separate dish.[88] I no that the women have generally ruled their husbands and their children rules their mothers. But when a woman undertakes to rule me I want them to be smart enough not to let me catch them at it.[89]

Brigham Lays Down Sanitary Rules

---

[88] Such remarks were typical of Brigham Young's sermons.
[89] Later, in Utah, Amelia Folsom did rule him. See *"Wife No. 19"* by Ann Eliza Young.

Now I don't want the brethren from my remarks to abuse their wives ·but treat them kindly, do their heavy lugging but don't wash their dishes as some do. We have enjoyed ourselves first rate brethren, now I will leave it to a vote whether we will continue speaking, have music or dance. Decided that they dance as a change for exercise. The room was soon prepared and a set on the floor led by Pres. B. Young. The assembly danced before the Lord till about 11 o'clock when Pres. Young called the house to order and was dismissed by benediction from Elder I. Morley. I presume every heart was filled.

Winter Quarters, O. N., Wed. 17th, 1847.

Morning clear, warm and pleasant. About 8 o'clock Pres. B. Young was taken very unwell, being much distressed in the stomach and bowels. Fainted away, apparently dead for several moments and it was with much ado that he could be kept from falling asleep to await the resurrection morn. At 11 I was in. He appeared some revived. His words to me was that I have frequently [*fainted*] away but never died before. Asked me if his family had commenced assembling. At 8 morn. the Pres. Isaac Morley, his 2 counsellors, the Co. including their officers (1st 100 B. Young's) met and deliberated some time after reading the names of the Co., then voted that the whole Co. should go.[90] At 11 meeting dissolved to R. Cahoon where the officers with the Pres. and his 2 counsellors were to meet and deliberate on what they had done in the forenoon. At 12 the 2nd Co. of Pres. B. Young's family commenced gathering. Presant of the 12: H. C. Kimble, O. Pratt, J. A. Lyman and W. Richards. Pres. B. Young not being able to attend Elder H. C. Kimble was called to preside. The house having been called to order, the hymn The Spirit of God Like a Fire Is Burning &c was sung and prayer by

Brigham "Dies"

---

[90] Refers to the Pioneer emigration.

Elder O. Pratt. Pres. Kimble addressed the multitude. Said that on account of Bro. Brigham's ill health placed me as his representative to instruct you today. I am his brother and we are both heirs to the priesthood. How did we know it? Jos. had a vision and saw and traced back our bloods to the royal family.[90a] You have chose him for your leader but does that separate you from me? Ans. No. I have chose him for my leader long before you did, and so did the 12, so we are ahead of you and my interest is yours and if I thought that the law of the doctrine would sever the union of this people the Lord knows I should be sorrow[ful]. I look upon the law of adoption as being the means of uniting families together by the connecting links of the priesthood, still I am aware that many have had trials for fear that they had given away their birthright when in fact they had none, not having been adopted. Consiquently could not be heirs to the birthright. What you have done is the best thing that you could have done. For example you may take of all the different varieties of apples and graft them all in one tree. Will it change the quality of these different fruits? No, only it refines it and makes it better. Still the apples are the same kind, yet they all partake of the same nutriment from the same tree. But to urge anyone to be adopted or sealed to you it is like damming water to make it run up hill, it always breaks over unless [you] are all the time draining and is but dammed water at last. Then let it have its course. Elder O. Pratt said that he had been highly entertained with Elder Kimble's remarks and as Bro. Brigham said yesterday that no man has lost anything by being adopted, but every man has gained that have kept their covenants. We are or all will be of one family when united by the priesthood to Father Adam's. This has been a privilege that God has

Kimball on "Adoption"

[90a] The Mormon church maintains a large genealogical library, but revelation still plays a large part in the compilation of family trees. See example in Egan's "Pioneering the West," where the Egan family is traced directly to Adam.

91

offered to the children in all dispensations. Some have embraced it and endeavored to carry it out but the major part of the children of men rejected this privilege, consiquently subject themselves to become the children of wrath to wander in darkness doing evil deeds instead of good until their cup of inequity is full and the Lord comes out and says that you shall not afflict nor oppose my handiwork any more; your career is ended, your agency you have forfeited, hence you have no more power to act, let your inclinations be what they may. And that is the torment of the wicked to want to do anything and cannot. But to return; the priesthood is from all eternity and will head back to all eternity and we must fasten on and hold to it as the people did to the rod of iron that Father Lehi and Nephi saw while in their vision and while we hold on to the chain and keep traveling we are still advancing. Although we may pass through dark valleys of sorrow and dispair yet we'll triumph, but when we let go are soon in darkness until we are lost while in that condition &c. Evening's services. After supper was over and the congregation seated the music cheered us with their sweet melodious sound. Dr.

Remarks by Richards

Richards (the Historian) addressed the collection. Said that was it not that the Pres. always delighted in a variety and I know of no greater variety than to present the Dr. before this people as I but seldom ever address this people. I have been well entertained from the instructions that has been taught in this house yesterday and today. One item that caught my attention was this thing of jealousy, fearing that some now is rising or gaining power and influence faster than what I am. Therefore jealousy will arrise which causes an envious feelings in our bosom and we imagine that man is lexeering [*electioneering*] and using unlawful measures to gain an influence. This is soon whispered from one to another and in the meantime it comes to the ears of the Pres. and thereby does that man an injury

92

when in reality he is as innocent as the man who reported him and perhaps a great deal more so. Is not that principle wrong? It certainly is, and was we to indulge that little, jealous, selfish, envious, devilish spirit we would soon go down to hell. But for example let every man that sees any man is going ahead of him jump and pull him back, directly another starts and someone pulls him down and so continue this throughout the church and soon our union would be dissolved and we would soon be destroyed and that would be the result of our labors. But to push each other ahead and do all that we can in righteousness admitting that we get no reward for what we do here, and all my brethren gets up before I do, will they forget my faithfulness and good works? I answer no. No good man will ever neglect a friend and leave him in the rear. He will labor as hard to pull that man up as that did to push him up. Elder W. Woodruff said he never before enjoyed himself as well as he did under the instructions of yesterday's and today's while my brethren were reasoning upon the law of adoption, seal of the covenant and priesthood, a subject of deep and thrilling interest to us all. Yet I have had but little instruction on this important subject although I have much desired. I have never had the privilege of having anyone adopted into my family. At the time those ordinances were attended to I was absent on a mission, consiquently have never lextioneered much and I do not know that I have ever asked a man to be adopted into my family. And as for jealousies, I believe that I am free from them and am determined to walk acording to counsel and always have been &c. Elder G. A. Smith [91] said he and Bro. Amasa Lyman have just returned from a mission on the other side of the river but he durst [not] say as Bro.

General Discussion of "Adoption"

[91] George Albert Smith, son of Patriarch John Smith, and an Apostle. In 1857 he was sent to southern Utah to rouse the Mormon settlers against Gentile emigrants, and fanned the fanatical flame which resulted in the Mountain Meadows Massacre, for which Lee was executed.

Pratt and Woodruff has, that he had not lextioneered, for I have with all my might, but if I have lectioneered to the injury and hurt of any man I am ignorant of it. I always lectioneered but for the good of this cause and so does Bro. Pratt and all my brethren. But there is one thing that I don't like to see and that is this thing called jealousy stirring up family disturbances and broils because we are afraid that some man is gaining favor and I am not advancing as fast as they are. And in order to keep back or stop their influence we go to those that have been sealed and discourage them saying why dident [you] go come with me where none but the respected are? Was you not as capable of holding the keys of presidency yourself as Bro. Lee who has probably 10 or 15 men sealed to him? Certainly you (I use Bro. Lee present because he is the 1st man I see) were. Then you should have gone to serve the 12 and thereby caused dissatisfaction. For example suppose I was to jump every man and be sealed to the Great God and have 3 only sealed to me. I don't think my kingdom would be very large or my glory very great. Not more so than it would be was I sealed to the most obscure Saint in this Kingdom. I could get no more. I should be dependent on the exertion of those who were sealed to me. But was I sealed to the most obscure individual in this church and I had 10s of 10,000 sealed to me, would not my glory be greater than it would be was I sealed to headquarters with my 3 only? Certainly it would. It does [not] matter so much where we are sealed provided we form a part of link the Priesthood. Then let jealousy stop and be united that we may speedily build up the kingdom of God on the earth, &c.

Elder A. Lyman followed lastly and offered a warm interesting exhortation. Concluded with the previous observation of his brethren and continued to considerable length, but the weakness of my body and eyes somewhat

94

sore rendered it inexpedient for me to note his remarks. About 11 a vote of the house was taken and decided in favor of shucking off some of their traditions by dancing. I replied that I could not participate with them in the evening's recreation from the fact that I did not consider it a time to dance but a day with me of deep solemnity and prayer for the recovery of the health of my file leader and father who this day has been near yielding up the ghost. Having made those remarks I left the room and entered the place where the afflicted lay. Found [him] more comfortable than in the forenoon. He asked me how we enjoyed ourselves in the meeting through the day and was it closed, &c. He requested me to ask Bro. E. Ellsworth to come in as [he] wanted to be washed and anointed. I complied with his request and returned home. The party continued till 2 a.m.

Winter Quarters, O. N., Thurs., Feb. 18, '47.

Morning clear, warm and pleasant. President still on the mend. I occupied the fore part of the day in writing. Bro. Thomas Woolsey was crowded with visitors inquiring after their friends in the army. About 3 eve. Bro. Stewart and I walked to Pres. B. Young's, found still gaining. I took him arround the city in a carriage on a pleasure ride. In the meantime he said to me that I must go and lay my hands wherever I could find a good span of mules and a waggon for T. Woolsey to bring his family from Pizgah to this place forthwith as he wanted him to return back to the army as it was important to send messages to them as soon as possible for their salvation.[92] I accordingly went

---

[92] That Brigham Young considered himself commander in chief of the Mormon Battalion is evidenced by the following extract from the journal of Thomas Bullock, dated at Ft. Laramie, June 3, 1847: "President Young read some instructions which he had previously written to the brethren, and gave them to Amasa Lyman. He told the brethren that they had accomplished their design in getting the Battalion to Mexico, but the brethren at Pueblo must not follow Brown to Mexico, but go to California. If the officers will not do right, he instructed Amasa to call out the men and choose officers who would do right. If the Battalion brethren are at Santa

95

about and obtained one mule of Br. Magee Harris and another from Bro. J. M. Flake [93] and a waggon from Bro. Job Hall. About sunset I went to see Bro. David Young who was low of the consumption. Spent an hour in conversation with Mary.[94] Returned and went to the basket factory accompanied by Rachel. The room was thronged, yet we enjoyed ourselves first rate. After a few hours had passed in mirth and recreation I was called upon to address the young people. Taught them to reverence the priesthood and our sovereign and eternal benefactor in the dance as well as in the pulpit for this would be pleasing to him. About 11 I returned, found it very dark insomuch that it was with much difficulty that we could find our way home through the rain. Leaving Rachel at her residence I took the lantern and conducted the 2 Sisters Vances and Lovina Young home.[95] Staid about an hour with Father D. Young's who was sick. About midnight wind changed north and began to snow.

Lee Goes Courting Again

Winter Quarters, Friday, Feb. 19, 1847.

Messages for the Battalion

Clowdy, W. N. Somewhat cold. About 9, in at Pres. B. Young's. Had some conversation about the Bat. Said that he would send messengers to Puerblo and to the Bat. with proper credentials to carry out the counsel of the church;

Fe, these brethren should go there and bring the Battalion there; if the Pueblo command has gone from there, to pursue them and bring them back, and if General Kearney is there and objects to their return, according to our agreement, tell him we are bound for California, and throw all Gentile officers out of the Battalion when you come up to it." The original destination of the Mormons was California, as attested by numerous early references. Thomas L. Kane persuaded Brigham Young to change his plans after the Battalion had left. The "new revelation" instructing members of the Battalion that the Saints would locate in the vicinity of Great Salt Lake or on Bear river, was carried to the Pueblo Saints by Amasa Lyman, guided by Tippets, Woolsey and Roswell Stevens, who left Brigham's party June 3, 1847, at Fort Laramie. Kane's influence in changing Brigham's revelation is partially verified by Lee's entry of Feb. 19. (See "Thomas L. Kane, Friend of the Mormons.")

[93] James M. Flake, who later acted as guide over the Southern Route between Salt Lake City and San Bernardino. (See Henry Bigler's Journal. MS.) He was the Flake of "Snowflake," Arizona.

[94] Mary Vance Young, later Wife No. 13.

[95] Left Wife No. 6 to court future Wives 12 and 13.

that a letter had been sent to Washington in care of Friend Kane,[28] petitioning the President through the secretary of war to discharge the Bat. that they may return and assist in removing their families in the spring. Requested me to borrow $10.00 and let Bro. T. Woolsey have it in part for a mule. I went and done as I was commanded. About [?] Bro. Woolsey left camp for his family. The remainder of the day I was employed in writing. In the evening Bro. A. P. Free and Magee Harris hauled me a load of hay gratis. Wind still N. Bro. Stewart assisted to write till 10 when he returned. I continued till 3 morning.

Winter Quarters, O. N., Sat., Feb. 20, 1947.

Clowdy, W. N. Cold, occasional showers of snow. At 8 in at Pres. B. Young. Found him rather feeble. Sat and conversed about 1½ hours with him on different subjects. He invited me to come in frequently whenever I could and see him. About 10 Bro. Stewart and John Green left camp for Tenn.[72] Took a mail of 10 or 15 letters. On leaving me I gave him $30.00 in cash to defray his expenses.[72] Blessed him in the name of the Lord and told [him] to go and prosper and return in safety. About 11 the storm increased rapidly and continued all day. W. high North.

Winter Quarters, O. N., Sund., Feb. 21, '47.

Morning cool, W. N. Snow drifted from 4 to 6 feet but on the level about 15 inches. About 9 began to fare off and grow milder. Pres. B. Young still on the mend. My teams not having returned from Mo. rendered it quite a task for me to keep up 4 fires[96] in such severe cold weather. Employed the remainder of the day in writing. In the evening went to Bro. Free, administered to his wife that was sick of the winter fever. Returned and visited Bro. B. Young. Found him on the mend. Sat and wrote journal history till 12 midnight.

---

[96] Lee was apparently maintaining four separate establishments.

Winter Quarters, O. N., Mon., Feb. 22, '47.

Morning clear and pleasant. W. S. Till noon I was engaged in getting up a cord of wood, then confined to writing till 4 when Pres. B. Young came in a sley and took me with him arround the city. His health improving. Told me that he wished me to take hold and assist Bro. J. M. Grant to organize his Co.

Winter Quarters, O. N., Teus., Feb. 23, '47.

Lee Assists the Pioneer Organization

Morning clowdy, W. S.E. Warm and mild. At 9 o'clock I had conversation with Bro. J. M. Grant with reference to Pres. Young's wishes. At [?] Bro. Grant and myself met in council with Pres. B. Young in Dr. Richard's office. He there told Br. J. M. Grant that he had spoken to me to assist him with the Co., that it was his privilege to have 2 counselors and if he wanted another to take Bro. George D. Grant. I am, said he, going on with the pioneers and will have to leave my family, therefore I want you, Brother Lee, Bro. G. D. Grant to take my family on with the 1st Co. Bro. Grant is not acquainted with doing business and keeping books but he understands all about rigging waggons. Bro. Lee is acquainted with doeing business and organizing cos. &c. The Pres. then told me that he wanted me to send 1 team of mules and 2 pioneers and that should I want more waggons or teams that he would suply them out of his teams and waggons. I read him a letter from Lieut. Pace in the Bat. stating the situation of the Bat. Pres. Young was highly pleased with the spirit of the letter, said that it contained some noble ideas and words that mean something. In the meantime he said that he would hold them by the prayer of faith until they would return and that good would result out of the present moves. Elder O. Pratt, W. Woodruff, E. T. Benson, W. Richards in the meintime came and spent about 3 hours in conversation. At 1 p.m. the widows . . . .

Winter Quarters, O. N., Frid., Feb. 26th, '47.

Morning clowdy, W. N. Light snow flying all day. My teams were employed in getting up wood and storing grain. I was engaged in arranging the affairs of my house. Had some conversation with Sister Nancy Gibbons, who had come to see me for that purpose. She told me that she was without a friend that she could in reality claim as a counselor or lodge the secrets of her breasts with, and that she had thought rather hard of me for I was one of the first elders that brought the gospel to her and a man in whom she always reposed the most exquisite trust and confidence in and that I had never been to see her and advise her since her exudous to the mountains and why I should treat her so coolly and be a stranger she could not account. She had often thought of speaking to me and asking me the reason why I was so distant to her. I told her that I always had the warmest feelings of friendship for her and the reason for my not being more familiar with her was that her sister Sarah was sealed to Bro. A. O. Smoot and that inasmuch as he had brought her (Nancy) from Tennessee that he likely had claims on her and always wishing to attend to my own business I said nothing to her for fear that it might cause feelings with Bro. Smoot. She assured me that it was not nor never had been her mind to be connected with him, that she traveled with his family through necessity because she was not acquainted with any other family and that she wanted I should take charge of her and her effects, that is if I considered her worth taking off. I asked her if she wished to be connected with me in marriage according to the seal of the covenant. She replied, I do, and am willing to fare as you do in all things in adversity. Your request shall be granted.

Nancy Gibbons Armstrong Proposes

Lee Accepts "Nancy the 2nd"

Winter Quarters, O. N., Sat., Feb. 27, '47.

Morning clowdy, cool wind N. At 20 to 9 I was at Pres.

99

B. Young's. Found him comfortably in bed. When I entered he immediately arrose, dressed himself and said that there was a meeting of the Capts. of Cos., Presidents and their counsellors and that he must attend and requested me to do the same. Told me that he and his lady would endeavor to pay us a visit in the evening and take supper. Called in at Bro. A. P. Rockwood's, took home a vessel of wine and brandy.[42] Sent some teams to the woods for fuel, others for hay. At 10 the Capts. of Cos. assembled and at 30 m. to 11 Capts. O. Pratt and J. M. Grant were sent to wait upon the Pres. B. Y. and notify him that the assembly were anxiously waiting his presence and counsel. Messengers returned and reported that the Pres. was engaged in listning at the sweet sounds of the flute and other instruments of music by a half blooded Indian, Mr. McGarry, musicioner,[141] but would be at their service soon. At 11 Pres. Young came in just as the house was called to order. 1st the names of the Capt. of 100s were called and answered to. 2nd, Elder A. O. Smoot reported that he had organized a hundreds with 95 families, 20 pioneers, 30 families to go. The whole No. of pioneers is 168 and perhaps 125 out of that No. will go from the 1st Co. and likely 100 will go from Bro. Heber C. Kimble's Co. The next thing is for the Capts. and the Pres. of Cos. to determine how many mule teams can be had in order to know whether we will be obliged to take ox teams or not and how many can go to a team. Some of the 12 met last night and raised 13 teams among themselves. After some deliberations on the subject decided that 3 men go with a team. Pres. (B. Y.) said that he approved the decision and that would supersede the necessity of hauling tents as 3 men could lodge in a waggon and that 400 lbs. of grain must be taken to each team. The provisions, clothing, spring seed and farming utensils &c will make a considerable load and that 50 waggons and teams will be required

100

Facsimile of two pages from John D. Lee's Journal. Entry of Feb. 27, 1847, showing record of his marriage to three women in one ceremony.

at least and that No. can be easily raised and if necessary teams can go to the Pawnee village with the pioneers to assist them that far, then return. The subject of building a rawhide boat was then agitated in the form of 2 large canoes and lash them together when used. Use the waggon boxes or rather the bottom boards for flooring and when done ferrying the boat could be used for waggon bodies.[97] Pres. Young said that 18 men could lodge in one of these boats and that we build one of those boats of sole leather well stuffed with bees wax and tallow, then when we are done with them the leather is still worth the cost to tap our boots and shoes, but for experience let us build another of rawhide which is said by some to be preferable to tanned leather. Lastly the above constructed named boats were decided upon. Pres. B. Young said that he would build the rawhide boat, decided that Pres. (B. Y.) superintend building of the boat. Bro. John Richards volunteered to saw the lumber. E. T. Benson volunteered to furnish a stick of white oak timber 22 feet in length, from 6 to 12 inches at the smawl end, and John Lytle will do the ironing. Edward Hunter furnishes the iron, and Bro. Weeks, Kesler, Ensign and Cooks . . . . and we will assist them in other things. Both boats will have to be building at the same time and those men can carry on better. Let the hides be furnished by the Co. wherever the Capts. can find them. Bros. Woodruff volunteered to furnish 1 beef hide, Bro. J. Vance 2, I. Morley 1, Chas. Shumway to secure the sinews. After deliberation it was considered preferable to build both boats of raw hide. Let Bro. Jas. G. Willey take hold and dress the hide for the boats and that Bro. Jas. Hart assist him. Let the Capts. of Co. pick up 12 hides from the Cos. and deliver them to Bro. Jas. Hart. Question by Pres. B. Y. that he has on hands 100 bushels

[97] Only one leather boat, the "Revenue Cutter" was taken by the pioneers. It did good service at Platte River crossing near present Casper, Wyo.

101

of seed corn, that I want the brethren to buy it and pay me $1.00 dollar per bushel. If you don't you will feed it to your mules but if you do you will say it cost too much.[98] I have also 300 bushels that I want the pioneers to buy and pay me for it. I have paid out well nigh $2500 dollars [99] to build a mill for the benefit of this camp having exhausted all my means to feed the poor and cannot go any farther without help. I am now in debt $300 for corn to Jumbo[100] that I must raise. The articles required for each team for

our outfit for the Pioneer Co. will be 400 lbs. horsefeed, 300 lbs. provisions and cooking utensils, 1½ bushel seed corn, 1 bushel oats, 1 bushel white beans, 1 peck of peas, 1 do. potatoes, ½ bushel flax seed, 1 peck of hemp seed, ½ do. barley, ½ do. of millet and garden seeds of every description, 10 prairie plows, 10 do. diamonds, irons suitable for waggons, horse shoes, farming utensils, &c. That every mule and horse be newly shod before starting and with 1 set of extra set of horse shoes with nails prepared. That everything be ready by the 15th of March. Added to the bill 5 sets of drag teeth, log chains, pit saws, crosscuts, axes, guns, 4 blacksmiths, 4 carpenters and let each Capt. of 100 select a place of deposit where every waggon and all equipage may be brought and inspected before starting. That the Capts. report on Sat. 10 morn. next at this place, and I want them to report 200 pioneers instead of 168 and 100 waggons instead of 50; mules and horses instead of oxen, for I know that they can be had, and should any refuse to let or send his teams and says that [they] don't intend going this spring, just cross out his name and tell him that no man can be attached to this Co. that will not help roll this cause on, and take no man that says he

---

[98] Although Brigham never overlooked a chance to profit, his psychology in this case was sound.

[99] A considerable portion was Battalion money.

[100] "Jumbo" refers to a half-breed French trader on the Missouri, according to Pulsipher's journal. Frenchmen were all nicknamed "Gumbo" by English-speaking settlers. It may possibly refer to P. A. Sarpy.

can't fit himself out for the journey, for such a man will not work when he goes. Let those that go as pioneers leave their families, but take the families of the brethren that are in the army,[101] for they will meet us at the mountains and should we find that our teams can be wintered in safety there, and that we can live on buffalo meat, then the pioneers can return and bring their families on in the fall. Otherwise we will necessarily have to send back our teams to be wintered on the rushes in the Mo. bottoms. Then when grass rises let them come on. Concluded by saying Mr. McGarry[141] seems to be willing to go according to counsel and that he may be a useful man after he has acquired a experimental knowledge. His skill on the flute cannot be surpassed by any musician that I have ever heard, therefore use the man with respect. 2 p.m. adjourned to Sat. next, 11, same place.

McGarry May Be Useful

Winter Quarters, O. N., Sat., Feb. 27th, '47.

At 30 m. to 7 evening Pres. B. Young and lady came into John D. Lee's to attend to the following ordinances (ss):

A Triple Honeymoon

Nancy Gibbons, born Jany. 7th, 1799, Noxville, Nox Co., State of Tennessee.

Mary Vance Young, born Nov. 10th, 1817, Jackson Co., Tennessee.

Lovina Young, born Sept. 25th, 1820, Jackson County, Tennessee.

John Doyle Lee, born Sept. 6th, 1812, Town of Kaskaskia, Randolph County, State of Ills.

Nancy Gibbons, Mary Vance Young and Lovina Young were all sealed to John D. Lee for time and all eternity in presence of Brigham Young and David Young.[102] Presi-

---

[101] This is a part of Brigham's "new revelation." It was later changed several times; the soldiers' families did not go with the pioneer company and only a few were taken west later in 1847.

[102] Married three wives in one ceremony.

dent Brigham Young officiate at 10 m. to 7 o' evening at the residence of J. D. Lee. After the above ordinances were attended to super was prepared, the Pres. (B. Y.) and lady, the guests and all those presant sat down and partook of the feast. After super the Pres. and lady amused the party by singing some sacred and sentimental hymns adapted to occasion. At 20 to 8 Pres. Young and I met in Dr. Richard's office. Elder G. A. Smith, E. T. Benson, W. Richards, J. M. Grant and the clerks were presant. Heard several letters read. Passed 2 hours in conversation principally upon the journey to the mountains. About ½ past 10 returned to my residence, found Sister Young quite unwell, but by mild nursing soon felt revived. While in conversation Pres. Young said that he wished me to prepare a waggon and load it with turkeys, geese, ducks, peafowls, guinea hens and dung hill fowls also some pigs of the best quality, she goats, sheep and &c. Blessed us and returned home. I acompanied them home at 11 o'clock and presented them $7.50 gold.

Winter Quarters, O. N., Sund., Feb. 28th, '47.

Morning clear, W. N., cool. About 10 morning Bro. Rufus Allen came in and quite a No. of families of my house were present. I reasoned with them upon the law of adoption. Bro. R. Allen proffered to go as a pioneer and take my team and that likely his father and connection would be attached to my family by the law of adoption. Visited Louisa [*No. 3*], found her quite unwell with a disease called the Black Leg which has been very fatal in camp. It is suposed to be the dregs of the ague and kanker that falls into the feet and legs and commences on the toes first with a pain, then they die away without feeling and so on continuing until the person expires. This and other pestilence have taken many to their silent tomb. However Pres. B. Young when wrought upon by the Holy Spirit pro-

Louisa Suffers with "Blackleg"

104

phesied that such calamities would come upon them as a scourge for their unbelief and murmuring and that the Lord would scourge them to prevent the Missourians from doing it. About 4 I spent an hour in conversation with Nancy. At 7 High Council met. Pres. related his vision which he had while sick. Appointed a meeting of the commanders of Co. at 9 the following morning (E.I.) the 2nd division.

Vision.

He saw Jos. sitting in a splendid mansion. On coming up to him embrased in his arms and kised him 3 times, asked him if he would return to the earth soon. He answered in the negative. He then asked the liberty of staying with him as he had long been deprived of his society. Jos. replied, you must return back and comfort the brethren, for I know their anxiety to learn their duty concerning the law of adoption and seal of the covenant. Tell them to be patient and not to grieve the Holy Spirit, but to live so as always have the whisperings of the Spirit and that will guide aright. This he impressed upon me three times and as I turned from him I went into the dark. Remarks: The vision I know to be of God and the same things that he has taught him he impressed on his brethren.

Brigham's Vision

Winter Quarters, O. N., Mon., Mar. 1st, '47.

Morning clear, warm and pleasant, W. S. At 8 I was at Pres. Young's. Found him at his breakfast. Had some conversation with him about company arrangements. At 9 we walked to Dr. Richard's office where Pres. Young in the presence of H. C. Kimble, O. Pratt, W. Richards, E. T. Benson, gave Bro. Jedediah M. Grant instruction relative to his mission east among the branches of the church. I then in Co. with J. M. Grant, walked to Nancy the 2nd [*No. 12*] and got $33½ in gold of her and let Bro. Grant have for silver. Took my mules from Charles Shumway that he had been using through the winter to fit them up for the Pioneer Co. Pres. B. Young not knowing that I had made arrangements to have Bro. Allen go as one of my pioneers counseled him to raise a team from his own neighborhood and bring to camp. Bro. M. Anderson concluded to fit up another team for the pioneers. Evening Sarah Smoot and Nancy the 2nd sat and chatted till 9 when Sarah returned. Nancy tarried till morning. She told me that she was perfectly willing to have me manage all her affairs as I thought proper, that she and all she had was at my command, all she asked was an interest in the family.

Winter Quarters, O. N., Teus., March 2nd, 1847.

Morning clear, W. N. About 10 changed S., moderated. This forenoon I let Bro Bliss have my mules and waggon to draw wood (conditioned) upon the ½. Still crossing on the ice. T. Johnson went for hay. Wm. Pace to rig up for Mo. At 6 I was at Pres. B. Young's, found him alone, stayed an hour or 2 in conversation about fitting up the families that were to go in the spring Co. Said that had Bro. Allen told him the whole circumstance about going with my team in the Pioneer Co. he certainly would have aproved of the course that I had taken and that he would yet advise that course and that should he fail to sell the mill that when Bro. J. M. Grant returned he would bring money for him which he wanted I should, in connection with Bro. Grant, purchase wheat and such things as his, mine, Bro. Grant and Rockwood families should want. That he would at a convenient time have me a list of what he wanted done. We then walked into the council room and partook of the super that had been prepared by the police, it being a day of recreation and feasting with them. Called by Bro. Free's on my return home. Found Sister Free gaining from her illness but Louisa [*No. 3*] growing worse. Had some sulphur, whiskey and blood root pre-

106

pared to cleanse and purify her blood. Reached home at 9.

Winter Quarters, O. N., Wed., March 3rd, '47.

Morning clear, warm and pleasant, calm and still. Bro. Wm. Pace, T. Johnson had some conversation, rather I had an interview with them. Showed the duties of parrents to their children and children towards their parrents acording to their covenants.[103] After conversation they appeared much better satisfied. Bro. W. Pace started for Mo. with 4 yoke of oxen and his boy. About 12 noon this morning I bought 1 yoke of oxen of B. Maginnis through George Laub. Paid him $25.00, 12 in a watch and the remainder in provisions &c. Took a contract of delivering 200 bushels of meal and corn for the 7th bushels from Bro. C. Bird for Pres. B. Young. Bro. Bird spent the night with me. Evening warm. Ice clearing fast.

Duties of Parents and Children

Winter Quarters, Thurs., March 4, 1847.

Morning warm, clowdy at sunrise. W. South. At 7 morning I sent 2 mule teams across the river. At 8 I was in at Pres. B. Young's, found him in good spirits. Presented him $2.50 cash. Spent some 2 hours with him. Requested me to meet at A. P. Rockwood at 2 p.m. Returned home and spent an hour or 2 in writing journal &c. At the hour appointed I met at Pres. B. Young's, G. D. Grant and A. P. Rockwood and after numbering the waggons and teams in his family circle he arranged them acording to the wants of his family after which we conversed some 40 m. then returned home. The boys returned with their loads of corn about sunset. Cut into the hub through the ice while crossing the Mo. river. Made 8 bushels of corn today. Evening pleasant. At 8 in Co. with Bro. Adolphia Young were called to lay hands on Sister Callahan who apparently was in great distress. Was relieved immediately.

---

[103] Refers to "adoption."

107

A. D. sat and chatted till 11 on the subject of the law of adoption.

Winter Quarters, Fri., March 5, '47.

Morning clear, wind south. Warm. At 9 morn., having set 1 team hauling wood I went with T. Johnson out for hay. Paid $2.50 per ton, making it worth $5.00 when delivered. About 4 p.m. Allen Weeks arrived in camp bringing with him Lucinda Pace and family from Pizgah. I purchased her a house near by of Bro. Chas. Bird. Read her the letter that I had received from her husband, Jas. Pace, in the army. Passed the evening in conversation.

Winter Quarters, O. N., Sat., Mar. 6, '47.

Morning clowdy and slight showers of rain. W. S. At 8 changed W. At 20 m. to 8 Bro. A. Weeks left camp for a part of his family that he left 40 ms. this side of Pizgah at Capt. Evens encampment. At 9 the officers of the 1st division met acording to adjournment. At 10 the house was called to order by the Pres. (Isaac Morly). 2nd. The Capts. reports were called for and examined. Pres. B. Young having been called away to preach the funeral of old Mr. Neff's son who had died the evening before, had not yet come in. The old man but a few days [ago] stated that his money should not go to support the whores of the 12 [104] when he was asked to loan a few hundred dollars to assist in building the mill. Refused by making the above remarks, when he had probably by him $10,000. Pres. B. Young told him that he should feel the hand of the Lord upon him and his family for his hard and foolish sayings and immediately sickness made inroads into his family. He remembering the prediction, became alarmed and sent for those men whom he once called whoremasters to pray the Lord that His hand might be stayed. At 20 m. to 12 noon

"Whores of the Twelve"

[104] Mormon converts knew nothing of polygamy until they arrived at Nauvoo. Mr. Neff expressed the sentiments of many when they observed its results.

RACHEL WOOLSEY

Married Lee in 1845 at the age of fourteen (Wife No. 6).
Was a sister of Agatha Ann Woolsey. Lived at Lee's Ferry,
Jacob's Lake, Upper Kanab and Moencopi. After 1877
moved to Lebanon, Arizona. Was Lee's favorite of
the three who remained faithful to the end.

Courtesy Edna Lee Brimhall

Pres. B. Young, H. C. Kimble, W. Richards, W. Woodruff, O. Pratt and E. T. Benson came in. The report of the captains of the first divisions were read by T. Bullock [105] as follows: 24 pioneers, 32 waggons, 33 horses, 24 mules with a complete outfit; and 42 P., 6 W., 5 H. and 2 mules that will want some help, making 116 P., 38 W., 38 H. and 26 M. from the 1st division. Pres. B. Young said to Bro. Bird that he would have some money for him within a few days as he had dreamed last night that he had $300 in gold given to him; while relating the dream his wife observed that a dream dreamed on Friday night and on Saturday morning told, will come to pass before one week old. A few weeks ago I dreamed a similar dream. My wife made the same remarks about it and before the close of the week I received $250.00 so I have the same faith about this dream and knowing that you was cramped for money to meet your engagements in behalf of the church I have made those remarks to satisfy your expectations. The bishops reports of the No. widows and women whose husbands were in the army togeather with their circumstances were read and found almost able so far [as] waggons and teams are concerned to remove themselves. Elder E. T. Benson said that he wanted to say a few words by way of expressing his own feelings, that others would likewise. The idea which he wished to suggest was this: Which would be the better plan, for the pioneers with the 12 at their head to go until we find the verry spot to plant the standard and build the Temple of the Lord before they stop to put in crops, that this people may have a place to geather, or whether will they stop short of this, plant and bring up the rear to that spot and then make another attempt. Some have manifested fears saying that this is a sickly place and we are afraid should we stay here another season that we will all dye &c. But my opinion is that the greater portion of the

Dreams

---

[105] Thomas Bullock was "camp historian" for the pioneer emigration.

disease of this camp were inhaled into their systems before they came to this place. The kanker seems to be more fatal than any other disease that has been in camp, which is certainly the dregs of colds, augues, which have been inhaled by exposures in an unhealthy atmosphere, but I do not think this is an unhealthy location. At least I would not be afraid to leave my family here. If they dye let them dye in the Lord and all will be well and in the resurrection they will overcome the kanker and all other fatal diseases by the resurrective power of the Lord. H. C. Kimble motioned to

Scientific Lecture by Dr. Richards

let the Lord [lead] us to the place and all will be well. Seconded by Bro. J. D. Lee. Dr. Richards said that he wanted to speak upon natural and scientifical and including physical principles. As far as natural principles goes this certainly is the most healthy location that is on this river. Some persons have been and are now troubled with rheumaic affections, cankers, and I was going to say the gout [black-leg], but the cause that has produced this effect is easily acounted for when we take in consideration the pregnated and impure air that this body of people inhaled into their lungs, filling themselves with diseases from the ponds and stagnated water about Nauvoo. All men of science and common sence agree that the air arround salt water is too pure for consumptive persons. We are now approaching the mountains which is pure air and water (the wells here are perfectly good and wholesome if or when they are kept clean, still the river water is better). Consiquently the principle of life is beginning to revive and the moment it does the canker and deep seated diseases rise to oppose it and causes a great struggle between the 2 principles (life and death). Sometimes the constitutions of many have become so much impaired from the power of disease that they have not strength to bear up under the counteracting principles (life) without the resurrective power of the priesthood, therefore they for a season sleep

110

in the dust to await the reserrection, and should I wish to shorten the days of my family I would rush them immediately to the mountains suddenly into the purer atmosphere, filled with disease as they are, where they would drop like the wind. I should prefer leaving my family here for a season on acount of their health, was this the object alone.[106] There [is] another cause for much of the sickness of this camp (E.I.) the exposure and fatigues through which the brethren have had to undergo in acomplishing the amount of labor that has been done in so short a time since we came into this region. Too much exercise is injurious to health. If we go 5 or 600 ms. to put in a crop this spring we shall probably be too late as the drought comes on much sooner in that region of country than it does here, thus you see we will have to be careful and select a locasion where we can irrigate [107] everything that we put into the ground, which will doubtless require considerable of labour to build a dam, cut races or make troughs sufficient to water a farm of that size and when this is done you can plant 2 acres here as easy as you could 1 there and one acre here well cultivated will produce as much as 5 would there and ½ the trouble will protect your crops here that it would 4 or 500 ms. west of this. I calculate to spend this coming winter over the mountains if my brethren will let me. Will it not be better to leave the families here this season where they have houses to shelter them from the storms and other necessaries prepared and let the pioneers go over the mountains and prepare the place, then return and bring the families over next season in perfect safety to the place of gathering without having to make and leave another stopping place for the devil. B. L. Clapp, A. Averett, W. Snow and

Dr. Richards Explains Principles of Life and Death

Irrigation

---

[106] This "scientific" opinion of Dr. Richards should be of historical interest to modern physicians.

[107] Earliest mention of irrigation. Richards learned of its use from trappers who had seen garden plots irrigated at Ft. Hall, Ft. Boise or Ft. Bridger, and from Tippets, Woolsey, Lee, Egan, Gully and Stevens, who had reported its practical use in Santa Fe. Irrigation was used at Spalding's Lapwai mission in Idaho as early as 1839.

Lewis said, let the 12 decide in these things and all will be right. Elder O. Pratt referred to the revelations and will of the Lord concerning the organizing and journeyings of the camp of Israel. Said it was his mind should any families go this season that the soldiers wives be the first as they have been absent longer from them. Pres. B. Young said that the brethren would all do just as he said notwithstanding the diversity of spirits now about the matter. Take the soldiers women along in the 1st Co. after the pioneers,[101] and when we find a place to put in crops then we shall take a Co. and go over the mountains.[108] But I will not be hurried for I am determined to do as I am dictated by the spirit of the Lord. I will go where I can consecrate the Gentiles [109] (when they come reading their authority) and strengthen the brethren. A man of God can disern the spirits that are here today. Just do as I tell you and all will be right. Let the officers meet on Monday night at candle light. Bro. G. Grant came in and said that in consequence of the thaw the water was rising so fast that the part of the mill dam that had broken away a short time since would be liable to go again unless several hands would turn out immediately and secure it. Upon hearing the news Pres. B. Young called for a general turnout immediately, 20 m. past 2 p.m. About 5 evening W. shifted N. W., blew a strong gale, turned cold as Greenland. This evening I was taken quite unwell and compelled to retire to bed about sunset. Polly Y. [*No. 14*] came in to see me, brought me a coat and pants that she and her sister [*No. 13*] had made me. About 7 I got up and wrote to near 1 in the morning.

"Consecrate the Gentiles"

Winter Quarters, O. N., Sund., Mar. 8th, '47.
Morning clear, cool, W. N. The health of my wife Ag-

---

[108] Brigham originally intended to stop and plant crops near Fort Laramie.

[109] In Mormon phraseology "consecration" of property meant unlawful appropriation for church use; to "consecrate" persons meant to kill them. See *"Holy Murder."*

gatheam [*No. 1*] rather on the decline. At 1 p.m. walked to Bro. A. T. Free's. Found Louisa [*No. 3*] gaining from her illness though she has been quite sick for 3 days past. Spent some 2 hours reading my journal to them. About 5 Almo, my eldest son, came requesting me to come home immediately as his mother was growing worse. Returned home, found her in great pain. I anointed her and prayed for her recovery and she soon felt relieved. About sunset Chester Loveland came in, took supper and chatted a couple of hours. About the same time Nancy the 2nd [*No. 12*] came in to spend the evening. W. high. Pres. B. Young I am told, preached old Mr. Neff son's funeral today instead of yesterday.

Winter Quarters, O. N., Mon., March 9th, 1847.

Morning clear, clowdy, W. N., cold, disagreeable. A solid bridge across the river. I set 3 waggons and mule teams drawing wood over the river on the ice. Aggatheam is rather better of her illness but Louisa is worse and I myself am almost down. This certainly is [*a*] time of deep affliction and sore lamentation with this people, for daily more or less of them are consigned to the tomb.[110] At 12 I was at Pres. B. Young's. His lady was quite unwell. 2 persons Bro. Groves said that he had been without bread for 3 days. I gave him ½ bushel meal and Bro. Collett [111] 1 bushel. This evening I am so unwell that I durst not venture out to the meeting of the officers of the 1st division. Yet severe cold, clowdy, W. still north. Information from T. Bullock, clerk of the meeting said that Pres. B. Young gave the Capts. of his division a considerable whipping for neglect of duty. Said that he had fitted 12 pioneers and 5 waggons and mules, that his whole division was only called on to fit out 100 pioneers, not to come again without re-

"Deep Affliction and Sore Lamentation"

---

[110] About 600 died at Winter Quarters.
[111] Sylvanus Collett assisted Porter Rockwell in the Aiken massacre of 1857.

porting an entire outfit and that every man and team be on the ground at the place of rendezvous (which is north of the council room) by Mon. next, duly prepared, ready for a march. He would then take them up or near the old fort [45] and set them to drawing out timber and fensing a field for those who stay back this season. Decided to leave Thos. Bullock to be the clerk for the 1st division. Adjourned to Sat. next.

Winter Quarters, Teus., March 10th, 1847.

Morning clear, wind sharp. W. N. Teams engaged in drawing wood over on the ice. At 9 Chester Loveland left my house for home with the promise that he would send 1 pioneer with an entire outfit by Sunday next. At 10 Pres. B. Young, H. C. Kimble, O. Pratt, G. A. Smith, W. Woodruff, W. Richards, A. Lyman, E. T. Benson and several others met in council in Br. Richards' postoffice. Bro. A. Gardner was advised by the council to leave all his notes and acounts in the hands of some trusty lawyer for collection and peradventure he might get something but never to go to law himself for if he did that he would never recover anything of himself. The amount of notes were about $1000.

Letter from
Nancy Bean

Just in time I received a letter from Nancy the 1st [*Nancy Bean, No. 2*] stating that she had not forgotten that in the moment of passion that I was the man to whom she was to look for salvation spiritually or temporally and that she would like a word from me to know what my feelings are, what she might depend on. I read the letter to Pres. B. Young. His counsel was to tell her that inasmuch as she claimed salvation at my hands that she must come to me and place herself under my guidance and control and protection and respect the priesthood and my standing as a saviour and if she does this she will have the sanction, blessings and protection of a saviour but on no other con-

114

siteration whatever. About 12 noon Bros. Alexander Mc-Ray,[112] Andrew Lawerans and Rodney Swasey arrived in camp from Charleston, Iowa. Reported that the mob had hanged 8 of the brethren nigh unto death. Little Rodney Swazey they hanged by the heels in order to extort from him something as evidence against the remainder of the Co. but found the boy knew nothing or was too true to reveal it, they let him down. Wm. H. Fulsome [113] and Charles Drown were 2 of the No. that was hanged, also said that Bro. A. McRae was taken by the mob and carried to Madison jail from near Mount Rose, was in custody 10 days in all, 3 days of which he was confined in the penitentiary. Finally bailed out upon a write of habius corpeas through the influence of the sheriff of the county. When released he broke for camp, brought with them Rodney Swazey, a boy about 14 years old whom the Pres. B. Young counselled me to take care of him, fit and send him as one of the Pioneers and keep his pony to chase buffalo on. McRay taken Feb. 8, '46 ['47]. Stated that Nauvoo had run down and looked indeed like a city forsakined. Louisa on the gaining ground. Nancy the 2nd sent me some linen for bosoms and collars. Evening moderate.

Rodney Swazey Hanged

"A City Forsakined"

Winter Quarters, Wed., Mar. 11, '47.

Morning clear, calm and pleasant. My teams went for hay. I also sent some cattle to heard by Bro. M. Harris, furnished him a mule to ride, settled up with Bro. Clayton and Whitney. About noon Sister Marcia Allen came to my residence. Said that all was well. The boy, Rodney Swasey that agreed to go as one of my pioneers has taken his horse away. I think he has been influenced by some selfish friend to do as before stated. At 10 I had Geo. Laub at work in the council house rigging up waggons for the pio-

---

[112] Two sons of Alexander McRae were murdered by Porter Rockwell in 1861.
[113] William H. Folsom was the father of Amelia Folsom, one of Brigham's later wives, at whose expense he built the famous "Amelia Palace."

neers. Louisa gaining. Word by Sister Allen that Caroline is well.[114] Called in at Pres. B. Young's, found him [at] prayer at the hour of 7 evening. Told him that Capt. Jas. Brown and Terrill had stated in a letter directed to D. H. Spencer that they had sent by me $200 in a check payable to Bayley and [Co.] at Ft. Leavensworth and that the report was in the mouths of busy persons that I have wronged Bro. Bayly out of said check which is as false as Lucipher for no such check was ever given me.[115] Furthermore there never was a sylable spoken to me on that subject by any man in the Bat. Pres. said that men lyed on him; it never troubled him as he knew there was a day of recompense. Pres. B. Y. said that I was expected to be on hand on the morrow to assist in selecting the location for a farm. He went into the council office and I went and settled up our accounts.

More Trouble Over Battalion Money

Winter Quarters, Thurs., Mar. 12, 1847.

Morning clear, warm and pleasant. At 10 morn. Pres. B. Young, H. C. Kimble, E. T. Benson, A. Cutler, D. Spencer, G. A. Smith and myself rode out around the city in search of a location for a farm but found none suitable save a small piece south of the city, about 1000 acres, which was decided should be put in cultivation for early crops. Adjourned about 1 p.m. and defered the search to another day, when we would likely go up to the old fort [45] and explore that country. Had some wagon work done. Prepared a dinner and invited in some of my family to partake, namely, Lucinda and Margarett Pace, Sarah and Nancy Gibbons, Sister Lytle, Patience Johnson, Bro. C. Bird, Marcia and Clarissa Allen, Wm. McClellan, Bro. David Young, besides those at home. After supper I sat and conversed with them and read from my journal several points

---

[114] Sarah Caroline Williams, his 15-year-old Wife No. 4.
[115] More trouble over Battalion money.

on principles of doctrine. About 8 Dr. Richards and E. T. Benson came in and spent an hour or more with us. Read a letter from Bro. Wm. Bird, Pu[e]blo, under date of about 26th Dec. 1846, giving an account of the country and game. Said that buffalo, elk, deer, antelope, mountain sheep and goats, white and grizzly bear, beaver and geese in great abundance and that salt are found in great plenty at the salt lakes in Bear River Valley. That a ridge of mountains is said to run through the lake [116] [*Great Salt Lake*] in which are large quantities of precious minerals. The conduct of Capt. Brown [117] toward his troops is outrageous and that many of the Bat. were as ungodly as the Gentiles. Evening pleasant. Thos. and Wm. has gone over the river for hay.

News from Pueblo

Great Salt Lake

Winter Quarters, Frid., Mar. 12, 1847.

Morning clear, warm and fine. Sister Allen and daughter took brakefast with us. I paid her $4.12 cts. and assumed payment for $24 more which closed the amount of her check sent her by her husband from the army.[118] Yesterday Nancy the 2nd sent me two shirt patrons and Rachel 2 apron patrons. About noon I finished writing a letter in answer to a letter written by Nancy the 1st [*No. 2*] in which I set fourth the law of the covenant and priesthood to her. At 4 p.m. Thomas and Wm. returned with the hay. Paid 2.00 per ton and hauled it 8 ms. At 3 p.m. to 5 I was at Pres. B. Young's, found him in good spirits. He told me that his dream had been fulfilled, that he had received $200 in gold as he saw in the vision.[119] On settlement with him he fell in my debt near $400 but I was perfectly

Lays Down the Law to Nancy Bean

---

[116] First reference to Bear River Valley and Great Salt Lake, into which Bear River flows. Bird got his information from Bill New, Timothy Goodale and other trappers wintering at Pueblo.

[117] James Brown, later first Mormon settler at Ogden, Utah.

[118] The only settlement with any of the Battalion soldiers' wives recorded in the Journal.

[119] Probably received from "Old Mr. Neff."

117

[*satisfied*] to let the whole amount rest and if he could assist me with some lumber, leather, meal or anything that would help fit out the pioneers should it be convenient, otherwise the whole amount remain. He replied that he could let me have what leather I wanted and anything else that he had and that he would not say that he would not let me have some money. I got 44 lbs. sole leather and 2 Morocco dressed skins. About sunset I walked to Bro. Free's, found Louisa [*No. 3*] quite unwell. Had suffered considerable from the pain in her legs. At dark Emoline [*No. 11*] arrived in camp from the rushes. Evening pleasant.

Winter Quarters, O. N., Sat., Mar. 13th, 1847.

Morning clowdy, occasional showers of snow. W. north W. At 9 a general rally for all the help to be raised to work on the mill dam as the water was crowding the work. I turned and rallied all men that came in my [*way*]. From 10 to 15 teams and about 4 men turned out. About 3 p.m. Pres. B. Young sent for me to assemble at Dr. Richards in council as the 12, Bishop Whitney, some of the High Council, the Capts. of 100s and their presidents were called to go there. The object of their meeting will be stated on the following pages. Louisa is some better. David Y. and *Polly Y.* [*No. 14*] came and spent the evening. Polly all night. At 8 Thomas and Wm. came home, left their loads on the opposite shore, being rather dark to venture. About 9 Bro. John Nay from the Booe river 30 ms. above camp came, he being a stranger. I told him that he was welcome to tarry with me and such as I had I freely would give unto him. He acepted the offer and staid over night. The following are the ques. and answers suggested by the council of the 12 for the benefit of the camp.

*Polly Y.
Makes a
Social Call*

[The following questions are in a different, more legible handwriting.]

1st. Shall there be a council left here? Yes. Presidents and captains of companies and when they leave appoint others.

2. Shall the houses be put on a line and this place picketed in? Let the people decide.

3. Shall they pay one tenth of their labor for the poor? Yes.

4. How much ground shall each family have for a garden? Let the council control this.

5. How much breadstuff to each person that follows after the pioneers? Not less than 200 lbs.

6. Shall the brethren labor unitedly or every man for himself? Unitedly and every captain of 10 oversee his own company.

7. Shall a record be kept how every man occupies his time? A record shall be kept.

8. What plan will be most beneficial to preserve crops and other property from Omaha aggressions? Take care of them.

9. May not every family have a garden of their own independent of public fields? Yes.

10. Shall a guard be kept up at Winter Quarters after 1st emigration? Council, that a guard be kept up and the people pay them.

11. Shall we take all the widows or only women whose husbands are ahead? Answer. Take the women whose husbands are in the army and as many more as can fit themselves out.

12. Shall Thomas Bullock be the Historian of 1st emigration Co.? Yes, fit him out and take him along.

13. Shall C. C. Rich be the military commander? Yes.

119

14. Shall John Scott have charge of the artillery? [120]
Yes.

15. Shall Hosea Stout be captain of the guard? Yes.

16. Shall Horance S. Eldredge be the marshal? Yes.

17. The Temple bell to be rung every morning to wake all up, then have prayers, breakfast, prepare teams. At the second ringing of the bell in 15 minutes afterwards start for day's journey.

Winter Quarters, O. N., Sund., Mar. 14th, '47.

Morning clear, cold, wind N. Through the day I indulged in resting and conversation. Thos. and Wm. went back some 2 ms. for their loads of hay that had been left the evening before. Visited Louisa, found but little change in her disease. About sunset Chester Loveland and Br. Downs arrived in camp with a span of horses and waggon. Brought with them Father Chancy Loveland with an outfit to go [as] a pioneer and drive one of my teams. About 7 Pres. B. Young, O. Pratt, H. C. Kimble, W. Woodruff, G. A. Smith, A. Lyman, W. Richards and E. T. Benson of the 12, Bishop Whitney and Miller of the bishoprick, besides several others met in Dr. Richards post office. At 8 we all walked over to the council room, heard the trial of Bishop John Murdock who had been arrained before the High Council by N. R. Knight. Upon examination Bishop Murdock was honorably exonerated from the charge but not until Pres. B. Young had shown the inconsistency and illegality of the charge and in fact the charge would have gone against Bro. Murdock had not the Pres. trimmed out the council for not doeing their duty. Showed them how to manage and decide in all cases (in righteousness) that come before them. The council acknowledged that they were in the dark about the matter. About 10 the council of the 12 returned to the post office and instructed the Capts of

Brigham "Trims Out the Council"

---

[120] The Pioneer company hauled a cannon with them across the plains.

100s with their presidents and counsellors respecting the order of the camp. After the departure of the 12 at 1 morning, desolved.

Winter Quarters, O. N., Mon., Mar. 15th, '47.

Morning clear, cold remarkably. At 9 morn. the Pioneers with the Capts of Cos. met at the council room. Pres. B. Young mounted the stage and said that he wanted the Capts. of 100s to report the No. of men ready to start on the morrow then let them go up to the fort and commence making a farm, that is, whenever a team and 3 men are fitted out and those that remain sustain the pioneers while they are at work in the field so that their provisions may be on hand when they start for the mountains. After hearing the instructions I marched my men to Bro. A. P. Rockwood where I gave them the necessary instructions and appointed Sat. for the day to start and Friday the day previous to meet at 12 noon in front of A. P. R. house for the purpose of being inspected and load up our teams, pack our waggons, &c. The same was reported at 6 eve. but few were found ready to start on the morrow. After the business part were transacted the questions that were propounded and answered were read and approved by the meeting. Pres. B. Young said that he wanted to be in council all that he could with the High Council, Capts. of 100s and 50s and their presidents and counsellors before he left them as he new that many things would arrise after their departure that they would want council on. Said that the Capts. of 100s and 50s togeather with their presidents and counsellors meet at the same place on Wed. eve. candle light. Disolved at 11 o'clock. Louisa quite poorly today.

Preparations for Farming

Winter Quarters, Teus., Mar. 16, '47.

Morning clear, pleasant, W. S. At 10 I was at Pres. B. Young's, had some conversation with [*him*] on the Co's.

matters. Received a letter from Bro. C. Bird stating that he had bought from 50 to 75 bushels potatoes for seed, all of which I could get by paying 56 cts. per bushel. I laid the subject before Pres. B. Y. He said secure them by all means. At 4 the Capts. of 100s and their presidents and counsillors were called togeather at Dr. Richard's office. Presant of the 12: B. Young, H. C. Kimble, G. A. Smith, W. Woodruff, W. Richards and E. T. Benson. Pres. B. Young suggested the propriety of taking ox teams. Deliberated at some length and lastly decided that the Capts. of 100s instruct their for such as wished to take ox teams and fit them out but at their own risk. Adjourned at 6. About 10 mor. Rod Swazey came back and insisted on going with the Pioneers and in one of my waggons. Said that he had been persuaded away and wanted me to forgive him. Strong wind S.

Ox Teams Permitted for Pioneer Company

Winter Quarters, O. N., Wed., Mar. 17, '47.

Morning clear, warm and pleasant. A general rally was again made to labour on the mill dam. Through the day I was engaged in fitting up pioneers' wagons. About 11 Bro. Jas. Bean came to my house, said that Nancy [No. 2] and her babe were both sick with a swelling in the throat, also wished to know whether I would pay for their board or not, and whether I intend to take her home or what she may depend on. (Answer) When I hire her board then I will pay for it, and that I have written a letter to her in which I have told her what she may depend upon. That when she considers where her interest is and where her dependence lies and does what justice requires of her then she may come to me and I will take care of her and nourish her and until then she need not expect anything from me. He returned but little better satisfied than when he came. Louisa [No. 3] some better. At 7 eve. pursuant to adjornment Pres. B. Young, O. Pratt, W. Richards, the

Nancy Bean Is Refused Support

122

Capts. of the 1st and 2nd divisions togeather with their presidents and their counsellors met. The house was called to order by Pres. Morly. Pres. B. Young said that he had but little business here this evening only to see the brethren and converse with them. Asked the Capts. what success they met with in fitting up the pioneers and getting the waggons ready. Reported favorably. Said that unless the pioneers get off this week that he would not stop to make a farm as he was determined to see the Loop Fort [*Loup Fork*] of Platt river by the 1st of April. The pioneers have done well today, they have got the dam so that the water is now running in the race and could we get about 100 men more on the morrow I think the dam might be secured and that the mill will start by morning. Called for volunteers; 26 offered their servises. While speaking a messenger reported that the mill had started. On hearing the news a general shout was raised. Bro. Phineas Young said that he wanted a horse to ride to the mountains to hunt buffaloes for the pioneers. Pres. B. Young said, Brethren, you have heard what Bro. Phineas has said and you that are in favor of his goeing by saying I. Unanimous. Bro. O. Pratt said that he had been helped to 5 waggons to take him to the mountains which were taken from him at Pizgah. He then was helped to 3 waggons to remove them here and yesterday the last one was taken away and how my family will be taken along I know not unless the brethren will fit them out and take them along. I sold 6 shoats which has helped my family to provisions and I have another that necessities will compell me to sell although twice the amount would not induce me to sell it was I not obliged to do so. Pres. B. Young said that some probably thought he consumed several thousands of dollars within a year. If I do I never have borrowed money upon the influence of no man but my own but I have borrowed thousands of dollars to lend to others. Just as I am

The Mill Starts

123

with my brethren now going to the mountains, not to benefit myself independant of my brethren. I feel as the apostle said, that they without the ancients could not be made perfect, neither can you be made perfect without me nor I without you. I never have wronged any man out of his money. Still I do not expect to pay all my debts before I

Brigham Will Pay Debts by Faith

go, but the borrowed money I will pay and I will do it by faith. I will liquedate (or see it done) the debt that is hanging over Bishop Whitney at St. Louis of $14,000. I have done more for this people this winter than would pay for bringing me 50 bls. of flour to the mountains then return for their family. I may be [*indebted*] to individuals that has helped me. Now I am going to the mountains and I want the presidents and counsellors, the Capts. of 100s see that the families of the 12 are taken along and that old Father John Smith and family be taken. Don't leave him. He has been with us from the beginning. He is of Joseph's family and we want him along. I have things written and I want them not to be neglected. It would be better for some young persons to remain than Father Smith to be left.

Pioneers Fitted Out by Those Who Remained

Bro. George A. Smith and family, Bro. Pratt, Richards and perhaps others of the 12 will need help. See that they are fitted out and brought on. Let the Capts. meet again on Friday even. if they choose, and we will clear out the room that the people may be seated and we will have meetings. Bro. Williard Snow reported that Bro. C. Bird had purchased from 30 to 50 bushels of potatoes which must be brought from there on the morrow or next day after. Pres. B. Young said that those of the brethren who wanted potatoes let them pay Bro. Lee the money in advance that he may procure them, whereupon about $7 was paid. Adjourned at 9 evening. Met at Dr. Richards office B. Young, W. Richards, E. T. Benson, O. Pratt, W. Woodruff, E. Snow, W. Snow, A. McRay and others met and chatted on various subjects. Disolved at 21 m. to 11. Went home. Evening pleasant.

Winter Quarters, Thurs., Mar. 17, '47.

Morning light W. south. Warm. At 7 Thos. Johnson crossed the river with our teams on the ice and drove to the Point & Poles where I bought 45 bus. of seed potatoes. Paid 40 cts. bus. for 30 bus. and 50 cts. per bus. for the remaining 15 bushels. Also bought about $50 worth of dry goods. Staid over night at John Gheen's. Prairies full of water, roads muddy, heavy wheeling.

Point & Poles, Pottowatomy Nation, Fri., Mar. 19, '47.

Morning foggy, warm and still. At 6 we start for camp, found it remarkably bad and heavy dragging for my mules. Traveled 3 ms., met Bro. Hendrixson who held a note on me for $14. I told him that I had expended my means in assisting to build the mill acording to council and that he must wait and could do so untill I met with an opportunity [of] getting the money. That he had 2 only in family to take care of and 5 yoke of oxen, 3 horses, waggons sufficient besides cattle and other stuff. That instead of pressing me that he ought to fit out some 2 or 3 families whose husbands are in the army and take them along and take at least 10 bls. of flour for Pres. B. Young and if you do this you shall never regret it but shall receive an 100 fould in the own due time of the Lord. He replied that he would [do] all that he could. Blessed him and told him that the Lord would throw means in his way inasmuch as he hear to council but if not he would regret it all the days of his life and his concience would lash him and be like worms that would naw at the root of his happiness and would destroy his comfort and prosperity for he would feel that this church was beholden to him as he had sought his own but not her interest. Consiquently he would not in justice have any claims on the privileges of the church. After a chat of an hour I left him and prosecuted our jour-

*Lee Pays a Debt
"By Faith"*

125

ney to camp.[121] I sent T. Johnson by Mr. Hildreth's mill while I drove both teams. It [is] about 2 ms. from the road. Returned in 3 hours. Reported that the 60 bushels of meal could be had the day following. Reached the ferry on the opposite side of the river (E.I.) about sunset. Drove our waggons under a shed covered with hay, covered up the potatoes as well as we could to secure them from the freeze as the wind had shifted N.E. Blew high and cold. We tarried at Bro. J. P. Harmon's. After supper I was called upon to administer to his wife who had been con-

fined mostly since September last. She was instantly restored and was the next morning up singing and prepared brakefast with her own hands. Rejoiced in the Lord and felt confident that she would survive her sickness, that she felt perfectly free and well. Dis. 18 ms. Evening clowdy, cool. Gen. C. C. Rich and family and Sister Huntington and family have just arrived from Pizgah assisted by 2 Pres. B. Young's teams and Bro. John Berry.

Winter Quarters, O. N., Sat., Mar. 20th, '47.

Morning clear, W. N. Cold, frozen considerably through the night. At 6 I got a waggon of Bro. Hyrum Gates. Sent Thomas back to Hildreth's mill with 4 mules. At 2 m. to 8 I crossed the river, went [to] Pres. B. Y., reported what I had done. He told me to keep him 5 bus. of seed potatoes, the remainder sell to the pioneers at $1.00 per bus. He by my assistance found the record of the Seventies which had been packed away. At 9 I went to the river and laboured hard till 4 p.m. when by the assistance of several of the brethren we brought both loads of potatoes over to my house. About sunset and before dark three-fourths of the loads were taken away. Pres. B. Young came along

No Potatoes for the Sick

while I was measuring up the potatoes, said that was the word circulated that the sick should must have potatoes,

---

[121] Mormon method of settling a debt; frequently used by Brigham Young.

126

but few would go west. I let the Pres. and family have 9 bushels free of cost. At 9 even. Dr. Richards stepped in and chatted a short time. Evening mild.

Winter Quarters, O. N., Sund., Mar. 21st, '47.

Morning clear and warm, wind S.E. At 11 the Saints assembled in a special conference at the stand by request of Pres. B. Young, notified or by the signal of the ringing of the Temple bell. The multitude called to order by Elder Alphius Cutler. The hymn The Morning Breaks, the Shadows Flies, &c. was sung and prayer by Elder A. Cutler who previous to prayer said in order that the people might have an understanding of this special call it was by request of Pres. B. Y. to . . . . Pres. B. Young said that the Saints would expect to hear from him, consiquently he would say what the Lord would give him. That he would like to spend a whole day with the Saints before he left them and would likely have a meeting on the morrow. Experience is the dear schoolmaster and many have served their time out though many have fallen and have been laid aside as we do the green herbs, implements of husbandry having done all that they could do. Still if the people were universally righteous they might overcome and not fall by sickness, yet the Lord takes some away before they arrive to years of maturity to acomplish His will. He giveth and He taketh away, and the time will come when every knee shall bow and every tongue confess His hand in all things and that He is the Christ and our Lord. I wish to exhort my brethren to humility and neatness that they may come unto the Lord and ask and it shall be done unto them. There is a principle that dwell in the heart of the Saints and always did that teaches them to know whether they did actually live so as to keep their hearts open to the whisperings of the spirit and do the work that entitles them to claim preveleges of the Kingdom by the light that lighteth

Parting Message to the Saints

127

every man that comes into the world. The Lord bestows upon his children a certain portion of the dowery that he has for them acording to the light which they have lived up too (which has been given to them) and says to them go and ocupp[?] upon what I have given and that is what the Apostle Paul had allusion to when he said the spirit of the prophets are subject to the prophets. Keep your hearts open and never bar against the spirit of the Lord. He then related a dream which he had a short time since while in the hour of affliction. The dream I have recorded as he related it before, and impressed upon the minds of the Saints to keep the spirit of the Lord that they may not be destroyed. This Jos. said to him while in the vision, repeatedly, and insisted to have him impress it upon the minds of the Saints. Be pure and holy for the Comforter will not dwell in an unholy temple. Said that he did [*not*] want to go into heaven (if he could) with a back load of sin but the feelings of the brethren are they have been driven from their homes and their feelings are good God could they have power over them if we dident use them up then I would tell it. What business have you with them? Vengeance belongs to the Lord. It is not for you to set in judgment. They have contracted the debt and they will have to pay it. This principle is in the hearts of some which is damnable and when the Twelve goes away you will see sights. Those characters will steal old spaven horses, waggon wheels, quilts, &c. Let such men go down to hell and if you do not understand what this means, cut their infernal throats. Never steal till the Lord tells you, and never steal that that should not be stolen. And when you hear of Brigham Young stealing you may know that it should be stolen.[122] There is another principle that is as

"Cut Their Infernal Throats"

Instructions on Stealing

[122] Stealing by Mormons, not their religious beliefs, was the real cause of their expulsion from Kirtland, Far West and Nauvoo. It was not considered wrong to steal from a Gentile. Brigham was perfectly serious in the above statement. His first speech in Salt Lake Valley was an exhortation to the Saints not to steal from each other.

damnable as stealing; that is this murmurings and saying that the rich does [not] feel after the interest of the poor. You should never covet the goods of any person and never find fault with your brethren. Be contented with your lot and station and stop your whining and babbling about the 12, saying that Brigham oppresses the poor and lives off their earning and that you can't see why you can't have some of his good living, and so on. Did Brigham Young ever get anything from you, did you ever help him to any of his fine living, you poor curses, or was it through Brigham's influence that thousands of the poor have been fed? You poor stinking curses, for you are cursed and the hand of the Lord shall be upon you and you shall go down to hell for murmuring and bickering. This people means to tie my hands continually as they did last year so that we can't go to the place of our destination. They are already coming to me saying can't you take me along? Don't leave me here, if you do I am afraid I shall die, this is such a sickly place. Well I say to them, die, who cares. If you have not faith to live here you will die over the mountains. This people will be subject to sickness and disease and death until they learn to be passive and let council dictate their course; without this their efforts are vain. I shall be glad when the time comes that this people will unanimously hearken to and be governed by council. We want to build up another Temple and then send out 1000 of elders to preach and gather out the honest in heart, by the power of their calling in the Priesthood and that the spirit that are in the Elders should beget the same spirit in the people and thereby draw them from among the wicked by the power of faith; but such men as steal, murmur and whine at everything and that nothing goes right will never feel the power of their calling in the ministry. They blackguard a little but can never preach. Closed by saying that he wanted to spend one whole day with the Saints before he left for the

"You Poor Stinking Curses"

129

mountains and that he wanted the sisters that comes to meeting to be brought in waggons so that they . . . .

Winter Quarters, Mon., Mar. 22, 1847.
Morning blustery with occasional showers of snow. W. N. About noon began to fare away. At 1 p.m. the Capts. of 100s with their presidents at their head by order of Pres. B. Young assembled at the Council House to take in consideration the next best policy relative to our move in the spring. As usual the Lord having proposed the better plan first for the promotion of the good of his people which they refused to comply with by withholding their substance, and of necessity the 2nd was introduced which was to send the Pioneers on to the spot with sufficient provision to last them 2 years and locate.[123] Leave all the families back untill the Pioneers should raise substance for them to come with the exception of smawl families that could fit with 2 years provisions. Such may go on this season, also bring on fresh suplies for the pioneers. Pres. B. Y. said that he was not going to ask any man whether he might leave his family or not for he intended to leave his women and some of the men and was going to take [care] of himself and family and [let] others do as they pleased with their selfishness, keep their old waggons and spaven horses and mules and worship them if they choose, and if the 12 did not rise up and exert themselves so as to bear their part he would cut them off and put in men that would and not be snubbed round by women to withhold their horses to draw their carriages. I have turned out every horse and mule that I have that is fit to go and would do it again if my wife had to ride on a bob sled. I have tried to get Bro. Pratt's horses to go in the Pioneers, but in vain. If we leave our wives here probably his horses can go. This Kingdom I am determined to bear off in spite of devils or wicked men.

Winter Quarters, Teus., March 23, '47.
Morning clear, wind S. At 10 the committee appointed to

Brigham's Revelation Revamped

---

[123] Brigham's only "revelation" undergoes another revision.

locate the city bounds met at the council house (namely) A. Cutler, Winslow Farr, Isaac Morly, Reynolds Cahoon, John D. Lee, Williard Snow, Hunter Edwards, Shadrack Roundy, Henry Herriman, Ira Eldredge and Bro. McCrary. Upon examination established the boundaries as follows (ss) The west side of the roe of buildings on Main street with the principle gates on the W. and that the S. side of E. Hunter Bishop be the south boundary with 2 principal gates and that the bluff be the E. boundary, 1 principle gate and that the N. side of H. C. Kimble's row be the N. boundary including A. P. Rockwood's buildings and that the houses that are without the specified boundary to be removed to the lines to form a part of the wall and such houses as are not suitable to live in also to be removed to the line and recovered. About 5 p.m. I removed Louisa [*No. 3*] to my room where I could take care of her. Evening pleasant. . . . .

Winter Quarters, Wed., Mar. 24th, '47.

Morning clear, warm. About 10 wind N., high. At 8 I was in at Pres. B. Young's who was then in the act of starting to examine the situation of the farm but defered it till some families should be ready to remove to the spot as he had previously examined it and pronounced it good and said that we would (the family) be well suited with it. He then rode in his carriage, took with him Bro. H. C. Kimble, N. K. Whitney, A. P. Rockwood and visited old Bro. John Neff. Contracted the mill in part to him, rec'd on $2500. At 3 p.m. he passed me in his carriage, told me that he would help me to some money and to send some teams for 60 bus. of seed potatoes. Bro. David Louis, his Bro. and Bro. Matthews has lately arrived in camp from Puncaw (Miller's camp)[18] with 2 waggons loaded with cedar vessels consisting of churns, pails, tubs, kegs, &c. I bought 3 churns and 2 pails. Bro. John Berry not being

News from the "Puncaw" Camp

131

able to return for his family from the fact that one of his horse were tired out, I let him take one of my best mules. Louisa still gaining strength. Wind high. Evening cool.

Winter Quarters, Thurs., Mar. 25th, '47.

Morning cool, W. high N. This morning reported in camp that 2 horses belonging to G. A. Smith had been stolen the night before, supposed to have been the Omahas that committed the theft from the fact that an Indian gun stick was found where the horses were taken from and that 7 head of catle had been killed the day before by them. Information came that the missionaries stirred them up to commit depredations.[124] This morning at 7 I was at Pres. B. Young's. He gave me $30 gold to pay for the potatoes. Said that he wanted his family to enclose themselves and stock that went up to make a farm so as to be guarded against Indian depredations and if we would do so at this and that and that point we would not have much more trouble. About 1 p.m. I sent the teams to Mr. Jumbo's for seed potatoes. Spent the day in settlement of book accounts. This day I received a letter from Nancy the 1st [No. 2] requesting me to bring her home.

Nancy Bean Asks to Come Home

Meeting of Pres. B. Y. Family.

Winter Quarters, Teus., Mar. 23d, '47.

At 7 evening acording to appointment the following members of Pres. B. Young's family assembled at Bro. Robert Pearce's, namely: Edmund Ellsworth, A. P. Rockwood, J. D. Lee, G. D. Grant, Isaac Morly, John Lyttle, Robert Pierce, Addison Everett, T. O. Angel,[124] Wm. Major, Wm. Weeks, Chas. Shumway, S. A. Dun, Thos Grover, Frederick Kesler, Phinehas W. Cook, David Davis, Jas. Busbee,

---

[124] Referring to the Methodist missionaries working among the Omahas, Pottawatomies and Otoes.

Solomon Angel, Millen Atwood, Samuel L. Sprague, Jacob F. Hutchinson, Sylvester H. Earl, Wm. Empy, Daniel Carns, Jos. S. Scofield, Moses M. Sanders, Hyrum Dayton, Jacob Wilder, A. P. Free, Edward D. Wooley, E. P. Dusette, Samuel Gully, George D. Grant, Benj. Brown, Isaac Chace and Sidney A. Hanks (37) and Chas. Decker (38). Meeting was called to order and prayer by Pres. B. Young who in addressing himself to the members said the object of our coming togeather this evening is to take into consideration the best plan to adopt for the promotion of the good of my family and the cause in which we are engaged. My plan is (seeing the brethren have been so backward in fitting up the pioneers and carrying out our council)[123] is to leave my family here for the present and take my adopted boys or brethren, fit up my own waggons and go over the mountains, find the place, plant the standard, put in crops, build houses, then come back and receive my family to myself, then remove them to the place of our destination and the preparation that we make. I design my family to enjoy first and then if I choose I will help others. I also intend to leave a part of my boys here to plant and raise a crop and fit themselves out to come on next season. I want Bro. Wm. Weeks and F. Kesler to come on this season. Their families are smawl and they can take 15 months provisions and come on. Just as soon as I find the spot I want Bro. W. Wm. to dig deep and lay the foundation of the Temple for I intend by the help of my brethren to build a Temple unto the Lord just as soon as the Saints by a united exertion can complete it. Bro. Robert Pierce and some others who have smawl families and can fit out with 15 months provisions may come this season to strengthen our hands and every family that comes over this season releases our cares that much. Come, brethren, who will be set apart to stay and farm? Here is Bro. J. D. Lee, G. D. Grant and David Davis that I will select to farm (Bro. J. Busbie also).

"My Family First"

133

Who will be your foreman or pres.? J. D. Lee said let our leader appoint the man to preside over us this summer and select the location for the farm and leave his blessing upon it and we will do as he shall advise. Pres. B. Young said let Bro. Isaac Morly preside. He appears to be good natured and will keep his men good natured around him. As for a location for a farm I know of no place to equal a piece of land lying a short distance above the old fort and about 16 ms. from this point. There is about 600 acres that has been cultivated which is just as mellow as an ash heap. We can enclose with a very little labour some 2000 acres including the broke land, where you can by industry raise almost any amount of grains. But this is my council that you build your houses and lots for your catle so as to be perfectly safe from Omaha depredations and that you boil all the water before using it and make beer as a drink. There are roots and barks in abundance in this country that is wholesome and if you will do as I have advised, you will have good health. I want to know the No. of Pioneers here. Whereupon 15 hands were held up, rather men raised up and were numbered, then were added to the farming department. I. Morley, Benj. Brown, M. M. Sanders, H. Dayton, Samuel Gully, Addison Averett, A. P. Free, John Lytle (who is to [be] our blacksmith), Chester Loveland, Thos. Johnson, George Laub, Daniel Kearns, E. D. Wooley and E. P. Dusett. Meeting desolved to Sat. evening next, 9 o'clock.

Instructions on Farming

Winter Quarters, Fri., Mar. 26th, '47.

Brigham's Advice on Nancy Bean

Morning clowdy, wind E. At 8 I was at Pres. B. Young's. We read a letter from Nancy Bean [No. 2] requesting me to bring her home. Pres. B. Young said that she was beginning to find out that I was independent of her, still I should not be in haste to answer her letter or bring her home. At 9 the bell was rung by the marshal for public meeting. While in conversation I started[?] A. Young's house to Pres. B. Young for a cow and calf. The night before Adolphia Young and wife gave me their names to be adopted into my family. At 10 the multitude was called to order by singing, prayer. Presant of the 12: B. Y., H. C. K., O. P., G. A. Smith, A. Lyman, W. Woodruff, W. Richards and E. T. Benson.

Winter Quarters, Sat., Mar. 28th, 1847.

Morning clear, warm and pleasant. About 10 I was at Pres. B. Young's. He said he wished me to take care of Sister Lytle until I should have a chance to send her on over the mountains to her husband that is in the army, which will not be this season. He also told me that when I were done measuring up the potatoes to the pioneers which occupied the major part of the day. About noon Pres. (B. Young) paid me $400.00 in gold which left about $300 still due. Nancy the 1st returned home at 3. At 7 evening pursuant to adjournment the members of Pres. B. Young's family met at the council house. 1st A. P. Rockwood called the house to order and upon motion of Counsellor Clapp the meeting of the Seventies was adjourned to the following Sat. The house having been called to order by Isaac Morley, the names of the members presant at the last meeting were read and answered too and then some 46 persons were added to the list. Pres. B. Young said that he did not tease any man to come into my family. Neither did he want any to do so on account of the farming organization. If I am able to save one man why cannot [I] save more, and sometimes I wish that I could say unto all the ends of the earth, come and be saved. I have no objection to receiving any man into this organization until he behaves like the very devil as Jos. Woodard did after teasing and whining around me for 3 days to have his wife sealed to me. I told him that they were both adopted to

Nancy Returns

135

me and that was enough, but that would not do. Now he wants to take my live. He is a poor miserable curse and he will be cursed, and when any man shall act as he has I will treat them like an enemy. About 80 names were entered. Pres. Young said that there were enough to commence with.

Now let old experience men head smawl cos., say about 4 to 10 men, and let each man have ten acres to commence with. My mind is that 10 acres of land well cultivated will produce more grain than 20 acres half tended. Pres. B. Young said Br. J. D. Lee is capable of heading a Co. and will likely raise 5,000 bus. grain with his own family.

> Isaac Morley, 1st Co.
> John Vance, 2nd Co.
> John D. Lee, 3rd Co.
> Consisting of 25 men.

Pres. B. Young said that he must withdraw and let Father Morley ascertain who can go on Monday to the farm and organize the remainder acording to the pattern. 9 Pres. B. Young withdrew. 10 names were recorded to remove on Monday morning next up to the farm.[125] Warm and pleasant.

Winter Quarters, Sund., March 28th, '47.

Morning clear and pleasant, W. S.W. About 10 morning quite a collection of the Saints met at the stand in public meeting and was addressed on various subjects and prophecies delivered. Pres. B. Young said while I am here the people can be controlled whether I have power or not. You will find when I am gone that rebellious and arbitrary spirits will arrise who will usurp authority that was never given to them and loose sight of the council that was given to them and will kick up the devil among the people. When these things takes place remember what was told you.

---

[125] Lee was thus doomed to remain behind. He had donated seven teams to Brigham Young for the Pioneer journey.

Through the day J. D. Lee was in company with his wife Louisa Free [No. 3], when she related the following dream. As I lay upon my bed pondering in my mind upon my past, present and future state, I fell asleep and while I was in the spirit I was commanded to arise and go to a large city at a remote distance, in which city was a variety of stores filled with all manner of merchandise, and by taking with me an order from the man with whom I was connected, I could have full access to all the rich merchandise of a certain store. After the personage disappeared I reluctantly did in part as he commanded me. On reaching the city I entered the store to which I was directed, found it filled with every commodity that heart could wish or desire. Still I was not satisfied, thinking that other stores might afford a greater variety of articles and if not there could be no great harm in going into other stores and looking, at least, so I concluded to satisfy my curiosity, went into a No. of large stores but none of them pleased me as well as the one to which I was directed. But inasmuch as I was so hard to please in the beginning and felt as though the best was not offered me, I would bye something out of another store from the one that I was sent too. So I concluded to take a pair of shoes; still they were not handsome and did not please me; the heels were high and sharp and did not fit me, still my dissatisfaction I concealed for a long time and felt much disappointed and how to help myself I knew not. My anxiety to return to the store where I was first directed too, became greater than it was to try new ones. But the difficulty was, in my ramblings I unfortunately had lost the order which was given me on that store; consiquently could not have any claim on it; and what was still worse than all, when I first entered the store to which I was directed, I had presented my order to the merchant who replied that it was good for any amount, and so, on the credit of it, I had taken up, or rather selected a variety

137

of articles and had them laid aside but did not pay for them. Looking arround me I discovered my father sitting by a desk writing, when new hopes began to revive; thought that probably he might have found my order. I stepped to him and asked him if he had seen my order. He replied in the negative. I was then in total despair of ever getting the goods, so I resolved to go to the merchant and tell him what had happened and that he would have to keep the goods as I had no other means of paying for them. The merchant then took me by the hand and led me to a private place where the names of faithful were registered and almost the first name that caught my eyes was John D. Lee written handsomely in large plain letters. The merchant pointed to this name and said I am well acquainted with that man, we are indebted to him, and although you have lost the order I will venture to let you have the goods feeling safe in his integrity and that he will settle the bill. Being overcome with gratitude I received the goods with thankfulness and my dream came to a close and I greatly marveled at what I had seen, not knowing the meaning thereof.

When she had finished relating her dream J. D. Lee, proceeding to give the following interpretation, said: Louisa, the vision is plain and the interpretation thereof is sure. The personage that directed you to the store where the names of the sanctified are recorded is Pres. B. Young who counselled you to be sealed to me, saying it [is] the voice of the spirit. The order which entitled you to everything that heart could wish for was the relationship that you sustain to me in the covenant and in the Priesthood. The goods that you were sent to obtain are the blessings of exaltation or in other words the reward of the faithful. The reluctance or difadence of feeling with which you set out in pursuit of the treasures was the feeling you had when you obeyed the voice of the spirit (partially). The goods

138

that you selected, which pleased you to a fraction which
you seemed not to obtain and yet did, are the blessings that
was promised you in the anointing, through faithfulness
to the end. The wandering visits that you made into other
stores in which you lost your order is an evidence that you
will become defected and your affections will be alleniated
from me to such an extent that you will seek to desolve the
union that is between us and that too without a just cause.
The order that you lost is the claims that you held on me
for salvation. The shoes that you bought in another store
that did not please you is an evidence that you will change
your condition and marry another man who will not please
you as well as the one that you now have, but that you
take him rather to justify you in the steps that you will
take. The anxiety that you had to return to the first store,
is an evidence that you will want to come back again to me,
but the way to get back will be dark to you and doubtful
for a long time acording to your knowledge of the dealings
of God. In fact you will despair of ever regaining your
first state, although you will make every effort but all will
be fruitless apparently to you, in vain. And finally you
will come to the conclusion to submit your fate and re-
linquish all claims, seeming no other alternative, when the
Bountiful Giver will cause you to know and see that I have
had favor with him all the time and that my name is still
registered in Heaven. And although you will have treated
lightly the offered favors and blessings of Heaven, through
me as an instrument in the hands of God and thereby will
have justly forfeited all claims to them through that channel, yet he has shown thee that I will redeem your pledges
and make good your contracts to your astonishment and
mortification. Now, Louisa, the Lord has warned you of
what will take place hereafter. My heart is filled with
blessings toward you, but a restless spirit will sieze you in
the day when I am oppressed and you will never stop until

139

you fulfil this vision. Contrast alone will ever reconcile you. My heart is pained when I think on the future.[126]

Winter Quarters, Mon., March 29, '47.

Morning fair. At 30 m. to 9 the officer and pioneer of the 1st division met at the council house. My name was called. Pres. B. Young said that I was packing up to move up to the farm and apointed Bro. E. T. Benson to act in my place (Capt. protem) [of] the Pioneers that reported themselves ready. Pres. B. Young sent with 2 of his teams to assist me to remove my family, making about 10 teams. About noon we left Winter Quarters. Just before I started Pres. B. Young sent for me. Said that he could not pay me the money that he had borrowed of me and the $60.00 that I had [of] Sister Lytle's I would have to charge, but, said he, you will prosper. But never consent to have a man settle with you unless he will hearken to council and build so as to fortify against Indian aggression. Fortfy your catle also. Dig a well and boil the water and use root bark. Be united, keep out selfishness, be humble and prayerful before the Lord, and you will have health and be prospered. Our teams were heavy loaded and some of them were low in flesh. About 8 at night we reached the creek 3 ms. and north of the fort where we encamped. Left Bro. M. Anderson about 8 ms. back, team given out.

Leaves Winter Quarters

Winter Quarters, Teus., Mar. 30th, 1847.

Summer Quarters

Morning clear. About daylight T. Johnson and I took our horses and explored the country for 5 ms. round. At length I found a splendid location for building and farming where about 6000 [600] acres of rich fertile land which can be fenced by 10 days labour, 2 creeks leading from a steep precipice which formed the W. line running to the

---

[126] Louisa did leave him to become the first wife of Daniel H. Wells.

Mo. river enclosed the N. and S. line and the river the E. with the exception of the foot of the N. and south precipice. About noon we reached the place of destination. Bought a bee tree of Bro. Arnold. Paid him $1.50 cts. At night I called my family togeather and prayed and consecrated and dedicated the location unto the Lord.

Summer Quarters,[127] Wed., Mar. 31st, '47.

Morning clear. After prayer I cleared off the ground for the foundation of one of my buildings. After brakefast A. D. Young and I commenced cutting house logs, Thomas and W. Woolsey to hauling. About 4 Bro. Wm. Pace and M. Harris came up. Bro. Harris assisted us till night to cut house logs. Got the lumber for 2 houses cut and for 1 hauled. Evening pleasant.

Summer Quarters, April 1st, 1847.

Morning clear. After prayers I laid the foundation for 2 houses. At about 10 I started for Winter Quarters. Reached that point about 4 p.m. Delivered up my bay span of mules and small waggon into the hands of C. Shumway and son, after rigging both them and the waggon and fitting them out with grain to go on with the pioneers of the 1st division, then brought my account up on the books with A. P. Rockwood. Evening pleasant.

Lee Fits Out Pioneers

---

[127] Summer Quarters, sometimes called "Brigham's Farm," was established for the purpose of raising grain for Brigham Young and his "adopted" families. Mr. E. G. Connely, of Omaha, who has definitely located the site, describes it as follows: "Summer Quarters is about 13 miles (by present highway) north of old Winter Quarters. The land lies between two streams, is perfectly flat, with good, friable soil, some of which had been previously cultivated by soldiers from old Fort Atkinson, and was the largest and best tract within easy reach of Winter Quarters. The buildings were erected at the north end of the tract near the larger of the two streams. The only tangible remains now existing, on the farm of Mr. Hineline, are a few scattered broken brick, fragments of limestone, and slight irregularities in the surface of the field. The courses of the two streams have been greatly altered since 1847 and the nearby marshes drained. The Missouri river has also altered the outlines of the land cultivated by Lee."

Summer Quarters, Friday, April 2nd, '47.

Morning clear and pleasant. About 9 I was with Pres. B. Young, told him my circumstances, how at present my feet were bound and hands fettered but to unloose them. That I could acomplish as much as the next man under no better circumstances. He said that he would untie them; asked me how much would relieve me. I told him $25.00. He quickly responded to my request with $50.00 in gold. Then said prosper. He also ordered my grain for the pioneers to be ground toll free and the first, that I might return to the farm. From noon till 9 evening I had about 22 bus. wheat ground and boalted (it was the first that was boalted) and 21 bushels corn, all of which I brought from the mill before I retired to rest. 20 bushels of corn I borrowed of Bro. McGee Harris who also donated 18 lbs. bacon and 10 bushels of corn for the benefit of the pioneers of the first division. Evening pleasant. Staid over night with Polly and Lovina Young [*Nos. 13 and 14*].

Donations for the Pioneers

Winter Quarters, Sat., April 3rd, 1847.

Morning clear, warm and still. About 8 clowded up, wind blew S.E. by sunrise. I took iron for 2 ploughs to A. Lamerou's shop. Paid $5.00 in advance, had some other repairs done. Dealt out flour and meal, corn and brand to the pioneers of my Co. and to the women whoes husbands are in the army (viz.) Sister Pace and Lytle, also David Young. About 9 Bro. E. D. Wooley took some 5 sacks of flour and meal in his waggon up to the farm. About the same time I left Winter Quarters, took one of my pioneer's teams and Rodney [*Swazey*] to bring it back. A short distance beyond the old fort I came up with Father Morly and Bro. E. D. Wooley. We traveled on togeather to Mudd Creek where we were detained some 3 hours in consiquence of my waggon braking through the bridge, and come nigh cripling one of my mules. By the time we

142

got out Bro. Pace came up with his family who was also moving to the farm. We all encamped here for the night. Evening clowdy and cold. Wind high S.W. Dis. 12 ms.

Mudd Creek Encampment, Sund., April 4, '47.

Morning clowdy, cool wind S.E. About 7 we took our march and about 9 arrived at our new location. Father Morly, E. D. Wooley and myself walked over the ground and after a thorough examination returned back to the spot where I had located, took brakefast and then called the brethren togeather. Told them that he was well pleased with the location and with the situation for a farm. He did not think that it could be surpassed in a new country and that he was as well pleased with the situation as though he had done it himself and that in as much as he was appointed to preside over them he would expect them to sustain him in that place and abide whatever decission he might be required to make and that it will be better to settle in block and fortify ourselves against Indian aggression and in fact it is the council of Pres. B. Young. In my absence Bro. Lee will take charge of affairs here and when he may be called to decide in anything that partains to this Co. let his decision be yea and amen and all will be right. I shall council with him from time to time. Bro. Brigham will likely be here before the Pioneer Co. all get away and will give us such instructions as will be for our good. Brethren, be united and prayerful that the Lord may bless us. About eleven Father Morley and Bro. E. D. Wooley started back, left me to measure and divide the land and set apart to each man his bounds, both for building and farming, choose the east line to place his building on. Wished me to sow some spring wheat for him and Bro. Wooley and when the crop comes to perfection to be paid out of it for putting it in. About 3 Bro. A. D. Young, Miles Anderson and myself measured the broke land, found that

Location of "Brigham Young Farm"

Lee Appointed Farm Superintendent

143

there was but 140 acres. Several horses and cows were pulled out of the mire today. About 12 at night a heavy storm of rain arose from the south and rained till daylight in the morning.

Summer Quarters, Mon., April 5, '47.

Clowdy with occasional showers of rain. About noon slacked up. We were engaged in cutting down trees for our cattle to brows on. We also built a bridge over a smawl stream, the better to haul our building timber over. Eve. clowdy.

Summer Quarters, Teus., April 6th, '47.

Morning clear, wind N.W., cool. About 8 I measured and laid off the city plots, then called my adopted family to-geather (I.E.) such as were presant. Gave them the liberty of having their land set off to them or working as one family. T. Johnson, Wm. Pace and Miles Anderson choose the former proposition; A. D. Young, David Young, Jas. Wooley, H. Wooley, Geo. Laub, A. Weeks, Allen, Wm. and T., Levi North, G. W. Hickerson and some others, the latter. Some sharp words passed between Bro. Arnold and myself because I reproved him and some others of his Co. for selfishness, for his hard speeches.[128] Bro. A. Young and myself got up some board timber and hauled a few logs in. Bro. Harris, Dun and Busby arrived in camp. Evening fine.

Summer Quarters, Wed., April 7th, '47.

Clear and cool, high wind N.W. The day was ocupied generally in procuring building timber. Bro. A. D. Young, myself by the assistance of Rachel, Louisa, Emoline, Nancy [Nos. 6, 3, 11, 12] and Rhoda Young raised the body of one house and hauled a part of a set. About [?] Bro. Isaac Houston and Jacob Secrest arrived here from camp.

---

[128] Beginning of the trouble, which continued all summer, over division of land.

AIRPLANE VIEW OF SUMMER QUARTERS—Showing location of the settlement, the land cultivated, and "Fairview" cemetery.   Courtesy E. G. Connely, Omaha, Neb.

Bro. H. brought his family and reported that the remainder of the pioneers started this morning and that Pres. B. Young, Kimble and Father Morley would be up here on the morrow. Evening clowdy, W. high N. Yesterday one of my mules died of the distemper.

Summer Quarters, Thurs., April 8, '47.

Morning clear, W. N.W. I was engaged in the forenoon in raising my cabbins. About noon Pres. Young, I. Morly, G. D. Grant, Chas. Kennedy, John Young and Jos. Young, Pres. B. Young's son, arrived from Winter Quarters, well pleased with the prospects of farming at our new locasion. We cut down an elm tree for their horses to brows upon after which we walked to my tent. I gave them some bitters which had been prepared by the direction of Sister Young, the Pres. lady, for the preservation of health. Pres. B. Young and John, his Bro. laid down and rested themselves as they were much weary from the fatigues of their ride. After indulging a short season in repose they arrose and took some refreshments. Pres. Young said that he had not eaten a meal in great while that did him as much good. He blessed us in the Lord. Before leaving he called the brethren togeather and told them that he wanted me and those that belonged to my family to have what land I wanted to till, then Father Morly and his 2 sons and son-in-law, and the remainder of the land to those of his family that would raise grain and prepare to winter his stock. Let others go down in the timber and some over the creek to till the ground, but all build in a square on the ground that has been laid [out] by Bro. Lee but let each man have his land set off to them.[129] He then

Brigham Leaves Instructions

---

[129] These instructions gave Lee and all Brigham's "adopted" family first choice of any quantity of land they wanted. It was in following these instructions that he became involved in continual strife at Summer Quarters. When Brigham returned in the fall of 1847 he denied having issued any such orders; but this entry, made at the time, is sufficient evidence.

said to me that Thomas Woolsey had just arrived in camp with his family and was dependent on me for an outfit and wished me to return with him to camp and fit him out. Said that I could ride with him in his carriage. At 20 m. to 3 p.m. we started back. Stopped 6 ms. N. of Winter Quarters 30 m. with the pioneers who had taken up quarters there for the night. Here I met some disagreeable feelings on the part of one of my pioneers, namely Rodney Swasey, who on hearing that his stepfather and his mother were out of jail wanted to return and meet them. I finally consented and let T. Woolsey take his place. Reached the main camp about sunset. Met Bro. A. Weeks who had just got in from Pizgah. When I met T. Woolsey he pressed me close for the liberty of having Miss Willis sealed to him. About 9 I walked to Pres. B. Young and asked him the liberty of giving T. Woolsey the girl which he granted and said that he would return from the Horn [130] about Sunday next and would then attend to it. Having communicated the same to T. W. and instructed him to tyle acordingly, spent the night with Polly and Lucinda Young [*Nos. 13 and 14*].

Winter Quarters, Fri., April 9th, '47.

Morning clear, warm and pleasant. At 8 morning the 12 met in council at Dr. Richard's office. Heard the report of Elder P. P. Pratt [131] who arrived the evening before from a mission to England. Said that he and the brethren that went with him had been prospered and that the spirit of the members in Parliament was to remove the Saints and colonize them in Vancoovers Island [132] at the expense of government, and that it is a current report at New Orleans when he came through that Santa Ana had hemmed in

Vancouver Island Suggested as Mormon Colony

---

[130] Elkhorn river, 16 miles from Winter Quarters; 35 miles by the old trail.

[131] Parley P. Pratt, whose death in Arkansas at the hands of an outraged husband, in 1857, was one of the indirect causes of the Mountain Meadows Massacre.

[132] The Mormons in England petitioned Parliament to remove them in a body to Vancouver Island.

146

Gen. Taylor's army and cut off all their supplies. They commanded him to surrender and upon Tailor's refusing to comply with the order a general engagement took place and the supposition was that Taylor's army have been cut off. About 11 p.m. Bro. A. Weeks started with his family for the farm at Summer Quarters. This morning I rode the city over in search of corn meal and bacon but failed to procure any for love or money. The fact was all the provisions that was in camp had been converted to fit out the pioneers.[133] About 12 noon Pres. B. Young, Kimble, O. Pratt, Woodruff, E. T. Benson, A. Lyman, G. A. Smith and Dr. Richards of the 12 beside several others of the pioneers started for the Horn (river). I started in Co. with them. I traveled about 10 ms. togeather. My 2 teams were in advance of the Co. When the waggons were all on the road in a line they made a sublim appearance. About 30 m. to 4 I took leave of them on the broad open prairie. I should like to have been in Co. with them, had wisdom ordered it so.[134] About 6 I with David Young and R. Swazey reached home. Evening pleasant. Today Chas. Kennedy and George Laub removed their effects in camp.

Pioneers Begin Their Historic Journey

Summer Quarters, Sat., April 10th, '47.

Morning clear. At 6 Bro. Secrest, A. D. Young, G. Laub, D. Young and myself commenced clearing off a garden spot. About 10 I sent a team for brick which are found about the ruins of the old fort and neighboring buildings.[45] We also cut some house logs. About 12 Bro. A. Weeks arrived in camp with his family and about 3 p.m. C. Kennedy arrived at Summer Quarters and about 8 eve. Bro. N. Night returned from Winter Quarters with 4 bus. meal and the remainder of his goods. About 8 morn. R. Swazey

---

[133] Those who remained have never been given due credit for impoverishing themselves to fit out the Pioneers.

[134] Lee mildly expresses his bitter disappointment at being left behind.

left S. Quarters. At 2 p.m. Bro. G. Secrest returned to W. Q. not being able to secure a team to go to Mo. for seed potatoes.

Summer Quarters, Sund., April 11th, 1847.

Morning clear, W. high, S.W. About 9 morn. Bro. A. P. Free, A. D. Young, Bro. Houston and myself walked down in the timber a distance of 2 ms. below our farm to examine the prospect for enlarging our farm. Found a large body of light loose land easy to manage and well calculated for the present purpose. While walking over it we fired the old grass. About 8 David Young returned to W. Q. with team to remove the family up. The evening I spent in conversation upon the subject of the advancement of the children of men. Sunset W. high W. Last evening Agathean, my 1st espoused, became highly offended at me and abused by hard speeches not only me but the remainder of the family. After requesting her to desist several times she railed out the more. I then told her that she should feel the hand of the Lord in chastisement for her speeches. She said she did not care how soon and that I should atone for what I had done. About 3 minets afterward she was taken with the most ecrutiating sickness at heart which well nigh caused her to yield up the ghost. When she was thus taken the whole family became alarmed. I told Sister A. D. Young not to be alarmed for the power of God would be made manifest in her sight. Agathean at 1st persisted and said that God for [?] taken her away but soon her feelings changed and asked what she would do. I answered, humble yourself and repent of your hard speeches. She soon became almost frantic, tumbling and rolling first from the bed then to the floor and when I saw that her spirit was right I called A. D. Young, took a bottle of oil that had been consecrated in the Temple of

148

the Lord at Nauvoo,[135] anointed her and rebuked the spirit that she had given up too, and prayed the Lord to stay his hand, and instantly she was relieved and fell asleep. Sister said that she was satisfied and felt grateful that such power was in our midst. The sequeal was the Lord loved her, therefore chastised her to bring her back in the channel of the covenant.

Summer Quarters, Mon., April 12th, '47.

Morning cool and clowdy, W. E. About 6 A. D. Young brought a crane and a goose [killed] yesterday morning. I have been employed in labouring on my cabbin. Cleared off some ground for garden and spent about 1 fourth of the day in pulling catle out of the mire. In the evening T. Johnson returned. Bro. Jas. Leavens and Markham came with him, who were going to the heard for catle. The Mo. river is almost level with its banks. Evening pleasant.

Summer Quarters, Teus., April 13th, 1847.

Morning clear and cool, W. N.W. About 6 and 30 m. A. D. Young brought in a fine turkey. This morning I broke 2 ploughs in breaking up truck patch. One of the ploughs I sent to W. Quarters to be repaired, the other was easily repaired by putting in a new beam after which I succeeded in preparing the ground planting some early potatoes and quite a quantity of garden seed and done some work on my cabbins. The girls done the gardening (vis.) Aggathean, Nancy the 1st, Louisa, Rachael, Emoline, [Nos. 1, 2, 3, 6, 11], Rhoda and Sarah Jane. About 10 quite a drove of catle went to W. Q. by Bro. Farr, Blozard, Allen, Merchants and others. Among [them] I discovered one of my heifers who I kept although she was claimed by Bro. Merchants. Bro. T. Johnson I sent to the upper heard for my catle the distance of 25 or 30 ms. Bro. Jas.

---

[135] Olive oil, blessed in the Temple, is still used in anointing the sick.

Lemons went up with him. Evening clowdy.

Summer Quarters, Wed., April 14th, '47.

Morning clow'dy, wind high. This day was ocupied in building and planting. About dark David Young arrived in camp with his 2 sisters [*Nos. 13 and 14*].

Summer Quarters, Thurs., April 15th, 1847.

Morning clear, N.W. This morning a No. of the brethren united and enclosed a piece of ground for a garden spot. About 9 Bros. Jos. Busby, Sanders, Dun and Arnold went to W. Quarters. About 4 p.m. Bro. Isaac Morley arrived, walked from Winter Quarters to this point. Evening pleasant. This morning Bro. A. D. Young brought in a fine turkey.

Summer Quarters, Friday, April 16th, '47.

Morning clowdy, W. N.W. At 30 m. to 8 the brethren assembled togeather at my tent by request of Bro. Isaac Morley, who said, Brethren, I have called the brethren togeather to consult your feelings about the division of this land. Bro. Brigham has given me some general idea of what he wanted and my feelings are to carry out his designs. He said that he wanted Bro. Lee [*to*] have what land he wanted to tend for himself and those of his family that would work with him, also that Bro. Grant and myself have what we wanted, the rest to be divided among those that he first selected to farm, but let all settle here although they may have to go down to the timber or the lower end of the lake to till their lands. J. D. Lee said that his intentions were to carry out Bro. Brigham counsel and views provided his brethren would let him. The majority of the brethren said that they wanted his views carried out. About 9 Pres. Morley, Knights, Houston, Gully, Anderson and J. D. Lee measured off the grounds, left about 70 acres to J. D. Lee and Co., 30 to G. D. Grant and Co. and

150

15 to Isaac Morley, the remaining 45 acres were divided among 20 persons [136] (vis.) Jos. Busby, G. Arnold, S. A. Dun, E. D. Wooley, W. Pace, Thos. Johnson, M. Anderson, A. P. Free, J. F. Martin, W. Martin, M. G. A. Harris, Levi Stewart, I. Houston and N. W. Knight (and son), S. Gully and son, M. M. Sanders, after which I. Morley with the rest of the Co. went [to] J. D. Lee's tent and gave some general instructions. Said to him I want you to organize those men into Cos. of 5 and appoint a Capt. over them then let the Capt. of each Co. draw for their men. About noon Pres. Morley returned to W. Q. The same evening I organized a part of the Co. Evening cold, W. N. A. D. Young brought in a good deer in camp.

Summer Quarters, Sat., April 17th, '47.

Morning clear, cold, W. N. Ice an inch thick. At 7 J. D. Lee called the members of the camp togeather and laid before them the propriety of having our catle guarded of nights to secure them from the Indians. They all responded by going to build fense. Evening cool.

Summer Quarters, Sund., April 18th, 1847.

Morning clowdy, cool, W. high N.W. About 11 Stewart, Arnold, and Woolsey's heard passed down on their way to W. Q. I took my catle from among them (E.I.) what I could find, but about 6 out of 15 were missing, suposed either to have [been stolen?] or killed by the Indians. At 30 m. to 2 p.m. I started for W. Q. with 4 yoke of catle for provisions and to remove some families up whoes husbands were in the army who were left in my charge (ss.) T. Woolsey and A. Lytle. Bros. M. M. Sanders and G. Lemons rode down with me. A little after dark I arrived in camp, found provisions scarce but fortunately saw a

---

[136] Lee took 70 acres, George D. Grant 30 acres, Isaac Morley 15; the balance of 45 acres was divided among 20 persons, an average of a little over 2 acres each. This was the cause of the trouble which followed.

151

young man from over the other side of the river who informed me that a load had come in from Mo. since dark. About 12 I retired to rest at Sister Woolsey's. Evening mild.

Winter Quarters, Mon., April 19th, '47.

Scarcity of Supplies

Morning clear, wind S., warm. By 6 I succeded in getting over the river and getting 12 bus. meal, 5 bus. of corn and about 6 lbs. bacon. Paid 50 cts. for the meal and corn and 8 for the bacon. Then by the help of Bishop Night, Lameraux and another brother I succeeded in getting over on this side in 2 canoes though the river was high, current strong. In the meantime Sister Woolsey was loading up her goods. About 12 noon I started for Summer Q. Removed Sister Lytle and family, also at Mud Creek we met Bros. Sniders and Co. heard, the best looking heard that I have seen this spring. Here we came up with Bro. Dunn and Busby, Br. D. having upset his waggon, hurt one of his children. Then encamped for the night. About 11 we arrived safe at our location and about 12 night Julia

Another Miracle

Woolsey was delivered of a daughter. She was taken before we left W. Q., but was held by the prayer of faith till she would [reach] her destination. Day and evening warm, lightning in the east.

Summer Quarters, Teus., April 20th, 1847.

Morning clear, warm, W. high, S.W. J. D. Lee was employed in covering one [of] his cabins assisted by A. D. Young, Allen Weeks and David Young, they also finished out his chimney, ploughed and planted garden seeds. At 7 eve. the brethren of the camp met at J. D. Lee's quarters, took into consideration the propriety of building a lot to secure our catle. Decided that the N. and E. line should build and occupy the North lot, and that the W. and S. line build and occupy the W. lot and both parties

152

build a bridge and watering place. J. D. Lee said that his instructions were to organize the Co. of farmers at Summer Quarters in Cos. of 5 and appoint a Capt. over each Co., then let each Capt. draw the land for his Cos. Jos. Busby and S. A. Dun, T. S. Johnson and G. Arnold manifested a spirit of dissatisfaction to the present arrangement. Censored Pres. Morley and J. D. Lee of acting partial and doeing injustice in the dividend of the land. Said that the brethren were not satisfied and would leave to go to Mo. sooner than bear it. J. D. Lee said so far as righteousness and council would satisfy them he was always ready to render satisfaction but to sacrifice principle and disobey council to appease the wrath of men he was not willing too,[137] and should any man feel dissatisfied, stir up strife and conflict by inflammatory speeches and cannot submit to the council and authorities that has been placed here and elsewhere to manage the affairs of this Kingdom, and wish to leave, they have the liberty of so doing, for unless we are united we cannot prosper and that he would sooner undertake to fortify against the Indians with 20 families well united than to risk 100 that are not, and that he knew that Father Morly had done according to council and should not be censored as the man that does it will have to atone for it. Samuel Gully said that he believed Father Morly and Bro. Lee were men that would do just right and that he considered that we have as much right to complain of Bro. Kennedy for having 10 acres as we have of Bro. Morly and Lee, but that he did not consider that we should meddle ourselves with it at all for it was none of our business to inquire into the whys and wherefore. Do as we are councilled and be satisfied and all will be right. About 9 the contention ceased. The feelings generally were expressed by Bro. Busby and Dunn. Evening pleasant.

A Spirit of Dissatisfaction

---

[137] Lee refused to disobey Brigham's orders, even to keep peace.

Morning clowdy, warm. About 30 m. to 6 a war party of about 40 Indians (Omahas) after skulking some time on or rather behind the brow of the hill rushed down into camp, showed some hostility, made signs that we were tilling their land and wanted a beef steer. Upon refusal to comply with his request 3 men were dispatched to shoot and butcher a beef. When J. D. Lee saw that they were fully decided to shoot he ran in their midst with hoop pole [138] drawn over them saying, at the same time to them, that if they did shoot any of our catle that he would kill every devil of them. The chief, seeing that he was in earnest, stopped the operation suddenly and held out his hand for friendship. The brethren were all on hands, that [is] those that were in camp, which were about 10 men. The savages finding that [we] were not to be frightened by them promised peace and said they were in persuit of the Sious and left. Seeing that they were about to go peacibly J. D. Lee told them (the brethren) to give the thieves some bread and poder. About noon report came to us that this same party had killed 7 catle the day before while on their way to this point and that depredations were commited daily by them at W. Q. and in the settlements round about and that the Indians said that they intended to kill all our catle and then live on our crops or make us leave. This they were urged too by the missionarries.[123] This morning, so says reports, that A Cutler, C. P. Scott and D. Spencer were sent to confer with them and know what their intentions were. About 9 Jos. Busby came to J. D. Lee, the Capt. of the 1st 100 (pro tem), and said that he wanted to know whether he would give him, Dun and Arnold 10 acres each. J. D. Lee said that he would divide with them provided that he was going to farm for Pres. B. Young

Trouble with the Omahas

---

[138] Hoop-pole: a heavy sapling about twelve feet long, from which barrel hoops were made.

but that Dun and Arnold must be contented with the divisions that were made by Father Morly and that he wanted Bro. J. B. to stop sowing the seed of discord and censoring him and Father Morly. Busby replied that he would take whatever land were alloted him, Dun and J. Arnold, and would drop the matter provided they could have it togeather. J. D. Lee said they should have the land as they wanted. [139] All hands after our visitors [*left*] turned to fortifying against any further aggressions. About 3 P.M. we had quite a gale of W. and heavy shower of rain from the N.W. About 6 Bro. Harris arrived in camp with his family. Sister Stewart and Arnold also arrived.

Summer Quarters, Thurs., April 22nd, '47.

Morning clowdy, W. south, warm. About 10 faired off, when Potter's heard passed down. This day the brethren of this place were generally engaged in the building of their lots. Evening pleasant.

Summer Quarters, Frid., April 23rd, '47.

Morning clear, W. south. A. D. Young and George Laub were employed in plow stocking, others were hauling logs, building and clearing land and so on. About noon Bro. Potter and Dalton came up from W. Q. Said that a treaty had been effected by the community with the Omaha Indians; that we were to pay them 500 bushels corn as soon as we could haul it from Mo. for the use of their land and they would let us live in peace and stop killing our catle. Evening pleasant.

Summer Quarters, Sat., April 24th, '47.

Morning clear, warm and fine. About 6 I, with several of the brethren, went 2 ms. above our quarters to meet the

---

[139] This quarrel over land seems ridiculous in view of the fact that the whole country, from Winter Quarters to the Rocky Mountains, was unoccupied.

stray heard and search for strayed catle. I found 2 only. About ⅓ of the catle have been lost since last fall. About 10 the stray heard went down. About the same time Bro. Dalton received a severe hurt in one of his feet from the fall of a pole but was greatly restored by the laying on of hands and the prayer of faith. About 11 Bro. J. Busby, G. Laub, D. Davis, Dalton and Potter started for W. Q. and about 5 evening C. P. Lott with 9 men arrived on their way to meet and protect the heards from this Co.

Proposition from Omahas

We learned that a proposition had been made by the chiefs of the Omaha to let us remain this season by hauling them 600 bus. corn purchased by government and that we should have 30 bus. out of that amount to feed our teams while hauling, and report says through the press that an engagement took place about 2, 3 and 4 of Feb. between Gen. Taylor and Santa Ana in which about 1000 of Taylor's men fell and 2000 of Santa Ana's men. Evening pleasant.

Summer Quarters, Sund., April 25th, 1847.

Morning clear, wind W. S. W. About 9 Bro. Allen Weeks started to Mt. Pizgah for his family, Jas. Woolsey and Levi North. About the same time Bro. Samuel Gully and lady started for W. Q. A. D. Young and David Young started for some cows that had been left 10 ms. back by the heardsmen. A cow and an ox were pulled out of the mire today. Peace in camp through the day. Evening fine.

Summer Quarters, Mon., April 26th, 1847.

Morning cool, clear, wind S. W. About 7 J. D. Lee commenced plowing for corn. Started 3 ploughs. A. D. Young was plough stocking. About 11 Father Morly and C. Bird arrived in camp. Said that the chief of the Otoes had a council with our people at W. Q. Said that we were

156

living on their lands and not the Omahas. Their lands lies above the fort [*Old Council Bluff*]. They were permitted to come among us (continued the chief) because they were oppressed but now they claim our lands. When your people first came and settled on our lands we made a covenant that you should stay in peace until you could recruit to go on. That covenant we never have never broke. My young men has never killed any of your catle, neither do they intend to brake their covenant, but the Omahas have. Still you give them presents to make them keep their covenants. We do not ask this of you. We know that you are poor and so are we, still could you haul us 500 bus. of corn we would pay you 25 bushel out of it to feed teams while drawing it. This we do not claim of you to make us keep our covenant for we will not brake it, &c. Council decided the same evening and reported to them the following morning that as soon as an order could be obtained from their agent that was then at the Pawnee village that we would comply with their request also. About 2 P.M. Pres. I. Morley and C. Bird returned. Bro. Bird's errand was to know whether Pres. B. Young had left any money in my hands for him &c. Evening pleasant.

Treaty with Otoes

Summer Quarters, Teus., April 27th, 1847.

Morning clear and warm. General stir in camp about farming. About 2 P.M. Bro. Richards, Bro. F. Kesler and another brother from W. Q. came up in search of catle. About dark J. D. Lee arrived bringing old man D. Young and a part of his goods, also Bro. Busby, Dun, and Arnold came in, left Bro. Samuel Gully and Houston at Mire Creek. After dark a thunder clowd arrose from the S.W. and gave us quite a shower of rain.

Summer Quarters, Wed., April 28th, '47.

Morning clear, W. S. About 9 the parties concerned met

J. D. Lee. We measured the land and had their bounds set off to them, after having been organized into Cos. of 5s by J. D. Lee, and drew as follows: Capt. Isaac Houston drew lots No. 1, Capt. Jos. Busby No. 2, M. M. Sanders No. 3, and Magee Harris No. 4. In the evening Bro. Simmons, Murdock and Bro. stopped over night. About 8 the brethren met at J. D. Lee's who after calling the meeting to order said the hearding of our catle was the subject of conversation before the brethren, which is essentially for the safety and protection of our catle. A suggestion has been made to have but 1 heard which he said was worthy of notice. After a deliberation of 2 hours decided that N. K. Knight superintend the hearding and that the brethren till his land in exchange for his servis and that those who have boys send them in turns to aid him. Adjourned sine die.

Summer Quarters, Thurs., April 29th, '47.

Morning clear, W. S. At 11 Bros. Martin started to Mo. for 2 loads of provisions. J. D. Lee sent for 75 bus. meal. About 4 P.M. I received a letter from H. B. Owens, Pizgah, asking council to know what to do with reference to coming on this spring. Said that the rest of my family that are at Pizgah were calculating to start for this point about 25 inst. Evening clowded up and a light shower from the N. W. accompanied with hail. Wm. Potter came from W. Q. and tarried over night. Wanted the hearding of my catle although he lost 6 out of 13 head. But as he asked it I paid it.

Summer Quarters, Friday, April 30, '47.

Morning clowdy, W. E. About 8 W. Potter returned. This morning several ploughs were started. J. D. Lee has about 12 acres broke. About 6 darkened and rained from N. E. Evening D. Carns son came up to farm. Evening rainy.

158

Summer Quarters, Sat., April 30th, 1847.

Morning clowdy and cool through the day. W. N.W. Ploughing was carried on lively in camp. About 8 Samuel Gully started for W. Q. At the same time Bro. A. A. Lathrop's heard passed down and about 2 P.M. Pres. I. Morly arrived from W. Q. Brought up some seed potatoes. Returned about 4, took with him his daughter, Jos. Allen's wife. Near the same time Wm. Woolsey returned from W. Q. Brought with him a horse belonging to John Berry and one to David Young. About 6 Bro. Simmons, Murdock, Hate and Miles came down with the remainder of the stray heard and stopped till morning. 4 head of catle were drawn out of the mire. This evening cool.

Summer Quarters, Sund., May 2nd, '47.

Morning clear, cool, W. N.W. About 8 J. D. Lee settled his heard bill for himself and David Young amounting to $18.00 and redeemed a cow for D. Young. At 20 past 8 the stray heard passed down and at 11 the Saints assembled at Elder J. D. Lee's who delivered an interesting discourse to them upon the subject of the duty of every person that holds the Priesthood. Said that we are messengers of salvation and special witnesses to the nations of the earth and have been called from darkness to the marvelous light of the everlasting gospel of peace to perform a certain work in this the dispensation of the fullness of times according to the appendages and grades of the Priesthood which has been committed to them (ss.) The Prince of this world (according to the sayings of Jesus) has set up his Kingdom and introduced his deceavable plans of unrighteousness, persecuted light by transforming darkness to make it resemble the true light, until he had succeeded in spreading a veil and covering over the nations of the earth and as the Apostle Paul has said, he who letteth will let until it shall be taken out of the way. The Lord, after many centuries

A Sermon by Lee

159

have passed away has called four of his servants to remove the covering and unlock the mysteries of inequity that the secret works of darkness might be made manifest to all men that those who would might have an opportunity of decerning between truth and error, light and darkness, that those who choose salvation might arm themselves with the whole armor of righteousness and thereby be prepared to fight the good fight and keep the faith, in patience endure to the end. Having thus attained to this knowledge the Lord holds us accountable and we are amenable to him for every evil that is done that we could have hindered; in fine it is the duty of every elder in Iseral (the sisters not excepted) to wage an everlasting warfare against principalities and powers and spiritual wickedness in high places, and instead of cherishing and fostering a spirit that militates against the work of the Lord we should always use our utmost endeavors to suppress everything that tends to disunion or that would give place to wrath whereby the adversary of our salvation could gain an ascendency over us. For when we suffer him to come into our hearts we are cherishing and strengthening his hand which enables him to gain ground . . . .

Summer Quarters, Mon., May 3rd, '47.

A Fishing Trip

Morning clear, W. N. W., cool, heavy frost. Ice near ½ an inch thick, nipped beans and other vegetation. Camp generally employed in ploughing and preparing to plant. About 4 P.M. Bro. Burgess and Co. passed up with their saine to fish in a lake about 3 ms. above this point where there is fish in great abundance. About 6 F. K. Fuller with 4 waggons rolled into camp. Evening pleasant.

Summer Quarters, Teus., May 4th, '47.

Morning pleasant. About noon wind blew strong gale south. As usual today general exertion in the farming line.

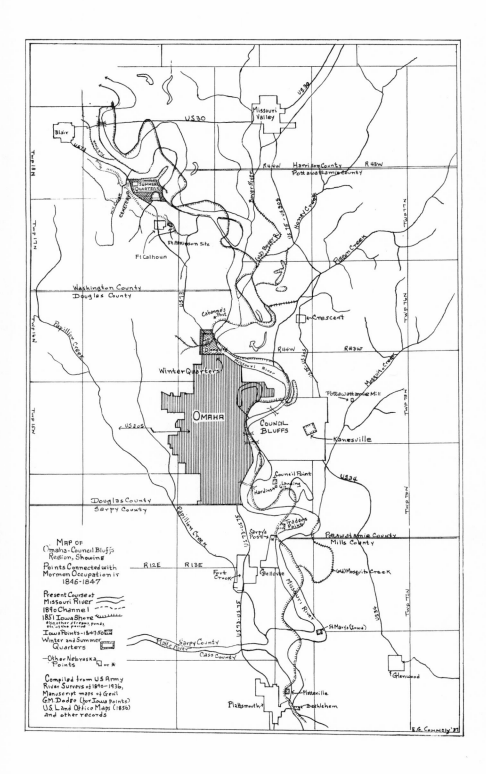

MAP OF
Omaha-Council Bluffs
Region, Showing
Points Connected with
Mormon Occupation in
1846-1847

Present Course of
Missouri River
1890 Channel
1851 Iowa Shore
also other streams, ponds,
etc. of the period
Iowa Points - 1847.50
Winter and Summer
Quarters

Other Nebraska
Points ▫ or *

Compiled from US Army
River Surveys of 1890-1936,
Manuscript maps of Genl
G.M. Dodge (for Iowa points)
U.S. Land Office Maps (1856)
and other records

E.G. Connely '37

J. D. Lee runs 4 ploughs and a harrow, 4 of his men are out as teamsters, besides some are gardening, &c. Evening clear. At 7 J. D. Lee and lady took supper with Bro. G. Laub's, the morning previous with Jacob Woolsey's and dinner Magee Harris. Since preaching the feelings of the whole camp appearantly are revived and more united. At 30 m. to 8 the brethren of the camp met at J. D. Lee's, the meeting having been called to order by the Pres. pro tem (J. D. Lee). The hearding of our catle was taken into consideration and after much deliberation M. M. Sanders profered to heard all of the catle of the camp at this place for $1.50 cts. per day payable in the fall at harvest time in such things as our land produces at the mill prices at Winter Quarters, the catle to be well hearded, and should any catle stray away or let out through his neglect the damage of hunting and loss of the milk to be deducted out of the hearding, the catle to be out of the lot at the 2nd sounding of the horn which will be precisely at 1 hour by sun, the horn to be sounded 15 min. previous to the 2nd sounding to notify the milk maids to wind up their milking, the catle to be brought in at ½ an hour before sunset in the evening. And should we fail (E.I. the camp) to raise good crops, or have them destroyed by the Indians, &c., he is to suffer equal loss with us. Assented by the majority presant. 2nd. Voted that Wm. Pace, Anderson and all those who have sheep at this place, heard through the day and pen them at night and from this time fourth that they may be accountable for all damage done by the trespass of their sheep. 3rd. Voted that the members of the [?] turn out on Sat. next and build a bridge over Mire Creek so as to turn our catle off our ploughed lands. 4. Voted that Samuel Gully serve in the capacity of clerk; that a daily record be kept showing how every man employed his time, according to the request of Pres. B. Young. 5th. Voted that the firing of 3 guns in succession should

Arrangements for Herding Cattle

161

be the signal alarm when the camp wants help. Adjourned sine die. J. D. Lee, Pres. pro tem.[140]

Summer Quarters, Wednesday, May 5th, '47.
Morning clear, W. S., high. All hands were employed in preparing for planting. About 4 P.M. Jas. Allen returned from W. Q., brought Sister Binley to S. Gully. About 11 commenced raining.

Summer Quarters, Thurs., May 6th, 1847.
Clowdy, wind high S. Occasional showers of rain till noon, also again in the evening.

Summer Quarters, Fri., May 7th, 1847.
Cool, clowdy, W. N. The evening previous report came from W. Quarters that the Saints at that place were reduced to 1 meal per day (E.I.) many of them on account of the scarcity of provisions and that Geo. Miller and a part of the Puncah camp are going on to join Lyman Wight and McGarry the Indian prophet [141] and that the ferry is thronged continually with waggons to cross, that the scattering has become so general that Bro. J. Taylor and P. P. Pratt put a vetoe on any teams crossing without a certificate from Pres. I. Morly to show his approval.[142] Evening cool. W. high. Continued at the same point.

McGarry, the Indian Prophet

Summer Quarters, Sat., May 8th, 1847.
Clear and pleasant, W. low. At 7 o'clock a majority of

---

[140] This Journal, beginning at Summer Quarters, was kept as an official church record of activities there, omitting much personal matter. For that reason Lee always refers to himself by name.

[141] Members of the "Puncaw expedition" were disgusted because of having been ordered back to Winter Quarters. George W. Miller left Brigham to join Apostle Lyman Wight, who had led a company of Mormons to Texas in 1845. McGarry, the halfbreed Indian flute player, whom Brigham hoped to take west with him, seems to have developed into a prophet on his own account and probably for that reason Brigham withdrew his former invitation. This journal contains the only known references to "McGarry, the Indian Prophet," and his subsequent activities have not been recorded.

[142] The "Council of Twelve" represented supreme authority in Winter Quarters and exercised their power in this instance, although food supplies had been exhausted in camp.

the brethren in camp met at the creek east of the square and commenced building a bridge. Succeeded in getting the timber togeather, raised the butments and put the stringers. About 2 P.M. Bro. G. D. Grant, Jos. and Brigham Young, Pres. B. Young's sons, arrived from W. Q. Brought with them 18 head of catle to be hearded, said that a party of about 30 Omaha Indians drove 12 catle from a heard and butchered them, loaded the beef on their poneys and made their escape before a sufficient force could be raised to pursue them. However a few men came up with a part of them but were without arms. The Indians seeing the advantage that they had over them, cocked their guns and ordered the brethren to return, which they did. Evening clear. Bro. M. Harris started for W. Q. about 8 morning. J. D. Lee wrote a letter and sent by him to John Young (B. Young's Bro.) in answer to his request in which he said that he was not only ready but willing to render him all the assistance even to the last dime within the reach of his cobble toe.

Summer Quarters, Sund., May 9th, 1847.

Clear, rather cool, W. S. About 9 G. D. Grant, Brigham and Joseph returned. About 2 the day before Jos. Busby started for W. Q. At 11 the Saints met (that is, about ½ of them) for public worship at J. D. Lee's. The meeting called to order by J. D. Lee, Pres. pro tem, after which the brethren spoke in turns. Lastly J. D. Lee said that peace and union which is so essential to the happiness of all but more especially the Saints, was what he pled for, hoped and prayed for, and that our prosperity and safety depended upon it. Good feelings prevailed. About sunset J. Busby returned and at 7 the brethren met at J. D. Lee's and looked into consideration the proprity of dividing of the land down in the timber. Busby, Dun, Arnold, Kennedy, Johnson, Pace and Teeple had already taken claims

163

and run around their land [143] as they called it before a division could be made which caused some hard feelings with some of the brethren. J. D. Lee guarded the brethren against suffering their feelings to be aroused while speaking on the subject, consider it better to bend to each others interest, as Bros. should, and there would be no danger of doeing wrong.

Summer Quarters, Mon., May 10th, 1847.

Committee to
Divide Land

Clowdy, W. W. About noon cleared off. At 7 at the sounding of the horn the committee to divide the land met at J. D. Lee's and reported ready for business. Some hands were employed on the bridge, others ploughing. J. D. Lee was planting. About 6 Bro. M. Harris returned from W. Q. without success, the mill having been stopped to repair some of the troughs. Left the whole city measurably without bread. ¾ of this square is within [*fence?*]. Evening clowdy.

Summer Quarters, Teus., May 11th, 1847.

Clowdy, cool, W. N. Nothing worthy of note to record for today. Evening clear. At noon Samuel Gully started for W. Q. J. D. Lee received a letter from Bro. John Young asking for help to fit him out for the mountains.

Summer Quarters, Wed., May 12, '47.

Clear, cool. First camp generally employed in ploughing and planting. About 12 noon S. Gully returned from W. Q. Said the mill had started. Evening clear.

Summer Quarters, Thurs., May 13th, '47.

Morning clear, cool. About 7 Bro. M. Harris and W. Stewart started for W. Q. The camp in general employed in preparing for crops. J. D. Lee is planting, his women al-

---

[143] "Run around the land"—a squatter's custom in establishing a claim.

most unitedly affords him quite a help. Good feelings prevails in camp with the exception of J. Busby, J. Arnold, S. A. Dunn, Kennedy, T. Johnson and Wm. Pace, who have from the beginning rebelled against, doubting the authority of those that were appointed to preside, finding fault with everything that is done. Evening clear.

Many Wives Are a Great Help

Summer Quarters, Friday, May 14th, '47.

Clear and warm. J. D. Lee and family were planting corn, the remainder of the camp ploughing, clearing, &c. About 3 P.M. A. Weeks, G. W. Hickerson, Jas. Woolsey, Levi North and their families (all members of J. D. Lee's household) arrived from Mt. Pizgah. Their arrival produced no smawl stir among the connections. They came up like good and dutiful children, told their adopted father in the priesthood (J. D. Lee) that they and their effects were subject to his council in all things. Evening clowdy and warm. At 7 Hickerson, Weeks, North, Jas. and H. Woolsey, A. D. and David Young and their families met at J. D. Lee's and spent the evening in music and dancing before the Lord. At the close of the recreation J. D. Lee called them to order and after instructing them in the order of mirth and recreation bowed down in prayer before the ruler of all things. Adjourned at 11. Good feelings prevailed. At 8 M. Harris returned but with verry little meal. The mill was so crowded that it was almost impossible to get grindings. Rain about 12.

"Order of Mirth and Recreation"

Summer Quarters, Sat., May 15th, '47.

Lowery, warm. J. D. Lee took his family and Jos. Allen, S. Gully, M. Anderson and son and finished the bridge. The rebellious party were sleeping and working on their houses. About 2 started in for an evening rain. Just before dark Wm. Pace and Thos. Johnson met J. D. Lee while on the bridge with verry insulting language and

165

came nigh unto blows.[144] He told them if they did not repent speedily in the name of the Lord that they should atone for what they had done.

Summer Quarters, Sund., May 16th, 1847.

Still raining. This morning the range of the heard was changed over the N. side of the creek. At 12 noon about ½ the members of the camp collected at J. D. Lee's for public meeting, who addressed them upon the subject of union in the discharge of duty, after which Bros. Allen, Free and Houston bore record of the same. Evening rainy.

Summer Quarters, May 17th, '47.

Clear and cool. About 7 Bros. G. Laub, Miles Anderson, Mary Woolsey, David and Samuel Carns, started for Winter Quarters. G. Laub for Mo. About 1 P.M. W. Stewart and Alanson Allen came up. A. Allen wished to know what to doe. J. D. Lee told him to remove his father's effects and goods and assist him in putting in a crop, then [go] with him next spring. Evening clear.

Summer Quarters, Teus., May 18, '47.

Clear and cool. Quite a sevier frost. About 2 P.M. Father Isaac Morly, Bro. John Young, lady and little Jos. arrived from W. Q. Bro. Young and lady stopped with J. D. Lee's. Felt much pleased with our farm. Said that we had more land broken and corn planted than all the camp at W. Q. and the regions round about. Said that he was almost persuaded to remove up and stay with us. In the evening Pres. I. Morly, Jos. Allen, A. Weeks, I. Houston, G. W. Hickerson, Jas. Wools[ey] and several of the sisters met at and passed the evening at J. D. Lee's, dancing and

---

[144] In his *"Confessions"* Lee says there was a fight; he probably did not wish to describe it in this semi-official record.

enjoying the music. Adjourned at 9 by prayer from Pres. Morley.

Summer Quarters, Wed., May 19th, '47.

Clear, still rather cool. About 7 by request of Pres. I. Morley the brethren of the square were gathered at J. D. Lee's. Pres., in speaking said that so far as progressing in the crop line, he was highly pleased, but to learn that there was and still are feelings in and among some portion of the brethren in this camp, although those that are refractory and cherish bad feelings are but a smawl minority, still such things remaining among us is calculated to destroy the peace and happiness of the whole camp. It is wrong, brethren. Be united, yield to each others circumstances and when a general call is made for the good of the public by the man who has a right to council you, turn out, if it is to build a bridge or lots to secure your catle or any other public work wherein the whole are concerned, always do your part. Bro. Lee is the man to council you especially in my absence. Hearken to his council and all other men that God has set in authority to council in the things of this Kingdom, and if you do not, the day will come when you will regret that [*you*] did not. Pres. Morly said that would covenant with him to be united and endeavor to walk upright from henceforth. Jos. Busby said that [*he*] wanted to speak. Said that it has been intimated that all the members of this [*camp*] were first rate fellows but 5 or 6, and that means myself, Bro. S. A. Dunn, T. Johnson, Wm. Pace, J. Arnold and C. Kennedy, that we are the refractory persons. Now since the subject has been called in question I want the boil opened that we may see the extent. Samuel Gully said that he would prick the boil. Those five men that has been designated by 1 of their No. has been and are in all probability dissatisfied and cherished feelings against both Pres. Morley and Bro. Lee about the division

Morley Pleads
for Peace

Samuel Gully
"Opens the Boil"

167

of this land. Said that Bro. Brigham Young never gave
such instruction, and used an influence both in public and
private to cause dissatisfaction among the brethren to make
them revolt against what was done. This I no to be a
fact. Furthermore they have murmured and found fault
with every move that Bro. Lee has made since they have
been here and are now trying to slander him whenever they
are togeather. This I also know to be a fact. And when
by a vote of the camp we all agreed to divide the brethren
into 2 parts to build 2 separate lots for our catle, Bro. Lee
and those that occupied the N. and E. line of this square
built our lot, but they have not built theirs yet, but has
crowded their catle in our yard for 4 weeks past, and when
it was necessary that a bridge should be built, the men
that built the lot met and would have finished their portion the first day if those men, with some others, would
have done their part. The bridge lay still until the Sat.
following, about as we left it. Bro. Lee, finding that the
work dragged as usual, took his own family, Bro. Allen,
Anderson and myself joined him, and we finished it. Those
5 men worked on their houses. This I know to be a fact,
also. Still they have been imposed on according to their
story. S. A. Dun arose boiling over with rage, pooring
out the feelings of his heart; was checked by Pres. Morly.
He at first smote his hands togeather and positively affirm-
ed that he would not be interrupted while speaking. Pres.
Morly replied, you shall, sir, where I am. He then rather
calmed and tried to justify his party in the course that
they had taken. J. D. Lee arose, corrected several of his
excited statements, showed to the brethren the course that
he had taken, and the opposition that he had to contend
with from those persons, which had been grevious and
painful to him, yet in the midst of all opposition he had
strove for union and sued continually for peace but with
the residue of the members in camp he had no cause of

168

complaint. Jos. Busby followed, filled with personating speeches and threats. He was also checked by Father Mor-ly, who rebuked his spirit; told him that his spirit was not of God. Busby said that he kno it is. Father Morly said but perhaps he could teach him the spirit, but he did not believe it, then continued to chasten them and exhorted them to humility and union. Bro. John Young said that he felt to bear record to what Bro. Morly had said and continued to exhort them. Said that he had discovered in times past that refractorus persons generally come out on the dark side of the light house. Father Morley said that it was an easy matter to preside over men that was disposed to do right but arbitrary persons always caused trouble. Finally covenanted by the show of the right hand that for the future that all would strive to do right. Disolved at 8. Pres. Morly, J. Young and lady brakefast with J. D. Lee, insisted to have him come down to lay Bro. J. Young's case before the brethren at W. Q. At 10 they started for W. Q. Evening clowdy. About dark Bro. Burgess, A. Stout, Ander[son] and Allen returned with 500 lbs. of fish which they caught in a lake about 3 ms. above this point. Some Indians were seen skulking arround.

"Personating Speeches and Threats"

Summer Quarters, Thurs., May 20th, '47.

Cloudy with occasional gentle showers of rain. Held up about sunup till about 3 P.M. when Burgess, Stout, J. Anderson, J. Woolsey, J. Busby and Samuel Gully started on a fishing expedition. About noon David Young found sign where the Indians had taken a horse from the camp that was in the care of J. D. Lee. They were a party of the Sious. About 9 the fishermen returned having had moderate success. Evening rainy. W. shifted north.

Indians Steal a Horse

Summer Quarters, Fri., May 21st, '47.

Clear, W. N., rather cool. This morning the fishermen

changed their range but without success. Returned about 2 P.M. and started again for their old fishing ground. J. D. Lee is ploughing and braking. Run 6 ploughs. John Holman came up to farm and joined C. Kennedy. Evening clear.

Summer Quarters, Sat., May 22, '47.

Clear and warm. J. D. Lee's family were planting corn, beans, peas, mellons, squashes &c. Some 20 hands were employed consisting of men and women. About 30 m. to 11 J. D. Lee, Jas. Woolsey, A. Stout and wife, Wm. Burgess and Bro. Colling started for W. Q. About 2 P.M. met Sister M. Allen and family moving up to S. Quarters. About 6 J. D. Lee reached W. Q. where he met John Berry from Pizgah where he spent the night. Evening clear.

Winter Quarters, Sund. 24.

Rather clowdy, W. S. J. D. Lee was engaged in the forenoon in preparing teams and loading goods belonging to John Berry and the Widow Boss. At 11 Berry, Widow Boss and Nancy Armstrong [*No. 12*] started for the settlement at Winter [*Summer*] Quarters. At 11 the Saints met at the stand for public meeting. Presant of the 12: P. P. Pratt and John Taylor The Saints were instructed upon different subjects by P. P. Pratt, J. Taylor, J. D. Lee, Isaac Morly and Father Smith. All in turns pled the cause of the poor. P. P. Pratt said that no person should be held in fellowship that left for the mountains without first securing a certificate showing that he had done his portion of the ploughing in the Big Field and those that left without this certificate should be considered as belonging to the anti-covenant and field party. J. D. Lee said that a people well organized and firmly bound togeather by union so as to harmonize with regularity from the head down always would prosper but for the want of that

Certificate Necessary to Emigrate

170

union, order and government company fail to flourish. Said that he with 2 men and 2 boys and by the help of his women had actually cleared, ploughed, harrowed and planted about 75 acres of land this season besides removing, building shelters, and feeding 65 persons consisting of women and children. He then said that Bro. B. Y's. last request to him was that he wanted his oldest Bro. to go on in the first Co. that starts for the mountains and as one who covenanted to carry out his council which was the rev[*elation*] of the Lord concerning the organizing and journeyings of the whole camp of Iseral felt determined to redeem his covenant. Donated $10.00 for Bro. J. Young's benefit, the remainder of the brethren $2.35 cts. J. D. Lee then gave a good substantial yoke of oxen for $37.65, to make out $50.00, which was the amount required in cash to secure his outfit. About 3 called in at Sister B. Young's, took some refreshments and received a map of Texas, Oregon and Uper California as a present from Col. Thos. L. Paine [*Kane*] of Philadelphia.[145] About 4 started for (S. Q.), walked on foot near 14 ms. Evening rained.

Maps from Col. Kane

Summer Quarters, Mon., May 24th, '47.

Rain all day.

S. Q., Teus., May 25th.

Clear and pleasant. About 8 Jos. Busby and T. Johnson started for W. Q. Camp again ploughing and planting. About 5 Bro. John Scott arrived in camp. Brought 25 gallons whiskey,[42] some tobacco and salt which I soon bought. Paid 50. for whis.

Summer Q., Wed., May 26th, '47.

Clear, W. S.W. At 8 Bro. Scott left camp and J. D. Lee removed a part of his family 3 ms. below the main camp

---

[145] Before leaving Winter Quarters Brigham Young had been been supplied, by Thomas L. Kane and others with all the latest maps of the west, Fremont's Report, and Hastings' Guide.

171

to put in more grain, having put in all the land allotted to him that was nearer. About sunset Busby and Johnson returned. Reported that a steamboat had arrived at W. Q. on Mon. 24th, and one on Wed. 26th, loaded with goods and passengers for W. Q. About dusk the camp were called togeather by J. D. Lee and the following resolutions passed. 1st, that no catle be turned on this bottom loos so as to damage the crops. Any man thus violating this ordinance shall pay the damage. 2nd, That the calves be kept from doeing mischief. 3rd, that the fence be made on the W. line by the party concerned on the morrow. 4th, that C. Kennedy's land be fensed by the camp on Sat. 29th. 5th, that J. D. Lee Co. fence the lower line of the farm, the remainder of brethren the W. point. Adjourned sine die.

Summer Quarters, May 27th, 1847.

Clear and warm. The camp engaged in planting. Evening clear.

S. Quarters, May 28th, '47.

Morning clear and warm. About 3 P.M. John and Barton Burrell arrived in camp from Indiana. Bros. to Sister Mary Woolsey. Wished her to go to some justice or judge and acknowledge the deed or dowry to her estate. Evening clowdy.

Summer Quarters, May 29th, '47.

Clear and warm. At about 12 noon J. D. Lee, Racheal [*No. 6*], and Mary Woolsey and the two Burrells started for Winter Quarters. Spent the night in W. Q. About 9 rain came like a torrent. J. D. Lee bought some clothing and provisions for Sister Lucinda Pace.

W. Quarters, Sund., May 30th, '47.

Clowdy with occasional showers of rain. About 1 P.M.

172

J. D. Lee and Co. crossed the Mo. river and traveled to Musketoe Creek. Staid over night. Clowdy.

Musketo Creek, Mon., May 31st, 1847.

Clear, wind south. Traveled 25 ms. and struck camp at a point of timber which we called Point Convenience. This evening one of our horses tired out.

Point Convenience, Teus., June 1, 1847.

Clear and warm. Started about 7. Reached Hunsacker's ferry about 6 eve. Attended to business, then returned and spent the night at S. B. Frost's.

In the Neighborhood of Austin P. O. office, June 2nd, '47.

Clowdy. About 9 J. D. Lee returned to the store and made a bill of $30.00. Returned to Bro. S. B. Frost's and tarried till morning. Found them a little disaffected and rather inclined to murmur, Sister Frost in particular. I reasoned and preached to them till about midnight.

Austin P. O., June 3rd, 1847.

Cloudy, misting of rain. Started for Winter Quarters about 7. Reached Point Convenience about sunset where we encamped for the night. Evening clear.

P. Convenience, Fri., June 4th, 1847.

Clear and pleasant. Heavy dews. Started about 7 having been detained on account of my team being out the way. About sunset reached Musketoe Creek and took up camp. Cloudy.

M. Creek Encampment, Sat., June 5th, 1847.

Cloudy. Started about 6. Called at Bro. Bean's and got Nancy the 2nd [*1st*] [*No. 2*] goods. Reached the ferry about 5, found about 60 waggons waiting to cross. About sunset reached Sister Pace where we tarried till morning. Bought about 15.00 worth of goods at the new stores.

Winter Quarters, Sund., June 6th, 1847.

Rather cloudy. Succeeded in getting some grain ground. Got a mule in place of my tired horse of Bro. M. Harris. Heard that Bro. L. Stewart had arrived. Brought with him Sister Gilliam [146] and Drusilla Holt. But every sweet has its bitter. This morning Sister Allen was murmuring because she was not fit out to go over the mountains. Reached Summer Quarters about 5 P.M. Found all well and prospering and doeing well. Met Bro. L. Stewart and Sister Gilliam firm in the faith. I had considerable conversation with them about their mission and what plans they laid in order to get away without suspicion &c. About 9 commenced raining and continued nearly all night.

Summer Quarters, Mon., June 7th, 1847.

Cloudy and occasional showers through the day. The brethren in camp employed generally in building. Evening pleasant. About 3 P.M. Comstock, T. Johnson's brother-in-law from N. York arrived.

Summer Quarters, Teus., June 8th, '47.

Clear, warm. About 10 Samuel Gully, Nancy the 2nd [No. 12], Mary Woolsey the 2nd, Clarissa Allen, 2 Mrs. Gulleys and James Young started for W. Q. The day pleasant. Planting and ploughing was the general occupation of the day. About 6 evening verry [heavy] rain. Wm. Swap came to camp.

Summer Quarters, Wed., June 9th, '47.

Clear, yet the earth covered in water where it is low. Nothing of note to record. J. D. Lee closely engaged in build-

---

[146] Levi Stewart had been successful in his "mission" (see note 72). The "bitter" refers to Drusilla Holt. Sister Gilliam, the "sweet," was the wife of Isham Gilliam. Lee had converted her to Mormonism while on a mission to Tennessee.

ing. About 8 S. Gully and Co. returned. Reported that the mill dam had broken away the night before.

Summer Quarters, Thurs., June 10th, 1847.

Clear, W. N.W. J. D. Lee and some of his family were ploughing and harrowing corn (namely) A. D. Young, Allen Weeks, G. W. Hickerson, Jas. Woolsey, Levi North, Wm. Swap, Jacob Woolsey, Hyrum Rheu[??] and Woolsey, Allanson and Marshal Allen, Wm. Woolsey, David Young and Eli Bennett; of the women Nancy the 2nd [*No. 12*], Nancy the 1st [*No. 2*], Racheal [*No. 6*], Lovina [*No. 13*] and Nancy Ann, Emoline [*No. 11*], Lucinda and Louisa Free [*No. 3*]. About 2 Pres. Isaac Morly arrived in camp and returned same day. Evening clear.

Summer Quarters, Friday, June 11th, 1847.

Clear. Ploughing and planting was the occupation of the day. About 4 P.M. Bro. Wm. Pace returned. Had to cross the river before he could get meal or stuffs at 63 per bus. Br. Gully's boy returned with him. About 5 rained.

Summer Quarters, Sat., June 12th, 1847.

Cloudy, about noon rain, light shower. At 3 Wm. Swap started for W. Q. The day previous I had [*made*] a mortar with a spring pole to beat corn into meal, it being the only alternative left by which we could get bread without going some 150 miles. Trouble in camp. The [*stock*] destroying our crops.

Trouble in Camp

Summer Quarters, Sunday, June 13th, '47.

Clear. About 10 A. Weeks, Levi North and A. Weekses son started for the settlements in Mo. with 2 waggons, 4 yoke oxen for provisions. Levi, Wm. Swap were to labour for eatables while the other 2 boys were to return, having money to buy the first load. At 3 P.M. the Saints met at J. D. Lee's for public worship. The congregation ad-

175

dressed by Levi Stewart, Johnson and Lee. Good feelings generally prevailed. Adjourned at 5 P.M. The brethren were requested to remain that were presant and those that were not were sent for. At 15 m. to 6 the brethren were called to order by Pres. J. D. Lee who said the meeting was called for the purpose of taking into consideration what policy, course or plan would be best to take that we may secure our crops. The ordinance passed 3 weeks since has not been complied with. The catle has been suffered to run over our ground and destroy our crops continually. I will say that there has not been a day nor a night but what there has been more or less stock turned off our crops. Since dark last evening I have turned out 26 head; 10 days hence that No. of catle within 24 hours time on our crops would positively destroy $500 worth. Now brethren I am not disposed to complain or find fault with any person although I have suffered more by the catle than the whole camp, still I never thought that any one [would] let their catle run at large designedly, but that it was through an over anxiety to put in all the grain that they could, thinking that that was no inducement for catle to run on the corn. Now let the past suffice and let us do better for the time to come. The subject is now before you. Speak your feelings. The deliberation lasted near an hour. Some were in favor of caning their work catle up at night but for the families that have gone down into the timber to remain untill they were done planting, others that all the catle be put in the common lot every night. J. D. Lee said that he should like to bend to all of their wishes could he do it without the risk of too great sacrifice. Past experience has certainly been sufficient to admonish us that nothing short of shutting down the gate and let no catle stay or stop short of being put in the lot or over the creek of nights and that no catle be permitted to be drove even through the farm without having them

176

yoked and if more than 1 loke, chain them togeather. Bro. [?] motioned that the gate be shut down, and carried unanimously, and was also carried that each man take care of their calves. Adjourned sine die. I passed [?] of the meeting in conversation at Bro. Harrises and had stew for the stomach's sake.

Summer Quarters, Mon., June 14th, '47.

Clear and warm. The camp still planting and plowing. J. D. Lee has finished planting corn and is today ploughing corn. Weeds ½ thigh high. Evening pleasant.

Summer Quarters, Teus., June 15th, 1847.

Cool and cloudy. J. D. Lee finished ploughing, harrowing 40 acres corn. The camp all contending with the weeds. Evening pleasant. At 6 Jas. Young (B. Y.'s nephew) . . .

Summer Quarters, Wed., June 16th, '47.

Cool and cloudy. About ½ past 6 J. D. Lee took 14 hands and 4 ploughs and went and cleaned out about 6 acres of corn that was in the weeds almost waist high for Bro. Martin and was to take shoe making in exchange. Evening cloudy.

Summer Quarters, Thurs., June 17th, '47.

Clear, warm and sultry. About 12 noon clouded up and about 3 a heavy storm of rain and hail from the N.W. run through our yards and gardens like a mill tail. Washed up considerable of the garden and stuff. Sister Caroline C. Saunders [147] has been employed yesterday and today tayloring for J. D. Lee making him a suit of Rusia Duck. Last evening I was called to administer to Sister Woolsey,

Sister Caroline Put to Work

---

[147] Caroline C. Saunders, later written C. H. Saunders, was Mrs. Caroline Hooper Saunders Gilliam, the runaway wife, daughter of Elisha Saunders, wealthy farmer and boat builder on the Cumberland River near Gainsborough, Tennessee. Lee had baptized her there in 1841, at which time she evidenced considerable friendship for him.

Rhoda Young and C[aroline] C. Saunders. Sister Woolsey the 2nd was suddenly attacked with a pain in her arm which was instantly made whole. The others were also benefited.

Summer Quarters, Fri., June 18th, 1847.

Light clouds flying. The earth almost inundated in water. We were employed in getting puncheon timber, hauling brick and finishing rooms. The brethren were generally at the same employment. About [?] Cobly came up from Winter Quarters. Stated that the bridge was washed away. Evening clear.

Summer Quarters, Sat., June 19th, 1847.

Clear and warm. About 9 Bros. Martin, Houston, Tuttle, and G. W. Hickerson started for W. Q. for provisions. Bro. Canida and L. Stewart having traced out a new rout on a divide heading the creek that the bridge alluded to was on. All hands generally working on their houses. About 2 Pres. I. Morly arrived from W. Q. Stated that he had been at the Horn and that about 500 wagons had already crossed ready for the mountains.[148] Evening clear.

Departure of More Emigrants

Summer Quarters, Sund., June 20th, '47.

Clear, warm and comfortable. All the Saints met at my house for public meeting. House was called to order by Pres. J. D. Lee and prayer by L. Stewart. The assembly was addressed by Pres. J. D. Lee on the subject of the dealings of God to his people, there duty and relationship to him, followed by A. P. Free, L. Stewart, J. Allen and J. Busby and others. After meeting J. D. Lee had some conversation with Sis. C. C. Saunders with reference to her intentions. Found that Bro. Wm. Pace and his lady

Ascertains Caroline's Intentions

---

[148] This was the second company of 1847 Pioneers.

Margarett had been trying to alienate her affectionate from him by fals statements which eminated doubtless from an evil and corrupt heart. The statements however Sister C. C. Saunders could not credit. About 5 Bro. Dunn, Martin, returned from W. Q. Reported that the mill was clear. Co. started and one of the brethren was shot through the hip [by] an Indian supposed to be of the Sious while on his way to the Horn. Pres. Morly also reported that a party of Sious had taken 2 horses and 2 head of catle from Bro. Kimble's farm 2 days since. Since writing the above I have been informed that Bros. Frances Weatherbee and Lampson were togeather when a party of 3 Indians evidently Omahas, naked, armed with guns, attacked them, cocked their guns. The 2 men without guns sprang at them and seized 2 of their guns, the 3rd Indian stepped off about 15 feet and when he saw that our brethren were using them up, shot Bro. Weatherbee as above stated. At the fire of the gun they all ran for life.

Summer Quarters, Mon., June 21st, 1847.

Clear and warm. The camp generally weeding their crops. About 9 Emoline Lee [No.11] started for W. Q. in Co. with Elizabeth Fairchild. J. D. Lee followed them and overtook about 6 ms. from S. Q. Told them the impropriety of such steps. Emoline promised reformation and returned home again.[149] Evening about 3 G. W. Hickerson returned from W. Q. with a load of provisions.

S. Quarters, Teus., June 22nd, '47.

Clear, warm. Ploughing was the general occupasion of the camp.

S. Quarters, Wed., June 23rd, '47.

Clear, W. S. About 9 J. D. Lee commenced ploughing for

---

[149] She left Lee later in the summer to live with Charles Kennedy, his bitterest enemy at Summer Quarters.

buckwheat. He and A. D. Young were employed in finishing room, the other hands plowing and howing. Evening clear.

S. Quarters, Thurs., June 24th, 1847.

Clear and pleasant. About 8 J. D. Lee took little Wm. Woolsey and Eli Bennett, Rachael, Emoline and Nancy and went to the old Ft. for a load of brick. Stopped and built by the way a bridge over South Mire Creek. Cut 10 stringers 20 feet long with the help of J. Berry. Bedded in and coupled the bridge so as to cross with safety. Day remarkably warm. Returned about dark.

Bricks from the Old Fort

Summer Quarters, Frid., June 25th, '47.

Clear, remarkably warm. J. D. Lee's teams went again for brick. A king boalt of one of the waggons broke while crossing the creek. About 5 Pres. I. Morley, Bro. Whiting and F. W. Cox arrived in camp from W. Q. Said that the agent upon hearing the depredations that had been committed by the Omaha Indians ordered 50 men armed and equipped to meet them at the town of Belle View to join a force of 150 men which he would raise from the other side of river. Accordingly the men were raised and put under the command of Capt. Stout and marched on Thursday morning to Belle View. Was met coldly by the interpreter and agent. Said that Jesus Christ could not hinder them from killing the catle. Finding that they only wanted a pretext to justify them in calling the militia on us, Stout and Hyde and Stout told the agent that they would make no . . . .

Expedition Against Omahas

Summer Quarters, Sat., June 26th, '47.

Clear and warm.

S. Quarters, Sund., June 27th, '47.

Cloudy. At 11 the Saints at the sounding of the horn met

at J. D. Lee's for public meeting and 30 m. to 12 noon Pres. Morley addressed the meeting upon the subject of self government, followed by J. D. Lee, Samuel Gully, F. W. Cox. Good feelings prevailed. Meeting closed by J. D. Lee. After the close of the forenoon services several children were presented to be blest, whereupon Pres. I. Morly instructed them uppon the order of blessing children, after which the names, ages and birthplaces of those that were blessed were recorded by J. D. Lee on this and the following pages. At the close of the meeting the table was spread and Pres. I. Morley and lady, L. Stewart and lady, F. W. Cox and lady, G. W. Hickerson and lady, Sister C. H. Saunders, Drusilla Pearson [Holt], Nancy Gibbons [No. 12], A. D. Young and lady and J. D. Lee's family sat down and partook of the rich festival that had been prepared by J. D. Lee. After which Magee Harris and lady who also dined and C[aroline] H. Saunders received their blessings.

Adolpha and Rhoda Young, parents of Adolpha Allen, born Nauvoo, Hancock County, Ills., March 12th, 1846, blessed by Pres. Isaac Morley and F. W. Cox at 12 m. to 3 o'clock P.M. Levei and Arminta North, parents of Levei North, born Mt. Pizgah, Pottowattomy Nation, November 7th, 1846, blessed by Pres. I. Morly and F. W. Cox, 10 mi. past 2 P.M. Frederick Walter Cox and Cordelia Cox, parents of Lovina Emoline Cox, born Mt. Pizgah, Pottomatomy Nation, Sept. 21st, 1846, blessed by Pres. I. Morly and F. W. Cox, 15 mi. to 3 P.M. Allen and Sarah Ann Weeks, parents of Sarah Ann, born Nauvoo, Hancock Co., Ill., Jany. 18th, 1846, blessed by Pres. I. Morly and F. W. Cox, 18 mi. past 2 P.M. Allen Weeks and Malissa, parents of Williard Wilbur, born Mt. Pizgah, Pottowatomy Nation, March 13, 1847, blessed by Prest. I. Morly and F. W. Cox, 22 mi. past 2 P.M. George W. Hickerson and Sarah, parents of Joseph William Hickerson, born Nauvoo, Hancock County, Ill., March 21st, 1845, blessed by I. Morley and F. W. Cox, 20 mi. to 3 P. M. Thomas and Julia Ann Woolsey, parents of Margarett, born Summer Quarters, Omaha Nation, April 29th, 1847, blessed by Pres. I. Morly and F. W. Cox, 15 mi. to 3 P.M. Samuel and Ovanda Gully, parents of Henrietta, born Nauvoo, Hancock Cty., Ill., Feby. 8th, 1846, blessed by Pres. I. Morly and F. W. Cox, 5 mi. to 3 P.M. Daniel D. and Cordelia Iam McArthur, parents of Andrew Bird, born at Liberty, Adams Cty., Illinois, Dec. 23, 1842, at 8 mi. to 3 P.M. Thomas and Sarah Fuller, parents of Thomas Eldridge, born Summer Quarters, May 10th, 1847, at 3 o'clock P.M. by Prest. Morly and F. W. Cox. Edward Meeks and Hannah, parents of Maroni, born Town of Providence, Saratoga County, N. Y., Sept. 27th, 1840, blessed by Prest. I. Morly and F. W. Cox, 7 mi. to 3 P.M. William Maxwell and Lucretia Charlotta, parents of James Baily, born Lex. County, I. Territory, Oct. 30th, 1843, blessed at 10 mi. to 3 P.M. by Prest. I. Morly and F. W. Cox.

Sister Caroline's
Patriarchial
Blessing

Patriarchal blessing rec'd of Isaac Morley, Patriarch, in the Church of Jesus Christ of Latter Day Saints, given at Summer Quarters, Sund., June 27th, 1847.

Caroline Hooper Saunders, daughter of John and Mary Saunders, born Jan. 3rd, 1813, in Buckingham Co. near the Town Marysville, Old Virginia. Sister Caroline, in the name of Jesus thy Redeemer, I lay my hands upon thy head and I seal upon thee thy Father's blessing. Thou are No. with the seed of Abraham and a descendant from Joseph who was sold into Egypt, and this thy Father's blessing shall be a comfort to thee, for the spirit of truth shall manifest to thy mind, and make thy duties known, and thy path plain before thy face for thy heart has been willing to make a full sacrifice for the sake . . . . [150]

Summer Quarters, Mon., June 28th, 1847.

Clear, W. S.W. At 7 by order of Pres. Isaac Morley,
Counsellor J. D. Lee notified the brethren in camp to make
their proportion of public fence, gates, &c. that our crops
be no longer exposed and liable to be destroyed by our
heards as it have been. But for the want of a general interest a part of the south and west line refused to attend to
the call, namely, Wm. Pace, T. Johnson, S. A. Dunn, J.
Busby, J. Arnold and C. Kennedy. The above named *More Trouble*
persons J. D. Lee called upon and plead of them by virtue
and authority of his calling and in the name of his Master
to secure their fences along their line and if they did not
the curse of indolence and disobedience should follow them
and not the whole camp. He then took his own family
and built the north gate of the city and placed G. W. Hickerson to superintend it, who did honor and credit to his
employer and neatly executed the work. Levi Stewart,
Samuel Gully, Magee Harris and Jas. Anderson he also
put under the direction of Jas. Allen who built the east
gate. J. D. Lee was employed in building chimneys, A. D.
Young laying floors.

S. Q., Teus., June 29th, '47.

Clear and warm. The brethren generally in their crops and
sowing buck wheat. Evening clear.

Summer Quarters, Wed., June 30th, 1847.

Clear and warm. The general occupation of the camp was
ploughing. About 4 P.M. some young folks arrived from
W. Q. for the purpose of gathering berrys. Evening fair.

---

[150] Sister Caroline (Mrs. Isham Gilliam) was "blessed" preparatory to being
"sealed" to Lee as Wife No. 14. The blessing was never fully recorded in the
Journal, but the words "full sacrifice" refer to abandonment of her husband to live
with the "Saints."

Summer Quarters, Thurs., July 1st, '47.

*Isham Gilliam
Comes for
Caroline*

Clear, wind W. At 6 J. D. Lee took a part of his hands and went to the lower farm and commenced ploughing corn. Sowed 6 'acres of buck wheat. About 6 P.M. Bro. John H. Redd and Isham Gilliam [151] both Rutherford Co. men (Tenn.) arrived in camp. Isham Gilliam was in search of Caroline [*Saunders*], his wife according to Gentile ceremonies. They were brought to this place from W. Q. by Horace H. Eldridge, Marshal of the camp.

Summer Quarters, Fri., July 2nd, 1847.

Cloudy, heavy storm passed arround westward. About 8 morn. ploughing and sowing was the business of the camp.

Summer Quarters, Sat., July 3rd, 1847.

Fatal Accident

Clear, warm and sultry. Ploughing was the business of the camp. From 12 noon till night J. D. Lee spent with his strange friends who dined with him about 11. Alanson Allen started for Winter Quarters taking with him old mother Lytle, Nancy Lee, Mary Lane and Julia Wool[s]ey who all met a fatal accident by the upsetting of the waggon in Mire Creek, throwing the 4 women into the creek with their children with the waggon bottom side upwards over them. Old Mother Lytle unfortunately fell on a leg, one of the women fell on her, and 2 or 3 sacks of grain, which bruised and mangled her shockingly, disjointing her hips and bruised her bowles. The others received no serious injury. About 2 P.M. S. Gully returned from W. Q. and brought the information. J. D. Lee immediately sent another waggon and team and brought them back to camp. Alanson, after drying his grain, went on to Winter

---

[151] John H. Redd, an old sea captain, formerly from South Carolina, had protected Lee when Mormon missionaries in Rutherford County, Tennessee, had been attacked by a mob. He later became converted and the prefix "Bro." indicates he was a Mormon at this time. Isham Gilliam, husband of Caroline, the runaway wife, appears to have been a Mormon, otherwise he would not have been directed to Lee's camp, and Lee would not have offered hospitality. If a Gentile, he probably would have attempted to kill Lee.

Q. About 6 Marshal Allen who was returning back with the broken waggon, saw some of J. D. Lee's boys on the prairie, who had been out on a hunt (of deer). Supposed them to be a party of Indians, left his oxen and fled to camp with the report, whereupon J. D. Lee took some 8 or 10 of the brethren and started to rescue the team; met the boys with it and told the joke. Evening pleasant.

S. Quarters, Sund., July 4th, '47.

Morning clowdy, W. S. East. About 11 Bros. John Lytle and E. P. Dusette arrived from W. Quarters. Found his mother dangerously ill from her hurt yesterday. At 12 noon the Saints met at J. D. Lee's for public meeting. J. D. Lee addressed them uppon the subject of individual duty and responsibility of the Saints, followed by Jos. Busby, Baird S. Gully, and A. P. Free. Left Bro. John H. Redd [152] considerably difficulted in his mind with reference to removing W[est]. After meeting, Bro. Redd, I. Gilliam and Caroline and several others dined with J. D. Lee. About 3 rained and continued showery till sunset. Late in the evening a steam boat went down.

Brother Redd Is "Difficulted in His Mind"

S. Quarters, Mon., July 5th, '47.

Clear, wind S.W. About 8 Friend Gilliam, Sister Caroline and J. H. Redd started for Tenn., their native land. Before leaving Sister Caroline presented Sister Lee with some table linen, work pocket, pin cushion and $3.00 cash. About 4 P.M., A. Allen returned from W. Quarters with some provisions. Evening clear.

Sister Caroline Decides to Return

Summer Quarters, Teus., July 6th, '47.

Clear, W. South East, heavy atmosphere which caused a stupor of feeling in camp. About 20 m. after 11 A.M. Mother Lytle took her exit from time to eternity. About 12 noon J. D. Lee wrote J. Lytle, her son, A. Lytle, to

---

[152] John H. Redd later emigrated and founded the Redd family of southeastern Utah.

come and attend to her interment by Jos. Young (Pres. B. Young's son). At 3 P.M. A. Week arrived with 70 bus. meal.

Summer Quarters, Wed., July 7th, '47.

Visit from Mrs.
Brigham Young
No. 12

Clear, Wind S.W. About 11 Bro. G. D. Grant and lady, Sister Emoline Free and Tilley Young arrived and about 3 returned, left Emoline in camp on a visit with her mother and sisters. In the same carriage Nancy Lee went to W. Q. for the purpose of going to her mother's for turnips seed. Day warm. About 5 Pres. Isaac Morly arrived. Notified J. D. Lee to be and appear at W. Q. on Sat. 10th of July, '47, with his Co. from Summer Quarters to be organized acording to the patron [*pattern*]. Evening clear.

Summer Quarters, Thurs., July 8th, 1847.

Clowdy, warm and sultry. About 3 P.M. an angry cloud arrose from the N.E. acompanied with a heavy W. and a refreshing shower of rain. About 4 L. Stewart arrived from W. Q. with pullets. All were soaking wet.

S. Q., Fri., July 9th, '47.

Clear, warm, light breeze south. About 4 Pres. Isaac Morly started for W. Quarters. All hands in their corn fields and buckwheat.

Summer Quarters, Sat., July 10th, '47.

Clear, warm and sultry. About sunrise J. D. Lee and all his boys, Jacob Woolsey excepted, and D. Young who was sick, started to W. Quarters. J. D. Lee stopped at the 3 ms. creek and sowed 3 acres of buckwheat. Reached W. Q. at 30 m. to 12 noon and recorded the following minets (ss.) The meeting having been called to order by Pres. Isaac Morley who requested to know the No. of the old Capts. who were here who had not gone west this season. 3 Capts. of 50s were reported, namely J. W. Cummings,

B. L. Clapp and Benj. Brown. The Capts. of 100s having all emigrated Pres. Morly nominated J. W. Cummings and B. L. Clapp for the 2 Capts. of 100s. Carried unanimously. Then nominated B. Brown, J. C. Wright, G. D. Grant and Daniel Carn Capts. of 50s, Wm. Major counsellor to Pres. Isaac Morley to fill the place of John Young r??ed west. The Capts. of 10s to remain (E.I.) as many as are here. Jos. Busby, A. P. Free, Miles Anderson, A. D. Young and Isaac Houston were the Capts of 10s in the 1st division. The 2nd division followed the patron. The meeting was then left in the hands of the Capts. of 100s and 50s to continue the organization. J. D. Lee then went to John Berry's, had some conversation with Martha, also with John about his horse that had been taken by the Indians, then with Sister C. H. Saunders [*Mrs. Gilliam*] who was about to return to Tenn. Seemed much concerned about her future fate. Requested J. D. Lee to remember her in a future day. Tarried over night with M[*artha*] Berry [*No. 9*].

Sister Caroline Leaves with Regret

W. Quarters, Sund., July 11th, '47.

Clear and warm, light W. S. About 8 J. D. Lee, Martha Berry, G. W. Hickerson, A Colby, J. B. Teeple and J. Laird, also started for Summer Quarters. Left Nancy 2nd [*No. 12*] to tarry with Sister C. H. Saunders till the following morning when they were to start. About 1 P.M. reached the 2 m. creek. We met one of J. D. Lee's teams with several of his family who were gathering goose and rous berries which were in great abundance along the bluffs. J. D. Lee and Martha joined them in berrying. Reached S. Q. about 4 P.M. At 11 Elder O. Hyde preached at W. Q. His text was, There is a way that seemeth good unto man but leadeth unto death. Said in his remarks that all disobedient and unruly spirits would be servants in the next world. The idea was very offensive to Friend Gilliam. Evening clear.

S. Quarters, Mon., July 12th, '47.

Clear and sultry, remarkably warm. J. D. Lee, A. Weeks, Jas. and Jacob Woolsey and boys melted down one of their oxen. Thunder clouds in the evening but no rain.

Summer Q., Teus., July 13th, '47.

Clear, warm, light breeze from the south. About 12 noon Pres. Isaac Morley arrived in camp. Evening clear. A. Tuttle and John Holman arrived about 2 P.M.

S. Q., Wed., July 14, '47.

Clear, W. S., light. About 1 P.M. G. W. Clark with 1 of Pres. B. Young's waggons, with him Nancy the 2nd arrived. A. P. Free and M. Harris layed by their corn.

S. Quarters, Thurs., July 15th, '47.

Clear and warm, pleasant breeze S. W. By sunrise J. D. Lee and Co. were in the field ploughing and about 11 J. D. Lee and boys finished ploughing about 100 acres corn. Crops look remarkably well. 5 persons in camp sick (ss) A. D. Young, Rhoda Young, D. Young, S. Gully, and T. Johnson.

S. Quarters, Fri., July 16th, '47.

Clear and warm, light wind S.W. J. Arnold taken sick. J. D. Lee sowed some turnips seed. C. W. Whiting and some of I. Morley's family arrived from W. Quarters. Eve. clear.

S. Quarters, Sat., July 17th, '47.

Clear, remarkably warm, but little air stirring. About 3 P.M. clowd arrose in the N.W. acompanied with thunder but passed over and arround without rain, leaving the air rather cool. About 9 J. Busby and wife and T. S. Johnson started for W. Q.

S. Quarters, Sund., July 18th, '47.

Scatering clouds are to be seen this morning in the upper hemisphere. About 6 J. D. Lee was called in great [haste] to administer to S. Gully who was cramped almost to death. When administered, lay speechless but soon recovered. Soon afterwards, D. Young was taken in the same way. A. D. Young and Rhoda but little better. Evidently a desease and pestilence not common to our country. About 10 A. Weeks and son with H. Woolsey started to Mo., J. D. Lee to Winter Quarters, who called by the way of H. C. Kimble's farm. Found some sickness in their midst. Crops fine. Grasshoppers troublesome on their buckwheat. Met Jas. Bean going to S. Q. Reached W. Q. about 3, he [Lee] being cited before the High Council by John Berry, appeared. The Pres., A. Cutler, proffered inasmuch as the evening was far advanced to let a committee of 3 of the Council decide between the parties concerned. J. D. Lee said that nothing very serious existed between he and Bro. Berry. That if other folks would attend to their matters and let him alone the Council would not have been troubled with the case now depending. Pres. A. Cutler nominated G. W. Harris, Isaac Morley and Winslow Farr for the committee. Carried. High Council desolved at 20 m. to 7. The committee proceeded, called J. Berry's charge, which read as follows: I prefer charges against John D. Lee for letting my horse be lost which I left with him and for refusing to make full and entire satisfaction for the same. Signed, J. Berry. J. D. Lee answered when asked (by the Pres.) what have you to say to the charge, the horse aluded to was left with me and lost or stolen by the Indians while in my charge. But there are circumstances connected with the loss of the horse that I wish to bring before this honorable council for your consideration when in order. John Berry in confirmation of the charge said that about the 1st of Mar. '47, he reached W. Q. from Mt.

Church Trial
Over a Horse

189

Pizgah with one of his horses tired out so that he was unable to return with him. Went to Bro. Lee who let him take one of his mules to return for his family and in the meantime agreed to keep his tired horse until he should return, and feed him 20 years corn per day with roughness and water for which he was to satisfy said J. D. Lee on his return for the same. The horse has either been stolen . . . . Thos. S. Johnson, witness for the plaintiff was called up. J. D. Lee by permission requested the clerk to pen down the testimony of the witnesses as they might be called for hereafter. Witness continued. Said that he knew but little about the horse or contract last winter or rather spring. He saw the horse running loose in J. D. Lee's lot and among his hay stacks. I tied him up and Wm. Woolsey said that J. D. Lee wanted the horse to run at large in the lot, but how much corn he got he knew not, but did not think that he got much and about 5 days or 6 after the horse came he was limping and that he saw no more of him until he was brought up to S. Quarters. The next he saw J. D. Lee's boys were laying off corn ground with him and all at once the horse was missing but where he went he knew not, only as it was reported that I had run the horse off. J. D. Lee, he was told, reported it. Jos. Busby testified that Geo. D. Grant sent word by him to J. D. Lee that if I did not get the horse away and feed him that he would die and that the horse did not cross the little Indian bridge as has been reported for Bro. Arnold said that he broke up the bridge 2 months before the horse was missing and that he and C. Kennedy had trailed the Indians for several ms. and that the horse track was not among those that the Indians had. There was a large track but was not shod and the tracks that were found at the bridge were made by Pres. Young's large horses and asked G. D. Grant if old Stogy was not shod. G. D. Grant replied that he took off the shoes before sending him up

190

to the farm. However I do not believe the horse crossed the bridge. My impression is the horse was not watered when turned out and was mired in attempting to get water. Mrs. Kennedy said that he was not watered. Pres. Harris called him to order. Said that they wanted facts and not hearsay. Defendant's testimony: J. D. Lee said about the 20th of Mar. '47 Bro. J. Berry arrived from Pisgah with a part of Bro. C. C. Rich's family.[153] One of his horses was entirely tired out and unable to return. He tried for about 3 days to procure another to return for his family. I at length pitied his condition, knowing that he had a large family on his hands. I went to Pres. B. Young and told him the circumstances and asked him if I would be safe to loan him a mule.[154] He replied if I considered him a safe man and that he would return with[in] two weeks to favor him. I acordingly let him one of my largest mules telling him at the same time that if he could not return within 4 days not to start, for I wanted the mule to send on with the Pioneers. Said J. Berry asked me to feed his horse as he has stated, which I agreed and did until about the 4th of April about which time I with my families removed to Summer Quarters. But previous to starting I left 2 bushels of brand, 1 of corn, and money to buy more should it be wanted before J. Berry should return, in the hand of David I. Young and told him to take good care of him. He and I kept the horse 25 days when the horse got away from him. He spent 1 day looking for him but did not find him, so removed his father's family to S. Quarters. When J. D. Lee heard the horse had got away from him he immediately set out for W. Quarters in search of him but failing to find him got Bro. Alexander's boy to take him to Bro. G. D. Grant with whom I had made arrangements to send him to me by the earliest opportunity.

---

[153] See *"Charles Coulson Rich"* by Evans. Rich was founder of the Mormon colony at San Bernardino.

[154] John Berry was Lee's father-in-law No. 7!

191

Within 6 or 8 days I recovered the horse again and kept him untill about the 1st of June when he was stolen by a party [of Indians] according to the supposition of the camp. Bro. A. D. Young ploughed him about 3 days. I turned him out as usual and went to dinner between 1 and 2 o'clock he returned to work but could not find the horse. Continued to hunt him till dark but without success. The following morning David I. Young started early and searched till about 11. Returned and said that the horse had been taken across the little Indian bridge. His tracks he said were plain. I then instructed him to follow on the trail which he did for several ms. but lost it on the prairie. Pres. Morley testified that he heard the 2 men state the same about as Bro. Lee has. They were both lying sick and I believe that they stated the honest convictions of their hearts. Allen Weeks stated that A. D. and David I. Young said that 1 or 2 days after the horse was taken they went and tore away the bridge, found it strong and amply sufficient to bear any horse over and that he watered the horse before turning him out. J. D. Lee then submitted the case into the hands of the Council, who decided

that they believed that Bro. J. D. Lee had acted in all good faith without any necromancing whatever about this and that the loss of the horse was an unavoidable circumstance and that Bro. Berry should lose the horse and we also feel that Bro. Lee is willing to bear a part of the burden, should not charge for keeping the horse nor the hire of the mule. Bro. Lee said that he never intended to charge anything and that he honored their judgment and submitted to their decision although the use of his mule 11 weeks and expense of keeping the lost horse was more damage than 3 such horses were worth. J. Berry said he would have to do the same although the horse once cost him $45.

P. S. The witnesses of the plaintiff were influenced by prejudice which caused them to make such wild state-

192

EMMA BATCHELDER

A later portrait, exact date unknown.

Courtesy Clara B. Lee

ments, such as Mrs. Kennedy saying that the horse was not watered, when she lived at least a ½ mile from the watering place and considerable heavy timber between her and the water, was to make it appear that through neglect the horse mired, the bridge having been torn away 2 months previous, and was for the same purpose. O prejudice and envy, how unjust are thy decisions, how unrighteous are thy judgments. Historian. Tarried till morning in W. Q. at Sister Lucinda Pace's.

"Prejudice and Envy"

W. Quarters, Mon., July 19th, '47.

About 5 J. D. Lee was in the store kept by Rolfe Wooley and Beach. Settled up his account. Mr. Beach told him that he could have what goods he wished. Bought $17 worth. Left W. Q. about 7. Met J. Bean about ½ mile below the old Fort. He profered to take Nancy [*No. 2*] and child, board them and take them on next spring for what help and Co. she would be to her mother.[155] Reached the lower farm about 11. Stopped a short time with some of J. D. Lee's boys who were working out a piece of late corn. Reached S. Quarters about 12 noon. Found David I. Young in a high state of mortification, often calling for J. D. Lee and when he saw him was overcome with joy, grasped him by the hand and said, I much wanted to converse with you before I feel to sleep. Will you baptise me for my death? Yes, if you are able. So great was his anxiety to be baptized that Bros. Martin and Allen came in, took him and placed him in a large rocking chair, but he was so far gone that he was not able to sit up, fainting,

Nancy Bean Abandoned

---

[155] Nancy Bean, unceremoniously thrown out of Lee's family for no recorded reason, came to Utah with her parents and infant daughter in 1848. She soon married Zachariah B. Decker, a returned member of the Mormon Battalion, and with him was one of the early settlers of Parowan. The daughter, born Jan. 15, 1845, at Nauvoo, is Mrs. Cordelia Decker Mortensen, living (1937) at Sanford, Colorado. Because of her bitterness toward Lee, Nancy Bean never told her daughter anything of her early history as a wife of Lee. Cordelia, 91 years of age, learned the facts from the original Journal, on Jan. 22, 1937, while on a visit to Salt Lake City.

asked to be put back on the bed and spoke but few words afterwards, yet his countenance bespoke that he wanted to say something but could not. Placed his eye steadfastly upon J. D. Lee who observed his anxiety, said, David, be at rest, sleep in peace. If the Lord spares me I will be baptized for you and attend to all the ordinances for you that I can. These words appeared to calm his fears. He soon stopped struggling in death and fell to sleep without a frown on his countenance at 20 m. past 4 P.M. Just before his death his aged father was violently attacked with the same strange desease or plague of the last days. When attacked a hot fever in head and bowels inwardly acompanied with sevire pains in head, back and bowels, vomiting and seviere cramping and distress in the stomach and bowels which if not checked causes an inflamation after which they soon mortify, hand, feet and legs cold as ice. J. D. Lee consulted Pres. Isaac Morly about the propriety of dressing him in priestly robes (acording to his request) seeing that he had not received the ordinance of endowment in the Temple. He replied, the priestly attire is a patron for such as has attained to that knowledge. Still there can be no impropriety in gratifying him and his friends request, for certainly his friend will be passed through those ordinances and bring him fourth to that attainment as he was a worthy and exemplary young man. Acordingly J. D. Lee had him dressed and buried in his [*Lee's*] own robes.[156] Considerable sickness in camp. About 5 P.M. Jos. Busby returned.

S. Quarters, Teus., July 20th, '47.

Clear and warm. At 6 after conseling Pres. I. Morly, J. D. Lee, Levi Stewart and A. P. Free walked south about ½ mile and selected a burying place on a very high eminence in the prairie which by J. D. Lee was called (Fair View)

---

[156] Burial robes of special Mormon pattern.

and laid it off and commenced berrying in the N.W. corner running south.[157] J. D. Lee and G. W. Hickerson made the coffin and painted it green. J. D. Lee paid L. Stewart for digging the grave. About 1 P.M. Squire Wells [158] from Nauvoo, Wm. Cutler, Miss Gheen, Golden and another lady whose name I have forgotten arrived, took dinner with J. D. Lee, seemed highly gratified with our new location. Returned about 30 m. to 4 and between sunset and dark David I. Young was buried. About ½ the camp attended the funeral. At the close of the interment Pres. I. Morly returned thanks in behalf of the deceased and gave good instruction.

David Young Buried

David Isom Young, son of David and Elizabeth Young, bornd March 24th, 1826, in Jackson county, Tennessee, on Indian Creek, whare he rec'd the Gospel. Was a member of the 21st Quorum of the Seventy's, but had not the privilege of the ordinances of endowment in the Temple, in consequence of the shortness of time. He lived the life of a Saint, his walk and conversation was worthy of imitation. He fell asleep to waite the resurection of the just. He felt much concerned about his future destany, insisted on J. D. Lee to have his woorke carried out and to be buried in priestly robes. He died at Summer Quarters (of a desease not common to our people) (resembling that of the cholera) on the 19th of July at 4

---

[157] After a great deal of research Mr. E. G. Connely succeeded in locating the old Summer Quarters ("Fairview") cemetery. He says: "It was located on an unwooded point of the high bluff above Summer Quarters, giving a splendid view of the whole valley for many miles. It was approachable by wagons from only one point in the Summer Quarters area, the slope ascending from the site of the Summer Quarters buildings. It was the most beautiful site that could have been selected. There are now no surface indications of the graves, but Mr. Hineline, oldest living inhabitant of the region and owner of the land, visited the site with me. He and his father, a pioneer of 1855, knew the graves to be those of white persons because of their regular arrangement in two rows, but assumed they were soldiers from old Fort Atkinson, never having heard of Mormon occupation. There were no markers when Mr. Hineline first saw the graves (about 1870) but the two rows of depressions were plainly visible then. Their location is definitely known, but no surface indications now remain."

[158] Daniel H. Wells, former "judge" in Nauvoo, later commander of the Mormon forces against Johnston's Army. He afterward married Lee's Wife No. 3.

P.M., 1847, and was buried on 20th at 7 P.M. acording to his request about half mile south of Summer Quarters on a high eminence in the prairie. The burying place was selected and laid off by John D. Lee, Levi Stewart and Absalom P. Free and was called Fair View by J. D. Lee. His grave is the first and was laid in the N.W. corner.

Summer Quarters, Wed., July 21st, '47.

Clear and warm, light wind S.E. Sickness increasing in camp. George D. Grant, Aunt Jemimah and Eliza Burgess arrived about 11 o'clock and returned about 4 o'clock P.M. with Emmeline Free [159] who had been in camp about three weeks. About 12 the wind raised. Evening clear.

Summer Quarters, Thurs., July 22, '47.

Clear and sultry through the day. Sickness still making inroads in the camp. About 10 o'clock George W. Hickerson, Sarah his wife, Rachel L. [*No. 6*] and William Martin started for Winter [*Quarters*]. Evening clear.

Fri., July 23rd, '47.

Clear, light breeze, atmosphere heavy and sickness raging. About six the brethren met togeather near the center of square by order of President Morley who said, Brethren, I have called you togeather to hear your grievances if any you have and try to have you put away all matter of differences that may be among you, that union may be in your midst. Some of you, I am told, are calculating to defer it till President Young returns, but I say you had better settle it before. You once covenanted before me that you would drop it and strive to be at peace that the spirit of the Lord might dwell in your hearts, but since that time

---

[159] Emmeline Free. one of Brigham Young's wives and sister to Louisa Free, Lee's Wife No. 3.

196

I have been told that some of you have maid threats, harsh and ungodly speeches and said that you would not settle it untill there was a proper and legal adjustment before President Young. Now, brethren, that spirit is wrong and is not of God and there is nothing that should ever exist to sever the union of Saints five minutes at a time and I am determined that you shall not break your covenants much oftener before I will cite you to Winter Quarters (some brother said will you cite us all to Win. Quarters), he replied probably I shall take some of you for crime and the rest for witnesses. I do not mean to frighten you with threats, brethren, still I mean to see if there is not power enough at Winter Quarters to settle your difficulties if it needs be that some of you be severed from this branch. After hearing what the President had to say they all agreed to drop all matters of diference and act like brothers for the future. About 10 Pres. J. D. Lee was suddenly attacked with the conjestic fever and about 1 P.M. A. P. Free, Elizabeth his wife and Louisa his daughter, the wife [*No. 3*] of J. D. Lee, started on a visit to H. C. Kimble's farm and about 3 P.M. G. D. Grant, Wm. Kimble and 2 other men came up from Winter Quarters. At 4 P.M. J. D. Lee verry sick and the most of his family.[160]

Sudden Illness of Lee

(Continued in Journal No. 7)

---

[160] Seventeen members of the Summer Quarters settlement died shortly after the conclusion of this Journal.

A list of those to be adopted into B. Young's family.

1. Jonathan Calkins Wright, born Nov. 29, 1808, Oneida County, N. Y. Rebeca Wright, Sept. 22nd, 1813, Penson [*Pennsylvania?*].

2. Jacob Secrist, born Sept. 18th, 1818, Franklin Co., Penn., petitioned April 1847.

3. John Kay.

4. Josiah Fleming Martin, born Dec. 15th, 1815, Huntington Co., Penn.

5. Wm. Martin, born Oct. 19th, 1811, Huntington Co., Penn.

6. Isaac Houston and lady.

7. Charles Dolton and lady. C. D. born Aug. 22nd, 1810, T. of Essex, Bradford Co., Penn. Elizabeth Dalton, born Feb. 10th, 18?6, Town of Walsworth, Ontario Co., N. York.

8. George S. Fowler and lady petitioned at Winter Quarters, Jany. 1847.

History of the 1859 Journal

❦

In the spring of 1859 Judge Cradlebaugh, accompanied by United States marshals and a company of soldiers from Camp Floyd, went to Cedar City, Utah, to conduct an investigation into the Mountain Meadows massacre. As a result, warrants were issued for the arrest of several leaders in the affair, all of whom went into hiding in the mountains. The first part of the following journal was written while John D. Lee was "on the underground."

After his death, the journal was in the possession of his wife, Rachel, who left it to her son, Ralph. It was kept with other old papers in a tin trunk in a shed at Lebanon, Arizona, where most of Rachel's descendants lived. Ed Richardson, husband of Effie Lee, a granddaughter, found some of the old papers scattered about the shed, realized their value as family records and replaced them in the trunk. The house was later rented to Mrs. Kate Rogers. When she moved away she found the journal among her books and returned it to Doyle Lee, brother of Effie, and son of John A. Lee. Doyle gave it to Mrs. Edna Lee Brimhall, granddaughter of John D. and Lovina Young Lee, his thirteenth wife.

When found by Mr. Richardson only a few pages were missing from the journal. Since that time other pages have been lost, so that the surviving portion is unfortunately fragmentary.

Other journals, of an earlier date, were at one time in the possession of Frank Lee, a son, living in New Mexico, but were destroyed when his residence burned. The journal of 1857-58-59, mentioned in the following pages, contained Lee's own story of the Mountain Meadows massacre, but has never been found. It was the volume immediately preceding this mutilated record. After his first trial in 1875, Henry Darrow, a son-in-law, with a stranger, went to Lee's home at the Ferry—presumably at the latter's request—took certain papers from his desk and ordered the rest destroyed, which was done by Emma Lee.

After his second trial and conviction Lee obtained a temporary release on bail and went to the Ferry to arrange his affairs. While there he wrote a story of the massacre and the manner in which he

201

had been "sacrificed," for the private information of his family. This paper was preserved by his daughter, Mrs. Amorah Smithson, until a few years ago, when one of her daughters destroyed it.

Diligent search has failed to disclose any other surviving journals and it is believed these two are the only records now in existence in Lee's own handwriting. The following journal containing entries for part of 1859, with the accompanying letters, have been copied by, and are here reproduced through the courtesy of Mrs. Edna Lee Brimhall, of Thatcher, Arizona.

JOURNAL OF 1859

❦

[*First sixteen pages missing. Page seventeen begins——*]

not as easy to scare as you are, and besides I was not in the country when it happened you g——d liars, Dam you, you are all engaged in it." Seeing that they refused to hear reason, he went on his horse and told them to kiss his ass: with that the sergeant ordered one of the Indians to shoot him. No sooner said than done, the ball whistling under his ears as he rode off. After their excitement was over a little they removed their quarters to the foot of the Santa Clara where they are waiting the arrival of Maj. Prince with 200 cavalry, escort and guard to the paymaster who has about one million dollars from California. Prince's division will then return and guard the 150 teamsters through to Cal. while Judge Cradlebaugh will return to Camp Floyd with the remainder of the troop; but before they return my scalp they want, let it cost what it may. They say that they would rather arrest me than to have all the Piedes, Haight, Bishop Smith and all other criminals, but catching is before hanging and my trust is in God.

Soldiers Want Lee's Scalp

Maj. Prince is expected up in 8 days. This evening passed off well. At 10 the brethren returned.

Pocketville is situated in a valley near the Rio Virgin river, valley narrow, mountains high and rugged, land sandy though fertile. Cottonwood timber in abundance, limestone rock generally. Range middling, the settlers industrious and every family has some fruit trees and corn, peas, beans, potatoes, etc., all look fine.

Wed. May 11th. Pleasant this morning. Bro. C. Hopkins left us with the intention of going north. D. C.[161] and Bro. also left to return to their planting. About 10 the Bishop, P. K. S.[162] and I concluded to change our quarters. Went into the settlement and got breakfast. I eat at Bro. Barney's. We then got up our animals and bent our course across the mountains up the Leverkins about 12 mi. distant from this place and camped by a precipice of lime stone rock.

Thurs. May 12th. We bent our course north up the Leverkin and at a distance of 5 mi. we ascended the mountain on the west side. Mountain is rough, rugged and steep, limestone. My horse is an exception for climbing mountains, going over rough country though he fell 3 times in ascending this mountain and slid down about 30 or 40 feet on a smooth lime stone angle about ½ pitch covered with a little gravel on top. But this however did not discourage him in the least. No sooner than he could get foothold than he was up and at it again, though he hurt himself badly in the fall. After I had ascended I found that I had lost 2 of my revolvers. The Bishop at this time was some ¼ of a mile north. I left my horse standing, saddle and bridle on, and started to hunt my revolvers thinking that I would find them on the mountainside, but I went back to camp following the trail, which was difficult on account of cattle tracks. On my way I met a large rattle snake. He offered fight and being the first snake that I saw in 1859 and according to tradition to kill the first snake is equivalent to conquering your enemies that year. So I blowed his brains out with my revolver.

---

[161] "D. C. and Bro." designates two of those implicated in the Mountain Meadows massacre, of whom we have no other information.

[162] Philip Klingen Smith, bishop of Cedar City, and one of the church authorities responsible for the massacre.

About 1 hour after dark I reached the summit almost tired out and famished for water and faint for the want of food. The wind blew like a torrent. I was in my shirt sleeves and my clothes wet with sweat. The change of atmosphere chilled me instantly and not knowing where my horse was, my blankets and coat was on him; traveling toward the place I left him, to my astonishment he was within 150 yds. of the spot and seemed glad to see me. I felt in my heart to bless him for his kindness. I fired off my revolvers thinking that the Bishop might be near by and return the signal. But in this I was disappointed. He supposing that I had gone ahead he pursued on; consequently I struck up camp without food and watter, having traveled near 30 miles.

Frid. May 13th. By day I was up, found my horse near camp, went to the brow of the mountain, asked the Lord to direct me to the spot where my revolvers were. I saw the spot and went to it, and there they laid about 100 yds. from where I stood. I returned thanks to God and mounted my steed and started in pursuit of my partner, P. K. Smith. Followed his tracks from range to kanyon over the roughest country that I ever traveled over before, and came up with him on Dry Kanyon some 6 mi. east of Harmony. Was much fatigued and worn, done a distance 20 mi. about 4 p.m. Here we encamped for the night.

A Miracle

Sat. May 14th. Pleasant. I stood on the summit of the mountain east of Harmony [163] about 12 noon and with my spy-glass looked over the whole valley. Saw some of my family; from this point I could overlook the whole country, from the tops of the mountains down to the base,

---

[163] Harmony, a few miles below Cedar City, was Lee's home at the time of the massacre, and was 12 miles in a direct line from Mountain Meadows.

205

and a more lovely and beautiful landscape I never saw before; the snow caped mountain on the south with the lofty pines on its summit clothed in their green foliage, gently sloping to the North and North East, tinged with red and blue down to the slopes of the mountain; the vale covered with green vegetation intermingled with shady groves of cedar, presented a romantic though majestic scenery. My residence and farm appeared more dear and lovely to me than ever; and above all, that of my family from whose society I was deprived by wicked and corrupt men, for the gospel's sake.[164] I saw the brethren and my family plowing, planting, hauling pickets, making fence, irrigating, etc., after which I descended into the field unobserved to a brother-in-law, Samuel E. Groves,[165] and sent him to Rachel, my second wife, to bring me some provisions, pen and ink and a pint of spirits; to meet me at the east end of my pasture fence, and let no person know my request, save it would be his father, E. H. Groves and Rachel. In a short time the old man came. Appeared glad to see me, offered his services in anything that he could. He then said that intelligence had lately reached here from G. S. L. C. that Gov. Cummings notified Pres. Young to prepare to defend himself against the troops; that the Judge was determined to hold court in S. L. City, and arrest him and his council the 12, and every other man that they wished, and that the Gov. Cummings could not control them. That all his efforts thus far in a measure was spurned at and had proved abortive and in vain. Pres. Young replied that the troops and officials were all in his hands and had been all the while and he by the help of the Lord could have wiped them out of existence long ago, but that he did not wish to shed blood if it could be avoided; but

[164] This entry indicates that Lee believed his participation in the massacre was "for the gospel's sake," and that the attempt to arrest him and others for the crime was purely persecution.

[165] Brother to Wife No. 15 whom he married in 1851.

if it must come we can control them and will do it, let them commence, and the first drop of blood or attack they make on any of the settlements or person belonging to this people their blood shall flow to atone for it. If this report is true it accounts for a dream that I had on the night of the 12th. (ss) I saw many of the cities of the Saints as though they were painted red as blood. Houses, roofs and all, even the fencing, railing, and everything was red. Again I saw as it were a river of blood. The blood appeared to be a little above the earth. I marvelled at the strange sight, yet I knew not the meaning thereof.

My wife having arrived with the articles that I sent for, father E. H. Groves returned. From her I learned that Jos. Johnson, a man that I hired for 8 months, became alarmed when the soldiers came,[166] and left for some more congenial clime, which to me was a great disappointment, as my crop was, and spring work was behind.

Rachel and I returned to camp, told Bishop P. K. Smith the news. We talked over Farnsworth vision, Pres. W. H. Dame's dream and our own, and said that the way things were shaping, it looked like bringing us to the test, etc. The Bishop then packed up, blessed each other and parted, he bent his way northward. I remained with my wife at the old camp ground.

Sund. May 15th. Pleasant. Some flying clouds. I arrose troubled in spirit, the cogitations of my mind through the night plainly indicated that I in connection with others were threatened with trouble, and that my eyes were not open to it, and that I must change my position, which I did after paying my morning's devotions to Him who rules all things, and asked Him to guide me through the day. Left my horse at the same place, hid my saddle, etc., took

---

[166] Soldiers accompanying Indian Agent Forney had visited Lee's home at Harmony searching for property and surviving children of the murdered Fancher party.

207

my position on an high eminence where I could overlook the country for the day, and to change my quarters when night would come.

Rachel returned. I spent the day in journal writing, reading, watching, etc. In the evening I returned to my old camp ground, saw the tracks of my horse where he had been around camp, but finding that I was gone, together with the camp equipage, he started out too, took my trail and followed it as far as he could track me for rocks. He then went to the field. I took my saddle and rigging to the field, turned my horse on the range and concluded to take the mountains on foot.

About 8 at night Aggathean, Rachel and Caroline, my first 3 wives, met near the east line of my pasture fence. They embraced me in their arms and wept with joy and sorrow. Brought with them excellent supper consisting of roast beef, short cake, pies, eggs, pancakes, butter and molasses. We sat down and eat together though my health was very poor.

I then blessed Rachel and Caroline and they returned home. Aggathean accompanied me to my retreat which was between two pinion pines and a cedar on a high eminence where we laid without fire to prevent discovery. After ascending the mountain I turned sick at the stomach and vomited several times.

Today I learned that one of my best cows fell dead a short distance from home, and while Bro. Tenny went to the house for a knife to skin her, a couple of pretended Mormons stole the hide and put off with it post haste. They were present when she died and knew that my wife would send Bro. Tenny to have her skinned.

Also learned that Father Groves and John R. Davies had been speaking lightly against those that the marshall had writs for. Said that travelers would impede the pro-

208

RACHEL WOOLSEY

A portrait taken in her later years.

Courtesy Edna Lee Brimhall

gress of the gospel. Fears were also entertained that should the troops visit Washington [*Utah*] in search of men, that one-half would turn traitors and go over to the soldiers. But such men are to be pitied and can only be looked upon as fair weather Mormons and not to be depended upon in the day of trial.[167]

Mon. May 16th. Pleasant. After sunrise Aggathean returned, took home my horse that was near the field.

Aggathean, Terressa and Jos., my son 13 yrs. old, were shearing my sheep. Have sheared 90 head in three days. Maryleah will help today. My pasture fence will also be finished today. The cost of my portion of it is about $3000.00 (Three thousand dollars). I sent word to Bro. Tenny, my foreman, to start 4 ploughs and put in the remainder of the oats, corn, peas, beans, squashes, melons, potatoes, etc., forthwith. Today I put on a pair of moccasins in order that my tracks might be taken for an Indian. This evening I took a shower bath for my health at the falls of Dry Creek. About 8 o'clock P.M., Rachel, Maryleah, Terressa, my wives, met me with hot coffee, beef steak, crab, custard, etc. From them I learned that I. Riddle and Wm. Slade from Pine Valley, had arrived. Reported the judge and troops at the foot of the Clara waiting the arrival of Maj. Prince from Cal. Had sent out a detachment to meet him. They are getting verry uneasy, and afraid too, for fear that the Mormons and Indians will cut them off. The fact is the fear of the Lord is fallen upon them in answer to the prayers of His people.

Rachel also informed me that Father Groves too returned. I had spoken to him for some seed corn, he being

---

[167] This and other entries definitely proves that many of the Mormon settlers in southern Utah did not approve of the massacre and were inclined to inform the soldiers of the whereabouts of those who were in hiding. Judge Cradlebaugh secretly received information as to the names of many participants, while in Cedar City, and when the people realized the enormity of the crime many of them expressed their contempt for the participants.

209

the only man to my knowledge in the country that has any to spare, and he is feeding his horses corn. I offered him 2 bushels of wheat for one of corn, which is double its value or $5.00 in cash per bushel for a little to plant, when it has never been sold for more than $2.00 per bu. He sent me word he could let me have 1½ bu. for a heifer, provided I would furnish him bran enough to feed his horses once a day through planting time; but $10 per bushel was no temptation to him. My wife replied that she would give him three bushels of wheat.

A Letter from Emma Emma, my English girl,[168] sent me a letter the better to express her feelings, as she was unable to come, expecting to be confined soon. The few words were as follows: My Dear Companion—It affords me joy that I cannot express to know that you are alive and have been safely delivered from the hands of your enemies thus far, who have been hunting you like a rowe on the mountain for the Kingdom of Heaven's sake. Yet I cannot but feel melancholy at times when I think of the sufferings and hardships that you must necessarily undergo in the mountains; saying nothing about the society of your family whom you love as dear as life. My prayers for your deliverance and safe return to the bosom of your family who loves you dear, has been unceasing. And although I cannot be with you in person to share your sorrows, yet the Lord knows that I am in spirit and I also bear testimony that your spirit visits us. May God speedily permit you to return home, for I feel as though I could not stay from you much longer. I am sometimes tempted to try to climb the mountains in search of you. God bless you, my dear, to live long on the earth to bless and enjoy the society . . . .

[*Pages 37 to 55 missing*]

---

[168] Emma Batchelder, a Handcart Pioneer from England, had been given to Lee by Brigham Young as "a reward for faithfulness" after the massacre.

and reported that Moore and Bennett were traitors and were supposed to be hunting me to kill me.

Rachel, Sarah C., Mary Leah and Mary Elizabeth and Henry took a ride on horse back to Fort Sydon. Apostate spirit manifested in different settlements.[169]

Mon. May 23rd. Fine. Today planted potatoes. Shell Stoddard took dinner with me, it being the first meal that I have eat in my house in 4 weeks.

Evening. Jos. returned from Pine Valley. Got 3 pecks seed corn from John Holley who kindly sent it without asking the price. I also exchanged my stallion Jim to C. Hopkins for a fine young stallion that I had sold him in the spring. Paid him $10.00 in the exchange.

Tues. May 24th. Planting potatoes, making water ditches, etc. Broke a plough stock.

Wed. May 25th. I with Bro. Hopkins stocked it again. Alma returned from Washington. Bishop Smith returned from the mountains; happy reception. Spent the night with me.

Thur. May 26th. All hands on the ditch taking out water. Drew an article of agreement with R. Woolsey, relative to our farming, etc.

Fri. May 27th. do.

Sat. May 28th. do. About sunrise Moquetas,[170] chief, and a number of Indians came in search of me at dawn, 5 mi. from home. They felt warm and greeted me with a cordial welcome. Related the bribes that had been offered them by Cradlebaugh for my head. $5,000.00 reward, a

---

[169] This "apostate spirit" refers to those who were inclined to inform against the participants in the massacre, and seems to have been more general than has been previously supposed.

[170] Moquetas was one of the Piede chiefs in command of the Indians at the massacre. When the cattle of the murdered emigrants left in Lee's charge had all been eaten, Moquetas and his band killed any beef with Lee's brand on it and made themselves a great nuisance at Harmony.

considerable reward for a man that is endeavoring to obey the gospel requirements.[164]

They also had a little squaw to trade me for a horse and wanted me to give them a beef and ammunition, flour, etc. Evening we all returned. Received a letter from a friend informing me that Cradlebaugh has offered a reward of $5,000.00 for my person or head, and that he intended to make an example of Haight, Higbee, Smith and Lee as well as myself.

Mr. Robb of Puragonah presented a note of $210.00 payable to Mr. C. H. Bright, which I sent the money to settle some time ago; but as the spirit of apostacy is so appalling I scarcely know in whom to confide save God, the arm that cannot be broken.

Sund. May 29th, 1859. This morning I gave the different chieves presents to the amount of some $20.00 in ammunition, shirts and provisions. I also gave Moquetus (chief) a young horse for an Indian girl some 8 years of age,[171] also traded for a buckskin. They having no regard for the Sabbath I was obliged to trade with them.

About 10 I went some 5 mi. with 12 persons and baptized 7 persons (ss) Nancy Emily, my daughter by Rachel, and Henry G. Birknell, Marcus Henry Darrow, a young man about 22 yrs. of age; and Louisa Evaline, my daughter by Aggathean; and Elnorah, a Lamanite girl about 13 years of age, also Alace, another Lamanite girl about the same age, of the Seebeets [172] tribe; also Rasmus Anderson Lynn, a young lad; and Mahonri, an Indian lad that is living with father E. H. Groves.

Returned home and had E. H. Groves and ladies, Bishop W. R. Davies and wife, John R. Davies and wife, Jos. Davies and Henry P. Young took dinner with me.

---

[171] It was customary among Mormons of that early period to purchase Indian slaves, but such purchases by Gentiles was prohibited by Brigham Young.

[172] Lee's spelling of the tribal name now rendered as "Shivwits."

H. J. Young was enrout from Cal. to Salt Lake City. At 3 p.m. meeting those baptized were confirmed and Sardle Jane Doldon's son was blessed by Bishop Davies, E. H. Groves, J. R. Davies and myself. I was then called to the stand and I preached to the Saints upon the fulfillment of prophecy—the apostacy and signs of the times; exhorted the Saints to faithfulness in the cause of truth.[173]

Evening I made arrangements with Bro. H. J. Young to take Sarah Jane back to Centerville to her husband.

Mon. May 30th. Pleasant. All hands on the water ditch except E. H. G. This morning I bought 250 lbs. salt of Hakes, paid him $20.50 in whiskey, wool, cards, etc., and sent to Parowan (36 mi.) for it. Sent Sarah Jane to Henry J. Young's camp; when she got there he declined taking her on account of his wife.

Bishop W. R. Davies and I regulated the distribution of water for irrigation. Ash Creek fell to me entirely and the ½ of Kanarah Creek.

Tues. May 31st. I with my help on the ditch. 4 Indians visited me and stayed over night with me. I gave them some ammunition.

Wed. June 1st, A.D. 1859. Planting potatoes, beets, corn, etc., irrigating and making ditch, etc.

Thur. June 2nd. do.

Fri. June 3rd. Planting corn, etc.

Sat. June 4th. Planting beans, squashes, melons, etc., irrigating, making ditches, etc., this morning. Bro. Sand Leigh stayed over night with me. Reported that I. C. Haight had returned; and that Judge Cradlebaugh was called, or rather removed from this Territory and that

---

[173] "Faithfulness in the cause of truth"—an exhortation warning the brethren not to betray those imvolved in the massacre.

an express had arrived from the States. Two men supposed to be peace commissioners had come in, but their business was not yet known. Troops rather uneasy for fear of the Mormons, etc.

Yesterday I had some sharp words with Bishop Davies and his son John about the water and his conduct towards my family while I was in the mountains secreted from the hands of my oppressors. He detained 24 hrs. of my water at a time when my crop was needing it. John, his counsellor, instead of comforting my family as a father in my absence, he would taunt them and intimate that it was just that we had to flee and hide—virtually accusing the Priesthood, for I with them was hunted for the same cause.[164] I told them that their authority and calling did not justify them in doing unrighteous deeds or acts, but rather they should be models of perfection or rather leading to perfection, etc.

"Accusing the Priesthood"

On Thurs. evening June 2nd, 1859, Elders I. C. Haight and Higbee returned to Cedar City from their hiding places. Alma returned with 4 of my cows.

Sund. June 5th, 1859. This morning at   o'clock, Mary Adaline, my daughter, once the wife of Don Carlos Shirts, was delivered of a son bearing the name of his father; but rather in honor of Don C., the Prophet Joseph's brother. She had a very hard time of labor to bring forth. She fainted away several times. Sister Davies officiated as mother in Isreal, who after the birth of the child asked my forgiveness for the hard sayings that she used against me to my family in my absence. She said that she was wrong and narrow and had repented from the bottom of her heart and had prayed to God to forgive her and enable her to overcome and to be more guarded in the future. Her request I granted and blessed her and commended her

214

for her humility and the honesty of her intentions. At 11 o' public worship.

Mond. June 6th. Tenney and all hands on the ditch planting, etc.

Tues. 7th. do.

Wed. 8th. do.

Thur. 9th. Samuel Hamilton arrived from G. S. Lake City, reported that Thos. Ivy killed Isaac Allred, both of San Pete Co. It seems that the parties got into dispute about herding sheep and Ivy struck him an unlucky blow on the head with a cedar stick which he drew out of the fire in the moment of passion, broke his skull. He lived 8 hours, but never spoke. Allred previous to this it seems had struck Ivy several times.

Hamilton brought me 2 letters on business. I had previous to this empowered him to collect some $225.00. Some $60.00 of the above sum was not collected, stating that they did not owe it all.

Fri. June 10th. Planting, irrigating, etc. About 12 noon I. C. Haight and Chas. C. Hopkins arrived.

My daughter Mary very low and not expected to recover, having taken a backset—thrown into spasms frequently. I prayed for her recovery repeatedly and every time she was relieved. But as soon as I would leave the house the Tormenter would return and she would be racked with pain until she would faint away and she would cry out, Oh Father, do come and rebuke him. I know that it is the Devil that torments me, and do pray cast him out, and I pray to God to forgive me of whatever I have done wrong, that he may not have power to affect me continually. I rebuked him in the name of Jesus, and he departed and I had to sit by her with my hand on her for 24 hours.

Daughter Near Death

215

Sat. June 11th. I sent a grist to mill and Aggathean went to Parawan for some goods. Haight and Hopkins went to Toquerville.

Sund. 12th. Meeting in my family hall. The Bishop and I addressed the Saints. The spirit of the Lord attended our remarks.

Evening. Agga returned. My daughter Mary considerably better, still she was only living under the faith of the Priesthood. Nature needed help. There appeared to be obstructions in the womb. I by the advice of the nurses sent to Parawan for Dr. Meeks. This evening Pres. Haight and Hopkins returned and came and lodged with me. Bishop P. K. Smith and 4 others took dinner with me. Elder Hopkins said there were feelings now between me and Elder Haight that ought to be settled. I replied that if Elder Haight wished to be friendly and drop the past, he must not turn a cold shoulder nor wear an air of scorn thinking that I would bow to him for I never would with my present feelings. I am the injured person. If I had injured him I would readily make restitution. I have been seriously wronged, notwithstanding I am willing to bury the past and say no more about it provided he will show signs of friendship.[174] Hopkins replied that we were both like bull dogs, too proud to yield. I replied that no man ever found me in the fault but what I was willing to yield when I knew it, and even a disposition to do right or make restitution was enough for me and even now if Bro. Haight wants to drop it and be on amical terms let him come to my house and be social as he once was, and I will receive it as a signal of peace. Hopkins said that he would inform him of my proposals, etc., and if it was accepted they

---

[174] This is an echo of the quarrel betwen Haight and Lee. Haight and Dame quarreled on the field after the massacre over accepting responsbility for the deed, and as a result it was saddled upon Lee, who had merely been acting under their orders. Lee was actually "the injured person."

would be back that evening to supper. Accordingly about 12 noon they returned, took dinner and supper, then Hopkins returned home. Haight remained hunting cattle till Wed. noon, remained eating with me every day and seemed more intimately friendly than what he had for 12 mos. previous.

Mond. June 13th. About 1 p.m. Dr. Meeks arrived. Mary still on the mend. This evening I bought a goat of Tenney. Paid him about $10.00. Bro. Haight helped me butcher it.

Tues. June 14th. Mary still on the mend. Dr. Meeks appears to facilitate her recovery by medical skill.

Wed. June 15th. Mary is still recovering. Dr. Meeks returned. His bill is $15.00. Bro. Haight unlucky in hunting cattle. I sent my son Joseph out, found his cattle by 12 noon. After dinner Bro. Haight returned. Left a pressing invitation for me and my family to make him a visit.

By mail intelligence reached us of the removal of Judge Cradlebaugh and other officials for their injudicious course pursued against the Mormons.[175] Also the protest by all the public papers against them for violating the treaty of pardon [176] of the chief executive of the nation, and governor of this territory. Thus for once the public print has taken up our rights and defended them. The storm that so recently threatened us with destruction has again been dispelled by the hand of Almighty God and the prospects of peace is again restored in fulfillment to the vision that I had. (See Journal 1857, 8, 9, page 109). I feel

---

[175] Judge Cradlebaugh, after making his investigation attempted to bring the guilty parties to justice. Under the circumstances existing at that time he found himself powerless to obtain convictions and resigned his office. He was not removed; but his wise policy in taking an escort of soldiers to Cedar City was not upheld by President Buchanan, whose knowledge of conditions in Utah was very limited.

[176] The pardon was extended to Mormons who were in rebellion against the United States, and had no reference to the murders at Mountain Meadows.

like exclaiming in the language of one of the old prophets who is like unto our God; He heareth our prayers and revealeth His secrets to His servants, the prophets. He confoundeth the wicked in their sercet devices and bringeth righteousness to pass to those who put their trust in Him." The scene that we have just passed through, to those that know not God but have been walking by the light of others have been to them dreary, melancholly and forboding, looking with fearful indignation for sudden destruction to come upon them. But to those who acknowledgeth the hand of God in all things, discerneth the signs of the times, for they understand the moving of the spirit, and like the ancients they rejoice in the midst of tribulation. Knowing that it worketh for them the peaceable things of the Kingdom of God in as much as they are exercised thereby.

A Prophecy

     I here note a prophecy that I delivered concerning I. C. Haight, Higbee and others, on Sund. evening, May 1st, 1859, at the time an express reached me advising me to flee to the mountains and take care of myself. The spirit fell on me while I wrote them the following words (ss) Brothern, be faithful and put your trust in God, and you shall be delivered out of the hands of those that now seek our lives. For the Lord God hath revealed it unto me, and hath shown me that you will yet be placed in a position where you will be compelled to put your trust wholly in the Lord, for all other means of deliverance shall be shut up against you. Then you will be constrained to acknowledge the hand of the Lord in your deliverance. Remember what I say unto you. I bear record of what I have said, I know it is true and that the Lord God will deliver us out of their hands.

     Wed. June 15th, 1859. Bro. Haight in relating his narrative declared to me that Almighty God had delivered him and the Brothern out of the tightest place that ever he

218

had been in. He said that when Cradlebaugh and the troops passed the Sevier they turned by way of San Pete; Haight supposed the way to be clear; returned to get in the rear of the hounds, figuratively speaking. Hamblin had reported the way clear; when to their surprise they rode right into a detachment of Cradlebaugh's troops, who were encamped on the Sevier River, near the bridge, and were taken prisoners and were detained till next day. Men came up and said, "I have certainly seen you before." "Quite likely," replied Wm. Stewart, "we live in Provo City and are in pursuit of stolen horses, and are losing time every moment you detain us." They however kept them till morning when report came that all their horses and animals were stolen, producing quite an excitement for a few moments. But soon their animals were found running to camp. At that moment the lieutenant cried out. "Let those prisoners go." They were 4 in No. namely Haight, Higbee, Stewart and Wolf, 2 of the principal men that they were in pursuit of, but knew it not, for the Lord had blinded their eyes. Thus fulfilling my prediction. (See on page 78) present journal.[177]

Thurs. June 16th. Irrigating, making water ditches, etc.

Frid. June 17th. do. On the 15th inst. finished planting corn and beans.

Sat. June 18th. I was at home. Aggathean, my first in the covenant, returned from Parawan bringing with her two dozen breakfast plates and 2 doz. cups and saucers for which I paid $30.00.

Sund. June 19th. Meeting in my family hall. Bro. John Hamilton, his son Samuel, I. Hunt's wife and the Hamilton families were here for meeting and dinner and supper with me. I addressed the Saints from the text:

---

[177] This circumstance is related in substantially the same words in Haight's own journal under date of May 29, 1859.

Many strive for masteries and are not crowned because they do not strive lawfully, etc.; backed up by Elder Hamilton and Davies who also bore record that I had declared to them some time in March last that the Lord had shown me the troops would be upon us in the south and seek the lives of many; but that the Lord would overrule it for our good and that the excitement would die away just as it has been, and felt to rejoice thru what he had heard and seen, etc.

Excitement
Dies Away

Mond. June 20th. My daughter Mary has measurably recovererd. Don C. Shirts, her husband is here but her feelings are still aleinated from him. He made up some brooms for us today. I have commenced overhauling my tannery; was compelled to sink my vats in a house some 40 ft. in length on account of the wind and dust. Sunk 5 vats 6 by 4 feet, 5 feet deep. Some $500.00 worth of my leather lost for the want of care while I was in the mountains. I also set N. C. Tenney to repairing my wagons.

Tues. June 21st. do. do.

Wed. June 22nd. do.

Thur. June 23rd. do. Today I sold 2 heifers to Wm. Flake for $35.00 each; also G. R. Cooley, Spronce, Dewel and Pettitts and their families all passed by enrout for Texas; running as it were to meet the troubles. I sold them some tobacco, butter and cheese to the amount of $7.00. My wife Agga returned from Cedar City with a part of our tools from the machine.

Frid. June 24th. Resumed hauling rock for the foundation of my barn which I had in contemplation to build 70 ft. by 30 ft. 15 ft. high. Also setting hire 2 of Jos. Horn's men here. Sent him 1 gal. whiskey for the 24th July.

About sunset I started to residence in Washington, my wife Rachel with me. Had a load of flour, cheese, tools,

220

etc., for the benefit of my family. Turned my mules at the Old Fort 4 mi. distant, Horn's men at the same place. This we did in order to cross the sands before the heat of the day following.

Sat. June 25th. Dry pleasing breeze, though this spring and summer thus far has been rather sultry. By daybreak in pursuit of my mules, they having run away. Trailed them over the mountain slopes back to Harmony. They were heard braying about day dawn, then went off to their range. I reached home at 6 and sent my son Jos. in search of them, who found them about noon. I started and reached Washington about 8. Found my family in good health, my crop that was in charge of Wm. Freem and my family is promising peas in abundance, melons as large as cups, but the crop pitched by R. Woolsey and sons rather indifferent.

Sund. June 26th. This morning I had an interview with Bishop Covington, preached to him the gospel of the Kingdom. At 11 I was invited to address the Saints in the open air. The sultry or hot winds from the desert sands together with the dust rendered it anything but comfortable or agreeable. So I offered the Saints my family hall to meet in. They accordingly adjourned to my residence where I addressed the Saints upon the necessity of living before God so as to know for themselves and not be in doubt and fears as many of them was. Bore record to the onward progress of the Kingdom of God. Exhorted them to send out teachers to go from house to house to wake up the Saints and to persuade them to come to the house of worship and be fed from the rich basket of our Father in Heaven. The spirit of God accompanied my words and melted many down to tears.

At 2 p.m. the Elders Quorum met and I was again requested to instruct them, which I did, showing them that they bore an appendage of the Holy P. H. and it was their privilege to have the heavens opened to them and have the will of God revealed to them and even all who had the testimony of Jesus abiding in them, had the spirit of prophecy. The promise was that the Lord would do nothing without revealing his secrets to his servants, the Prophets. Now if you do not know, it is because you live beneath your privileges, etc.

I also at night taught the Pres. of the teachers and others, upon the subject of economy and the power and policy of government, showing that we would be saved or damned upon our own agency, of our own free will and choice and not by constraint. The spirit of darkness which is the seed of apostacy in this settlement was appalling. In fact about 1/2 the people had gone away, and others would go if poverty would allow.[169] Elder Richey, Covington and others bore record to the truth of my sayings.

"Seeds of Apostacy"

Mond. June 27th, 1859. All hands was called out to work on the dam, I also was in their midst, preaching to them. This evening the Seventies had a social party in my family hall. I was appointed to preside over it; they agreed to deliver me 10 loads of stone for the use of the hall. Good order and a lively interest was manifested.

Tues. June 28th. I bought 2 loads of hay of R. Woolsey. I also took his crop to tend by leaving Thomas to assist Br. Freem and Geo. to work with me, and relieve him (Richard) and his family to return to Harmony, not being able to endure the bad weather. I also mowed some hay on my little farm, and had 4 loads of wood hauled.

Wed. June 29th. I finished making and hauling my hay; weather warm and sultry. This morning I settled with Judge McCullough, sold him a ewe sheep for $8.75. Paid Tenney tax, all some $50.00. I also sold a steer to

Hatfield for $35.00. Also some spare tobacco, cheese, etc., to the amount of $20.00 more.

Thurs. June 30th. About 12 noon I started back to Harmony in company with R. Woolsey, hauled a part of his load and family; took back 2 of my cows. Hired Thomas and Geo. Adair to assist me to build a barn. Agreed to pay them a cow each for 30 days labor. Camped at the Grapevine Springs.

Frid. July 1st, 1859. About sunrise resumed our travel. After returning thanks for the good success that we had up to the present, that moment Satan entered one of my mules and he fell to kicking and continued about 1½ hours.

Satan Enters a Mule

[*Pages 95 to 100 missing*]

through the week I with my hands were employed in building, attending to the crop, hauling lumber and shingles from Pine Valley, etc.

Sund. 10th. Meeting in the, or rather my family hall. I was called to address the Saints, which I did. The Bishop was at Pine Valley.

On Thursday morning at 1 o'clock, Emma, my seventeenth wife, was delivered of a still born son. The child was large and proper but the mother was hurt in a fall some days before its birth, which was supposed to be the cause of its death. By its mother's request I gave it the name of John Henry, after her father and myself. At 10 a.m. its remains was neatly interred in the Harmony grave yard.

Mond. July 11th. This evening my team returned with some 2200 shingles and 6000 feet of lumber. I also

223

borrowed 20 bushels of wheat of E. Hanks and was to pay him 50 cents on the bushel for a month's use.

Tues. 12th July. Pres. I. C. Haight came and stayed over night with me and preached to the Saints in this place. The spirit of God attended his remarks leaving an impression on his hearers showing them how easy they were to turn against the P. H. when trials assailed and that if a man did not carry the power of the P. H. with him he would be persecuted and hunted by our enemies.[178]

Wed. July 13th. Bishop P. K. Smith and others took breakfast with me, I sent N. C. Tenney and Henry Barney up Coal Creek for making timber to make a house mill.

Frid. eve. Returned on the 12th. Tues. morning Jos. Hatfield commenced labor with me at $38.00 per mo. (carpenter) and a book. By the latest advices from the States, we learn that the bulldogs of war are marching to the field of battle, namely France and Austria and some of the allied powers. Also the foundation for bloodshed and the desolution of the Union is laid by the North against the South in fulfillment of the revelation given to Jos. Smith foretelling the ruin and downfall of American liberty. Also Prest. Buckhannon's views and answer to the associate judges for Utah, St. Clair and Cradlebaugh, disapproved of their official proceeding, but approved of the course taken by the governor and district attorney, etc.

Sat. evening, July 16th. The first story of my barn is up and timbers on ready for the second story.

Sund. July 17th, 1859. Meeting in the meeting house. Elder H. Barney and E. H. Groves preached a good discourse. I was invited to dine with Bishop Davies. I was

---

[178] Isaac C. Haight, president of the Parowan "Stake," and the man—next to Brigham Young—principally responsible for the Mountain Meadows massacre. here cautions the Saints not to criticize or inform against the "Priesthood," thus admitting that it was the "Priesthood" and not a band of renegades, who were involved.

LOG CABIN AT LEE'S FERRY

Built in 1873. The only one of Lee's buildings still standing at Lonely Dell.

Photo by Charles Kelly

invited to Bishop Covington's to spend the 24th with them at Washington. Pres. Haight is also expected to join us. Some 40 acres of my wheat is ready to harvest. My corn, vines, beans, potatoes, etc., need working. This evening my boys riding Brown Co. horses . . .. Evening cloudy.

Mond. July 17th, 1859. From this day up to Frid. July 21st, lowering weather, although at intervals I had 10 hands in the harvest field and cut some 30 acres. About 4 evening Elder G. A. Smith, A. Lyman, their wives, J. N. Smith, R. Brown, J. H. Martineau, O. B. Adams and their wives all arrived and put up at my mansion. In the evening preached in the meeting house. Touched upon the signs of the times and the mighty revolutions that are now among the nations of the earth and spoke of the French and Austrian war. 37,000 slain in one battle besides many thousands that were daily falling out of battle. Meetings of a fiery and excitable nature are held all over the Union between the party cliques (ss) the Black Republicans, Democrats, etc., which indication is fast hastening to wars and bloodshed in our midst, which will terminate in overthrow and disolution of the Union in fulfillment to a revelation given and prophecy delivered by the Prophet, Seer and Revelator, Jos. Smith.

Apostles Smith and Lyman Arrive

Dec. 25th, 1832 (ss) Verily thus saith the Lord concerning the wars that must shortly come to pass beginning at the Rebellion of South Carolina, which will eventually terminate in the death and misery of many souls. The day will come that war will be poured out on all nations beginning at that place. For behold the Southern states shall be directed against the Northern states and the Southern states shall call on other states and nations, even Great Britain, in order to defend themselves against other nations and thus war shall be poured out on all nations and it shall come to pass after many days slaves shall rise up against

225

their masters who shall be disciplined for war. And it shall come to pass also that the remnants who are left of the land will marshall themselves and shall become exceeding angry; and shall vex the gentiles with a sore vexation. And thus with the sword will the blood be shed. The inhabitants of the earth shall mourn and with famine and earthquakes and the thunder of heaven and the fierce vivid lightning also shall the inhabitants of the earth be made to feel the wrath and indignation and chastening of Almighty God, until the consumption decreed hath been made a full end of all nations. That the cry of the Saints and the blood of the Saints shall cease to come up into the ears of the Lord of Sabboth from the earth to be avenged of their enemies. Wherefore stand ye in holy places, and be not moved until the day of the Lord come; for behold it cometh quickly, saith the Lord, Amen.

Lee Accompanies the Apostles

Sat. July 22nd, 1859. This morning Bro. G. A. and A. Lyman of the 12 apostles insisted that I and my family would accompany them to Washington City to spend the 24th of July. Accordingly about 8 o'clock we all set out. I had with me some 13 of my family, namely: Aggathean, Rachel, S. C., Sarah J., Mary A., Nancy, Louisa, Rachel, Olive, Mary Ann, Jno. A., Jos. H., Jno. Willard and Henry Darrow. On the way J. N. Smith had some trouble with his horses and carriage. I let him have one of my horses to work. Reached the Grapevine Springs about 2 p.m., took some refreshments and [baited] our teams.

Here Nephi, Bro. W. Freeman's son, was violently attacked with the cramps in his bowels and was near unto death. I called on the elders for help. At first A. Lyman was mouth; found some relief. Bro. G. A. Smith next was mouth. Instant relief was the result, and when within 8 mi. of the destined point we were immersed in quite a shower and a little after dark reached Washington. Bros.

226

Geo. and Lyman lodged with Bishop R. D. Covington. Distance 35 mi.

Sund. July 23rd. At 11 meeting at the Bowery. I was called to open meeting by prayer, then Elder Smith and Lyman addressed the Saints some 2 hours in a spirited manner to the joy and satisfaction of those who had been and were still trying to do right, but to the shame and condemnation of those that had availed themselves of the opportunity of the times to belch out the filth and corruption of their wicked hearts and have sought to betray and expose their brethren into the hands of their enemies.[179]

Apostles Approve of Mountain Meadows Massacre

Mond. July 24th. Washington. At sunrise the Stars and Stripes were floating in the breeze over the east end of my 2 story stone building. Also preparation was being made for the reception of the apostles and ([?] who were to dine with me. I had two goats dressed up for the occasion, also the production of the present season such as peas, beans, beets, cucumbers, green corn, melons, etc. Soon after another flag was hoisted at the residence of Bishop R. D. Covington.

At 9 a.m. the assembly met at the Bowery. Oration by Elder G. A. Smith and A. Lyman on the recent progress of the church, the crisis of the times in which we live and the necessity of living . . . . the test. Warn the Saints of associating with reckless characters; said that there was organized bands of thieves from Salt Lake down through all the settlements south, and right down here there is a band of thieves and I warn you . . .

[*Balance of Journal missing*]

---

[179] This is the most important entry remaining in this fragmentary journal of 1859. Apostles George Albert Smith and Amasa Lyman, representing the highest authority of the Mormon church, made a tour of the southern settlements to threaten and intimidate those who had "belched out filth and corruption" by informing Judge Cradlebaugh of the true facts connected with the Mountain Meadows massacre. It proves positively that Brigham Young and all church authorities had complete knowledge of the facts, approved of the massacre, and were exerting their official efforts toward keeping it secret and protecting the participants.

LETTERS

Amorah Lee,
My dear and affectionate child:

I received your very kind and touching letter under date Aug. 7th which came to hand on the 10th inst., found us both well, and you may guess that it made us glad and well all over to read your kind letter. I had not received your first letter when I wrote before; if I had I would not have expressed myself as I did with regards to my saying that you would have respect enough to stay with the children while your mother would come to see me; and if you had not, Nancy would come in the first place. I will say that your acknowledgments in your first letter bound up the wound that you made at the River. I accept the confession and forgive the offense. Again you said that you did not know why I should think that Nancy would do more for me than you would. I did not till you refused to do me a much less favor than this one. But in as much as you have seen your folly and have retraced your steps, that is all done away with and to be remembered no more.

When your mother got here I was almost dead. I had laid in the hot scorching sun near 18 hours unable to turn myself over and no one to give me a drink of water. The sweat poured off me like rain—except my loins and it was cold as death. In this situation I gave up to die and no one to see me breathe my last, when a strange bird lit within a few inches of my head and seemed to be sorry and tried to talk. This strange visitor startled me and I began to

---

[180] Moencopi, an early Mormon settlement in northern Arizona.

LEHI AND AMORAH LEE SMITHSON

Amorah seems to have been Lee's favorite daughter, to whom
he addressed the letters reproduced herein. She is still
living (1938) in Arizona.

pray and felt a little more encouraged and talked to the stranger and said these words as they came to me: "Go my sweet bird to my house in the cave and whisper this message to my loved ones at home. Tell her to come quickly, my own bosom friend, for I am alone in deep anguish and pain."

When I was done speaking, it started in the direction of the pools,[181] and I got up for the first time and walked to my wagon and washed myself in a tub of water. When your mother got here she told me of a similar circumstance of a bird at the pools, and for aught I know it might be the same bird that visited me as both occurrances happened on the same day. This however only serves to confirm us more in the overruling hand of Providence. Your mother certainly came in answer to my prayers and in a time when she was needed more than any other. Many is the time when I have looked upon the past and wept with gratitude to my Father in Heaven for blessing me with so good a woman for a companion who would leave all to come to my relief, and comfort me in my lonely hours; and for giving us such kind and thoughtful children, who are willing to stay alone without neighbors near them and insist on mother going to father and comfort him. Can a father and mother ever forget such children? No, never. I hope soon to find a better place where we can live together in peace. Be good children to each other and I will reward you for all your kindness.

Expressions of Affection

If Jacob should not pass before this letter reaches you, I would like for John Amasa to come out with him and help save the crop and bring out Hebe to Madge and one of the pups out as the wolves are very bad here. They have caught 2 of our hens and are destroying the corn bad. We

---

[181] "The Pools," now called Jacob's Lake on the highway leading to the north rim of Grand Canyon. Rachel lived there, tended a herd of cattle and made cheese in summer.

have 8 young chickens and Jacob has 1 Bremer. Your mother feels well and sends her love to you all. Mellons are just beginning to come on and we will have lots of them and all kinds of vegetables.

Visit to Chief Tuba

Your mother and me rode 8 miles on a visit to Tuby[182] and his lady and Taltee and his lady. We feasted on mellons and they got us a splendid dinner. Had tea and sugar, fried cakes and mutton steak, green corn, etc. She and I with an Indian went and visited the Cohoweenas. We were gone 4 days. They were very friendly. Gave her a bunch of beads and we got a deer and a turkey. I must close for the want of room. Kiss Ralph, John, Frank and Brig for me, so goodbye for a while.

YAUGAUTS.[183]

P. S. —Tell Ralph if that sow is about to have pigs before we come home to turn out the other lest she eats the pigs. Write any chance. I do not know when we will be at home. But will write again when we can.

[Part of a letter apparently written in 1873]

. . . . of supervision of Mohave County, instructing them to secure the right to her and to no one else, and for her to petition that board, and the right will be granted, etc. So I have concluded to send in the petition and secure the Ferry at once for the benefit of the Saints.

Emma is all right. Please say to Bro. Robert [?] Street I want him to send me the amount of corn that I got of Heath as I will want it to settle with Jacob Hamblin when he comes. I have been waiting to see him and learn something about the miner world and the present move, but I have not heard a word, only rumor through the In-

---

182 Chief Tuba, after whom Tuba, Arizona, was named.
183 "Yaugauts," meaning "cry-baby"—Lee's Indian name among the Piedes.

dians and Miners and that is nothing definite. Mr. Winburn, that old man that was at the house when you left, is an object of pity. He took down with a white swelling and is reduced to a skeleton. He is a great burden on our hands as he is confined to his bed and his leg swells terrible. And how much longer he will have to endure it I cannot say, but I pray for speedy deliverance.

I have had a letter from Willard. He says that David does not intend to let me have the horses that I bought of him and that they raised nothing much and do not intend to pay anything only as they raise it, etc.

I must close, hoping that you will come soon and write often. Goodbye dear children for a season. Peace be with you and God bless you. From your affectionate father,

J. D. LEE.

[*Part of a letter to his daughter, Amorah Smithson, written while in jail at Beaver*]

. . . . soon acknowledged by a flood of fast falling tears, we ate and we drank together; we talked, sang and praised God together, and thus we did rejoice exceedingly. It being New Year's day, through the courtesy and kindness of the officers and citizens of the Post, we had a fine treat of shampaigne, 3 bottles, one gallon of Dixie wine, brandy, apples, and nuts, grapes, sardines, pies, baked chicken, candies, sweet meats, etc. But to return—the future and past must not be forgotten. I am by no means free from slavery, anxiety and cares. A prison life is one of the most gloomy lives for me of all others. This evening the guard was forbidden to take anyone to meals except the regular boarders. This complaint was made by a little narrow minded sergeant. I have guarded against reactions of any

Prison Life

kind. The least little thing is liable to abridge my liberty. Sometimes I have the liberty of seeing my family without a pass, but all others must have a written pass from the Marshall to get in.

[*Missing*]

. . . . that foul demon disgrace that has followed me ever since that unfortunate and lamentable affair took place. I need not say to you that I am innocent,[184] you already know that as you have already manifested in your affectionate letter. Your mother and Sarah Jane started this morning for Panguitch to learn the cause of the delay of my team as my council is waiting for it to go south to look up my witnesses. She had a good carriage and horses furnished her by a friend.

"I Am Innocent"

Give my love to your husband and his father and all enquiring friends. Tell all to remember me before the Lord. My trust is in God, who has done as you said in your letter, softened the hearts of the people and has made me friends among strangers; and may God bless my family and friends in this kingdom and cause, that we may be enabled to stand fast with the vocation wherewith we are called that is in the day when He comes to make up His jewels here on this earth that we may be remembered.

JOHN D. LEE.

(To his affectionate child, Amorah Smithson.)

Write often.

---

[184] In his confessions made in court Lee admitted his part in the Mountain Meadows massacre, but insisted he had not personally killed any of the emigrants. This is what he means when he says "I am innocent."

Sugar House Ward,
Salt Lake City, Oct. 28, 1875, U. T.

My Dear Daughter Amorah:

I received your kind letter last evening and hasten to answer it this morning. I was glad to learn of your health and prosperity, but was grieved in my soul to learn that Ralph and John had left the Ferry and forsaken the interest that we had there and had perhaps the only team and wagon that is fit to be used, away working for molasses, when they should be at the Dell to take care of the stock and the Ferry. What is their labor at Pahreah working for molasses, by the side of being at home where all our stock and interest is? Besides you say that Emma has bread bought for to do her and all those little children that she has with her including ours and one of Caroline's, at least 100 mi. by road from settlement. If she has done all this, she has done well. But I know that she wrote to me that she had made arrangements for their bread at Long Valley and wanted me to send Ralph and the team home immediately as she had no wagon fit to use and that he was very much needed to help get the bread to the river before the snow stops the travel on the Buckskin Mts. and that he was needed at the Ferry as Billy and Isaac were not able to manage the large boat alone; and that Bro. Johnson was called at Conference on a mission. I wrote on the receipt of this letter to your mother and to the boys at Upper Kanab to send Ralph with the team right away by Long Valley and take the load with him to the Dell. As Emma said it was ready I advised her to try and get some of the boys to go with Ralph and haul a load or two before winter closed in. And I supposed that my counsel had been obeyed until I received your letter stating to the contrary.

I have written some 8 letters to Rachel, Caroline and one to the boys, but received no answer from any of them

233

except one from Caroline.[185] I have received one letter from your mother but not in answer to any of mine, and one from Willard. I could not find where she was till Bp. Dame came here.[186] He told me that he thought she had gone to Corn Creek and that Caroline had gone to Panguitch and that is all I could hear till Willard wrote and said that your mother was there. I wrote several letters to your mother to try and get those beef cattle that was at Upper Kanab drove to Beaver and cashed and bring me the money, and I gave her instructions how to travel, etc. As I was sick and no way to help myself to any little nourishment or medicine, I had made arrangements for her to stay near me. But have never heard a word in return. I have no hopes of another trial till next April and felt that her presence would have greatly aided me to while away these long, lonesome, dreary, disconsolate hours of confinement with associates many of whom are fiends in man form. But this comfort seems to be denied me. You seem to excuse the boys leaving home by saying that Emma could make her bread on the Ferry, and that the boys are working for bread to take to their mother who is living with Hebe and Nancy at Upper Kanab and that Caroline can do well enough at Panguitch with some 8 or 9 little children to work for and no one to help her but little Charles.[187] But Rachel must have Ralph and John, two young men with team and wagon and Frank who is equal to Chas. to work for Rachel and one child. (Brig thot any of the boys or family would be glad to keep him without pay). This inconsistency is not nor never has been my policy. Selfishness and jealousy will bring even more sorrow and wretchedness if it is possible to do so than

---

[185] In all this correspondence, only three wives are mentioned—Rachel, Emma and Caroline. The others had left him.

[186] William H. Dame was also under arrest and in the penitentiary awaiting trial at this time. After Lee's conviction he was released.

[187] Charley Lee, still living (1938) at Torrey, Utah.

even now exist. United we stand, but divided we fall. My advice is to keep our interest together for if divided it will soon go to the 4 winds and we will be left penniless without a hoof, and should I ever be fortunate enough to gain my liberty and my stock is not wasted away, we could soon recuperate again. Stock is very low now, but in a short time it may be high. I do not wish to find fault with Rachel. When she is with me she would die by me, but when she is away from me she is too easily influenced and led by bad counsel. If she can live with Hebe and Nancy without taking all or more of the help and team away from the Ferry and interest at home, she had better go there with the boys and help take care of things with them. If she remains where she is long, it will take what beeves I have there to keep them up. You may think that I have the blues. I don't know what to call it. I feel that I am forsaken by everybody. It certainly is the darkest hour . . .

Sugar House Ward,
Salt Lake City, Dec. 11, 1875.

My dear, kind and affectionate children:

Your truly interesting letter dated Nov. 22nd was received and handed to me by this mail, its contents was duly appreciated and I hasten to acknowledge receipt of the same by return mail. I was glad to learn that you were all well and that general prosperity prevails, that you were blessed with peace and a bountiful harvest. Your explanation and the purity of your motives in writing as you did was satisfactory to me. I was not vexed at you for writing as you did, but to the contrary I was pleased with the plain honest way that you represented things to be: they were the simple facts without evasion, which was the right way to do. It enabled me to know the true state of

235

affairs and give me the chance to correct anything that
should not be . . . .

[*Missing*]

Much anxiety is manifest by both parties in the next presidential election.   The Pres. message is much speculated
upon.

We had over a month of stormy weather, the snow
is very deep in the mountains but little in the valley.

*"A Man of
Sorrow"*

It can truly and justly be said of me that I am a man
of sorrow and acquainted with grief.

Remember me kindly to all enquiring friends. Kiss
little John Doyle for me. Write often and receive the confidence and love of your true and affectionate father,
though in tribulation deep.

J. D. LEE.

To Lehi and Amorah Smithson.

DENNIS J. TOOHY   U. S. Commissioner's Office
Attorney at Law   Territory of Utah
13 Federal Court House Bldg.

Sugar House Ward,
Salt Lake City, Jany. 18th, 1876.

My dear children:

I received your interesting letter of this morning's
mail bearing date Jany. 2nd inst. and I was truly glad to
learn of your health and the good feeling that you and the
friends manifested. I was sorry to hear that Judge Spicer
whom I took to be a gentleman would take advantage of
a woman in Emma's situation and persuade and influence
her to allow him to use up my means on his wild goose
hunt for the wealth of the earth and I am still more astonished at her for listening to his fine words while build-

236

LEE'S FORT

At Lee's Ferry, Arizona. Solidly built of stone with loopholes for purposes of defense.

Photo by Julius F. Stone (1909)

ing castles in the air. I have just received a letter from Emma and one from Judge Spicer asking my permission to allow him horses to prospect with and aid him otherwise and to tell him where those ledges was or is from which brought in some and saying that he had had bad luck with his mines, etc., and that the boys had scolded about his using my horses and I wrote back to them saying that the boys was right, that I did not want anything to do with Spicer's fortune hunting, that I wanted Ralph and John to cross the river and go to work at my place, the Mow Eabba,[188] lest someone would jump the claim and cause us trouble and let Bro. Johnson with Billy and Isaac keep up the place at the Ferry and take care of the stock, and have nothing to do with Judge Spicer's expedition; that a good crop at the river and at the Mow Eabba would be the best gold mine to us and that it would take all the available animals that I have to keep up these places and let Judge Spicer make his fortune independent of us; that he has only one wife and one child and is a free man and certainly can paddle his own canoe. I have paid him twice as much for his services as I agreed to. I owe him nothing, he got his pay down, Judge Houge has had but little as yet. Lehi, if you receive this letter within 10 or 15 days from date I wish you would ride to the Dell and see how things are going on at the Dell. Talk with Bro. Johnson about my wishes and tell him not to have my horses nor cattle traded for blankets or any other traps and not have them butchered for Judge Spicer or anybody else. Of course I want them to butcher meat for their own use but to do that sparingly and tell them not to allow my horses rode unnecessarily, and tell Ralph and Billy not to consent to lending my horses to explore or prospect on, and if Ralph goes over to the Mow Eabba that I want Bro. John-

---

[188] Moenavi, Arizona, near Moencopi. Johnson operated the ferry for some years after Emma moved to Holbrook, Arizona.

237

son with Billy to look after my interest at the river as an
honest faithful brother would. That Emma is not a judge
of the value of property and is too easily influenced by
flattery and big promises and that too from strangers and
you advise Emma to counsel with Bro. Johnson and to
make no moves without councilling with him and ask him
to advise her when he sees things are not going right. Do
this in a prudent, cautious, friendly way, that you may
have influence to do good. When I read Emma's letter I
felt impressed that all was not right and reminded her to
be on her guard and not listen to the fine promises of anyone. If the stock are not doing well at the river it had better be taken to the pools, Houserock Spring, that is. Wm.
Swap is there with cattle, the cattle should all go and get
in order; the horses had better remain at the river. John
I want to go with Ralph, its poor business for him to be
there working for stock and let what we have go to loss
for the want of care and when you return home write and
tell me how things are at the Dell.

Your mother reached here on the 20th of last month.
She had to borrow money to pay her way here. The four
steers got out of the corral at Beaver as you heard. Samuel
went in search of them but I cannot say whether they have
found them or not. Your mother made arrangements with
Col. Trotter at Cameron to take them and forward me a
check on Walker Bros. for eighty dollars and she came on
to me leaving her bed and luggage at the terminus of the
railroad, not having money to pay the freight. She is here
with me tonight, is well and is all that you expected her
to be, a true friend and comfort to me. I am indebted to
her as an instrument in the hands of God, she has purchased the liberty and favor that I now have. She works
as a cook with another from before daylight in the morning till 8 or 9 o'clock at night and I do chores and pay $5
a month cash and a 3 yr. old mare that I am to have from

238

Joe J. Smith for learning him to read and write. This, however, was my own offer and I feel under a thousand obligations to Capt. Burgher Maxwell and to Mr. Ward and lady, for heaven knows that I dreaded to go back in that prison. I feel so thankful that I am now on the outside that I scarcely know how to express my gratitude; I have paid for one month and that time is nearly up and where the next money is coming from I don't know but the warden is a kind hearted man. I have confidence in him that he will not put me back on that account.[189] I wish you would try and have Emma send me a little money as soon as you go there, if it is but $5.

Kindness of the Warden

I had liked to forgot to tell you that I have a school in the prison where I have taught several young men to spell, read and write a tolerable fare hand and through the kindness and good will of Capt. Burgher towards the prisoners I am allowed to go into the prison every day and teach them. The Salt Lake Tribune has highly commended the policy. Bp. W. H. Dame started to Beaver several days ago, he was allowed to return with a special guard by paying expenses, he was the best tickled man to go back I ever saw. For my part I cannot say that I am very anxious to return back to Beaver, unless I know what disposition would be made of me there. I enjoy a little liberty and quiet here and there might be a possibility of my not having any treatment there than what I have and perhaps not as good. If I could go home a free man it would alter the case very materially. But this I durst not think of till the setting of the court in April, in my own district. Gen. Maxwell has gone to Washington, he left some three weeks ago and we have not heard from him till we read in the Tribune where he has asked Congress to appropriate $75,-000 to build a penitentiary on Church Island. Thus we

---

[189] Apparently Lee made arrangements to live outside the penitentiary, with Rachel, but under what conditions is not clear.

239

see that he is still kicking and means business. I would like to see my old friend return again. I have several good letters from Caroline; when she last wrote to me she said John Blackburn's folks was talking of removing his establishment to St. George and run a boarding house at the copper mines as he own interest in them. She said that her children were all in school at Panguitch and were getting along fine.

Say to Robert that he has a cousin here in the penitentiary by the name of James Joseph Smith. His folks live in Summit or Santaguin, he is an easy kind of an inoffensive sort of a chap and it would be hard to make me believe that he of himself is a very bad man, but I should think that he would be easily persuaded to join with others, but not alone.

We have had a very mild open winter thus far, though abundance of rain in the valley and deep snow in the mountain, yet but little cold freezing weather in the valley. I see from the papers that the old rebel feeling has not died out in Congress, the party feelings show themselves more in this Congress than ever in any previous setting. The general amnesty bill has been defeated thus far as it requires a two thirds vote to make it become a law. If that is defeated the hatchet will not be buried between the North and South very soon. However, political matters but little concern me, yet I anticipate trouble ahead and that of a very grave nature, but we are all in the hands of our Father in Heaven, he will rule the destinites of all his children both good and bad and he will reward them in his own due time according to their merits or demerits and we cannot help ourselves, and when the cup of iniquity is full then their agency will be forfeited and then mercy will no longer rob justice for then justice will assert its just claims and each one will then receive from the hands of the Lord of righteousness retribution severally accord-

240

GRAVE OF JOHN D. LEE

Panguitch, Utah

Photo by Frank Beckwith

ing to their works whether it be good or evil. Still with me it is a dark time just now. Still my trust is in God and not in the arm of flesh. In fact I have nowhere else to put my trust for public opinion is against me, notwithstanding my innocence.[184] I must now close as Capt. is ready to start to the city and I am anxious to mail the letter that it may reach you soon. I must say that your letter has been quite gratifying to me and I thank you for it. May Heaven bless and protect you from all harm. Continue to pray for my delivery that we may see you soon. Your mother wept like a child when I read your letter. Be good children. All is and will be right. Trust in God. Your mother joins me in our love to you. Kiss little Joe for us.

J. D. LEE.

To Lehi and Amorah Smithson.

[*A letter given to George Wharton James by Emma Lee in 1899*]

Beaver City, Utah, Sept. 21st, 1876.

Mrs. Emma B. Lee,
Lonely Dell, Lee's Ferry, A. T.

Much Beloved Companion:

Knowing the suspense you are in to hear from me and learn of my present situation, and prospects in future, I hasten to write, as I cannot communicate to you in person. I reached here on the 4th instant, but was not wanted till the 11th, at which time my bondsmen appeared and surrendered me to the court, which placed me in an awkward position. I was left in charge of the officers of the court, and sent to prison, there to await the summons of the court from time to time. This strange and mysterious

241

move warned me that there was treachery and conspiracy on foot.[190] General Wells, or the "one-eyed pirate," as the Tribune calls him, was in Beaver, to advise and council and direct the Brethren how to swear, and those that composed the jury to be a unit in rendering a verdict of murder in the first degree. My worthy friend and able attorney, W. W. Bishop, felt that we were sold; he and Judge Foster of Pioche, who assisted him, had the promise that all was right from the leading men of the church here in Beaver, and even went so far as to mark the names of each man to be retained on the jury, telling him that if he would make up his jury with the names marked that they would be sure to clear me. Though fearful, he trusted them, which resulted in the jury's finding a verdict against me of murder in the first degree. Six witnesses testified against me, four of whom pergured themselves by swearing falsehoods of the blackest character. Old Jacob Hamblin,

the fiend of Hell, testified under oath that I told him that two young women were found in a thicket, where they had secreted themselves, by an Indian chief, who brought the girls to me and wanted to know what was to be done with them. That I replied that they was to old to live and would give evidence and must be killed; the Indian said that they were too pretty to kill, that one of them fell on her knees and said, Spare my life and I will serve you all my days, that I then cut her throat and the Indian killed the other. Such a thing I never heard of before, let alone committing the awful deed. The old hypocrite thought that now was his chance to reek his vengeance on me, by swearing away my life. Nephi Johnson was the last man that I could have believed that would have sealed his damnation by bearing false testimony against me, his neighbor.

---

[190] Brigham Young, violating a solemn promise, had decided to "sacrifice" Lee (at the second trial) in order to save his own skin, and this was the first notice Lee had of that decision.

to take away my life. The other two witnesses, Knights and McMurdy, swore that I committed the awful deeds, that they did with their own wicked hands. I own that I am perfectly whiped out, and have come to the conclusion that some men will swear that black is white, if the good Brethren only said so. But my expressing my feelings in this way will not change the verdict against me. This verdict has caused quite an excitement in Salt Lake City as well as here, among the honorable and thinking class of men. They all say that it is too thin and played out. When the verdict was rendered, my attorney asked for a stay of proceedings for ten days to prepare a plea of abatement for a rehearing, and an appeal to the higher courts, etc., which will sit in December next. My attorney promises to stand by me to the end, but must have a couple of hundred dollars within two months, to enable them to carry my case up to the higher courts. Dearest, do all you can to send me as much money as you can. I know you will do so. I have confidence in your ability to raise money. I have many warm-hearted noble-minded friends, whom I believe will never see me sacrificed at the shrine of imposition, bigotry, falsehood, and ignorance; my firm conviction is that all will come out right in the end, though it requires a little time to bring it about. Willard, Harie, and Darrow were here yesterday, and went away without letting me know that they were going to leave, a very foolish thing for them to do, as I wished to send my wagon-team and little Isaac back home. This evening Hellen came to the prison and told me that they had started for the Ferry to inform you and Rachel, and to bring Rachel. This, as I said before, was a strange move, but I suppose they thought from the verdict that all that wish to see me must come soon. This, of course, confuses my intended arrangements. I will have to wait until I hear from them before making a move in that direction; in all probability I will be sent

243

to Salt Lake Prison, as the supreme court sits in Salt Lake City. Dearest Emma, keep up good cheer. Say to friend Johnson that he must let you have all the money that comes from the Ferry, to help me in the hour of trouble. Tell Billy to remember Pa, and send him some money. My love to you and all the dear little children, to Warren and family also. Write immediately and often, for a word from you in your own handwriting carries joy and comfort to my soul. I have many things to say to you when we meet again. Joseph Wood is here in prison with me. He expects to get his trial soon. Miley is also here under indictment. Sarah Jane is at Jo Woods' ranch, taking care of things there, as Hellen was also indicted, and is here on bail, awaiting trial. I had to leave little Isaac with Sarah Jane for company and help her with the cows, as she was alone. Joseph Wood, Hellen and Sarah Jane all wish to be remembered to you. I will write soon and let you know how matters move along. So goodbye for the present. I trust that we will see many good days together yet.

J. D. LEE.

To Emma B. Lee.

INDEX

Numbers followed by (n) refer to footnotes on pages indicated.